FRANCO OF SPAIN

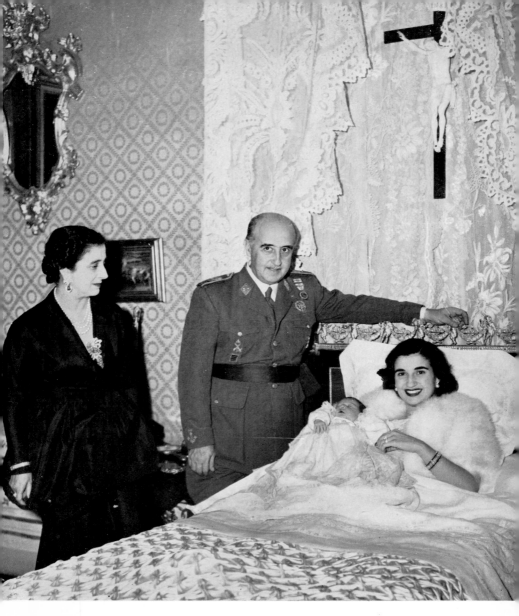

The Head of the Spanish State and Doña Carmen Polo de Franco, with their only daughter, the Marquesa de Villaverde, on the occasion of the baptism at El Pardo of the eldest of their three grandchildren   (*Photo: José Campúa, Madrid*)

FRANCO
OF SPAIN

a full-length biography by

S. F. A. COLES

THE NEWMAN PRESS

'Franco of Spain'
was first published in 1956 by
The Newman Press
Westminster, Maryland
All rights reserved
It was made and printed in Great Britain by
Page Bros (Norwich) Ltd
in 12pt. Bembo

CONTENTS

5

LIST OF ILLUSTRATIONS

TO SPAIN

AND TO ALL TRUE SPANIARDS

I DEDICATE THIS BOOK,

WITH RESPECT, HOMAGE

AND AFFECTION

FOREWORD

Although I lived and worked in Spain in the early thirties, it would be true to say that I had scarcely heard up to the outbreak of the Spanish Civil War of the General of Division, Don Francisco Franco Baamonde; and ever since that tragic event, indeed right up to the day when I addressed myself to the task of writing this book, I knew little more of the present Head of the Spanish State than has appeared during the past fifteen years in the conflicting and usually biassed or prejudiced articles in the world's press.

I was neither pro- nor anti-Franco, but I was pro-Spain and pro-Spanish people. While my sympathies in the fratricidal 'War of Liberation' had been definitely with the restorers of law and order—for I had both witnessed and experienced the absence of order and personal security under the Second Republic—I was, if anything, doubtful of Franco himself, having absorbed, like most of my countrymen, and, indeed, the greater part of the world, a good deal of the general propaganda line that represented him as a 'Fascist plotter against Democracy' and a sanguinary rebel against the 'legitimate Government' of his country.

Some indication of the reserved attitude I maintained towards the subject of this study for long after the Nationalist victory, if not of my actual bias, is provided by the fact that his name makes no appearance in the book on Spain which I published at the end of World War II.

I may justly claim, therefore, that when I started on the documentary research and personal enquiries necessary to the preparation of the present work I was certainly no Franquista, and that I began the writing of it with a tolerably open mind. As I progressed in my investigations, however, certain convictions were overwhelmingly borne in upon my consciousness, with the result that the 'absolute objectivity' with which I set out as the literary target became more and more difficult of attainment.

Nevertheless, throughout this interpretation I have kept to facts and established truths so far as I was able to discover them for myself; and I

9

now make bold to offer the fruit of a year's labours to those interested in the hope that my book may contribute something of value towards the better understanding by the West of Spain and her enigmatic Leader, which is of such obvious and vital importance in the critical times in which we live.

In all, I have read through well over a hundred books and published documents (Spanish, French, German and English) on contemporary Spain, besides a great many articles and news items in the British and Spanish Press. Not relying for persuasion either on friends or foes of Franco, neither upon participants and witnesses of the Civil War professing definite Nationalist sympathies, nor upon those who believe that the 'Legitimate Government' of the country and the cause of Freedom and Democracy were alike overthrown by the result, I have gone to all the sources I could find to sift truth from rumour, and fact from falsehood, or mere wishful thinking or self-deception. In the appropriate places I have given apt passages and quotations from the published accounts of Republican and Government supporters, and fighters for a Proletarian Revolution, such as Colonel S. Casado, who commanded the Central Republican Army before Madrid and eventually arranged the armistice with the Nationalists, "El Campesino", the late George Orwell who fought for two years and was severely wounded on the Aragon front fighting with Anarchist troops for a pure ideal, Hamish Fraser, a former member of the International Brigades, Arthur Koestler, author of the famous Spanish Testament, and others, as well as quotations from the works of such reputable authorities as the late Professor Allison Peers, Arthur Loveday, O.B.E., Robert Sencourt, and Sir Robert Hodgson, K.C.M.G., K.B.E., Britain's first Agent to the Nationalist Administration; while foreign authorities such as Paul Schmidt, the late Count Ciano, and the relative captured German Diplomatic Papers, have not been neglected.

At the end of Chapter 16 I give my own translation of the Manifesto published by General Franco in the Canary Islands on July 17th, 1936, only a few hours after he had left on his fateful flight to Spanish Morocco in a British aircraft. This, so far as I have been able to ascertain, has never before appeared in English.

*   *   *   *

I desire to place on record my deep appreciation of the assistance and kindness unfailingly accorded me by various departments of the Spanish Foreign Office—the Ministerio de Asuntos Exteriores *in Madrid—*

in particular, to the Technical Head of the Office of Diplomatic Information, Don Luis María de Lojendio, and to the Director General of Cultural Relations, Don Luis García de Llera, and to Don José Luis Messía, Secretary General of the Institute of Hispanic Culture at University City, all of whom honour me with their friendship.

I am under a debt of gratitude to the noble lady and fine artist, the Duchess of Nájera, Condesa de Oñate, and to my oldest Spanish friend, Don Leopoldo García-Durán y Parages, and his wife Carmen Marichalar, who generously offered me the hospitality of their homes during the preparation of certain sections of my book, and to the urbane and distinguished Director General of the Spanish State Tourist Department, Don Mariano de Urzáiz y Silva, Duke of Luna, for facilities courteously accorded for brief visits to State Paradors and Albergues and for cross-country journeys: and to Mr. Cedric Salter, Press Liaison Officer to the Department, for a key introduction.

My best thanks are due to friends and former colleagues in Madrid, M. Ernest Grimaud de Caux, Mr. Henry Buckley, *author of* The Life and Death of the Spanish Republic, *and Mr. W. T. Stuttard, for anecdotes and suggestions, and to my friend Mr. Bernard Malley, C.B.E., First Counsellor at the British Embassy in Madrid, with a knowledge of Spain and Spanish Affairs extending over nearly four decades, for his ready information and advice.*

Lastly, I record my thanks to Don Andrés Revész, Diplomatic Correspondent of A B C, *Madrid, for his help in obtaining illustrations and for his personal kindness over many years; and to Sir John Balfour, K.C.M.G., lately British Ambassador to Spain, for kind permission to reproduce on page 244 his hitherto unpublished translation of Góngora's great sonnet on Córdoba.*

S. F. A. COLES

Madrid,
April, 1955.

PROLOGUE

ONLY ONE MAN HAS HEARD from the lips of the Head of the Spanish State, Generalissimo Francisco Franco's own view on the immediate prospect for Spain should Fate bring to an abrupt or unforeseen end his eighteen years' leadership of the Spanish peoples. This man, too, although born in Cuba, is a 'Gallego', or man of Galicia, the green and pleasant north-west Spanish province abutting on Portugal and celebrated for its cool heads and competent brains. He speaks fluent English, having attended Manchester University for three years between the World Wars, where he excelled in athletics, and later having passed many years of his manhood in the United States and Haiti. For over a decade now he has accompanied Franco on all the *Caudillo's* sporting trips and expeditions and is, in actual fact, in charge of them—salmon fishing in the teeming Narcea, Sella and Deva streams deep in mountainous Asturias, deep-sea fishing off Corunna or tunny fishing in the Mediterranean from Franco's 500-ton yacht *Azor*, stalking the elusive and exclusive *capra hispánica*, or ibex, in the Cantabrian alps, Spain's central mountain ranges, or red deer in the Sierra de Gredos, two hours by a good motoring road from Madrid: shooting partridge in the foothills of the Montes de Toledo, or the Sierra de Córdoba.

Max Borrell—for that is his name—is, to tell the unvarnished truth, among the two or three intimates of the Spanish leader, for Franco has very few friends around him and, by deliberate choice, for reasons of authority and policy, none at all among serving chiefs of the Armed Forces.

One day last March I sat facing Borrell, with his clear and gentle grey eyes, whitening hair and fresh, healthy complexion in his *despacho* (study) in central Madrid, across a desk tidily crowded with publications and correspondence on sport and with office walls adorned with hunting and fishing trophies and a couple of framed photographs of a proudly smiling man, of Napoleon's

13

physical stature, standing with rod or gun beside some prone carcass or a score of salmon on a line. As I turned the pages of a red-Morocco-bound album containing a selection from the unpublished photographs taken of Franco by his personal Madrid *médico*, Dr. Vicente Gil, who, by invitation, joins all his shoots and fishing trips, I learned how Franco at sixty-two can easily outdistance and outlast all the diplomats he asks by protocol to his hunting and fishing forays, and even the most active and enthusiastic members of his entourage.

"He is tough," remarked Borrell, in his soft English cadences; "his staying power is amazing. With his short, sturdy legs he will climb all day, stalking an ibex or a big-antlered buck deer, pausing only for a brief picnic luncheon, and then return at nightfall to camp to deal with State papers until the small hours. . . . Once, after following him all day in the Gredos range, with the other members of the party left a long way behind—one of them, in fact, took to his bed next day—we surprised a herd high above the State Parador. I crept along to Franco's butt expecting to find him aiming to bring down the biggest buck; but he was quietly painting the scene! 'I will try for the big one,' he said, 'when he has a better chance.' And months afterwards he returned and got him in open country."

On these expeditions with Borrell, Franco eschews all formality. "I am just Francisco Franco now, Max," he tells him, and if an occasional "*Su Excelencia*" escapes from this boon companion it is countered with a solemn stare and silence.

"Franco loves the sea," my informant continued, for I was fortunate enough to have won his confidence. "In his boyhood, you know, he wanted to be a sailor like his elder brother Nicolás.* But there were no vacancies in his year at the Naval Academy at El Ferrol, and so he entered the Army as a cadet instead. But his first love is the sea, and being a good sailor he likes it rough; he likes to see the waves bursting over the low prow of the *Azor*, decks awash and the water boiling beneath him as he hangs on to a mast or cross-bar. . . .

"One morning, off Corunna, it was exceptionally choppy and the then Military Governor of his Household, 'Pablito' as we

---

* Rear-Admiral Nicolás Franco, since the end of the Civil War Spanish Ambassador to Portugal.

called him, came to me and said: 'Tell His Excellency that the sea is too rough to go out fishing today.' But I could not do that, for how could I say so to a man like Franco, when a yacht of less tonnage than ours was plunging into the trough on our beam manned only by two youths? So I did the next thing—I told him we were all anxious for his safety, and I added: 'Think, Sir, if you should drown what would happen to Spain?' He looked at me for some moments with his dark eyes and calm, direct gaze, and then quietly replied: *'Providence would look after Spain'* ". . . .

This touching belief of the Spanish Leader, sincerely held as it may be, is, however, pitifully inadequate—even if given sufficient publicity in a censored national press—to allay the deep anxiety shared by all classes in Spain, and the majority of foreign residents, about what will happen 'after . . .' Convinced Republicans have been known to remark that they would support the present régime indefinitely "if Franco would live for ever". No one knows with any degree of certainty what would occur in the country if he had to retire for health or other reasons, or in the event of his death, and it is idle to deny that this suspense engenders very real apprehension in the hearts and minds of all elements of the population, who, however, being by nature fatalists with a deep inherited belief in Spain's destiny, carry on without any panic-signs of their ever-present worry.

Before the marriage at El Pardo of María del Carmen, the only child of the Head of the Spanish State and Doña Carmen Polo de Franco, to the Marqués de Villaverde, a Madrid doctor, the happy bridegroom was seated in one of the Palace rooms with Franco's brother-in-law, and Spain's Foreign Minister during part of World War II, the lawyer Ramón Serrano Suñer, and other family intimates, when this very question of a successor to the Spanish leader was broached. "None of us know," the ex-Minister said on this occasion, "but I am certain that the security and well-being of Spain after his death, or after he has yielded up power, occupies first place in Franco's thoughts. After all, he has the safety not only of his wife to think of and daughter, but now of his grand-children." My informant heard the account from Serrano Suñer himself in a Burgos hotel.

The fact only partially allays the prevalent anxiety that Spain has been declared a 'Monarchy', that a Council of the Realm is in being, sanctioned by free and popular vote, the five Members nominated by statute with precise functions prescribed in case of emergency. With these men the decision will rest as to which royal candidate (if any) should be invited to ascend the throne and occupy the huge and empty Palacio de Oriente overlooking the shallow Manzanares and the royal 'Casa de Campo', where so many Madrid civilians were assassinated during the Civil War. It was through this royal park, now open to the public, that Spain's last Bourbon King, Alfonso XIII, sped by car at midnight on April 13th, 1931, on his way to embark in a warship at Cartagena after receiving an ultimatum from the Republican 'Shadow-Cabinet' and its nominated President, D. Niceto Alcalá Zamora, when the Leftist swing of municipal votes in the cities seemed to presage an over-whelming majority in favour of constitutional change (the final results were, in fact, by a substantial majority actually in the King's favour). For all know that the country's destiny is in the hands of the Armed Forces, that whoever, after Franco's disap-pearance, won the allegiance of the Army and the Civil Guard would rule Spain, and that without such allegiance no king and no regent could remain, even as a symbol of order and a rallying point of loyalty, for more than a nominal period.

"Franco is a Gallego; he knows how to wait." How frequently does one hear this sentiment expressed in club, hotel, restaurant or café in Madrid and the provinces! It is the *coda* of contemporary Spain, this almost fanatical reliance on the wisdom and astuteness of one man, who has survived every conceivable pressure, who has brought his country through every hardship and calamity, just by knowing how to wait, by simply "biding his time". He bided his time with the all-conquering Hitler, who had to go to the mountain as the mountain would not go to him, when, in an interview lasting ten incredible hours he gave nothing tangible away, and rather than go through which again Hitler bitterly announced to Mussolini later at Florence that he would "sooner have four teeth out". Yet, before Franco left Madrid for this fateful encounter—fateful not only for Spain, but also in its lasting influence on the direction and fortunes of Germany's war policy—he named three of the Government Ministers in Madrid to take over his power and high responsibilities "in case I am kidnapped at Hendaye", as Ferdinand VII had been kidnapped by Napoleon. Immediately after receiving Hitler's invitation (not 'summons' be it noted) to the Hendaye discussions Franco had asked the respective Government Ministries and Departments for Spain's exact requirements in armament, equipment, materials and provisions in the event of her being forced into the war as "a willing partner of the Axis". These figures he took with him to the discussions—and multiplied by four when Hitler asked what were Spain's requirements in return for co-belligerency.

There never *was* any question so far as Franco was concerned of a German land attack on Gibraltar, because both official and non-official records of the interview left by Dr. Paul Schmidt, the German Foreign Office interpreter, by Ciano in his diaries, and in captured German State Papers, all agree that Franco declared that it was against Spain's dignity to allow any troops other than Spanish to attack the Rock from the Spanish mainland. After this severe knock to Hitler's darling plan to close the Straits and invade North Africa two full years before the Allied landings, Franco then demanded guns to equip the Spanish heavy artillery of a calibre that he knew Germany could not then spare! . . . "He is a Gallego; he knows how to wait."

After two years of calm but determined discussion and argument between the U.S. General Kissner, and his team, and the Spanish delegation, which included General Vigón, Chief of the Combined Staff, the War Minister, General Muñoz Grandes, and the Air Minister, General Gallarza, on the terms of the U.S.—Spanish Mutual Aid Pacts, eventually concluded and signed in September, 1953, it was the American negotiators who gave way. "We approached Franco first through Admiral Sherman," one of them declared in a sudden mood of expansiveness after the signing, "but he has got everything he asked for. He just tired us out." An article by Michel Clerc, its special correspondent in Madrid, published in the illustrated French weekly, *Paris-Match*, in February, 1954, affords remarkable confirmation of this *dénouement*:

> Sur les quatre bases qui seront construites (par des ouvriers espagnols)—writes Clerc—*c'est le drapeau de l'Espagne qui flottera. Ce sont des officiers espagnols qui exercent le commandement. Mais Franco a obtenu mieux: les Américains se plient aux usages du pays, paient l'impôt, et ne portent pas l'uniforme dans la rue. La mission américaine du général Kissner est composée en majeure partie d'officiers d'origine espagnole,*

2

portant des noms à consonance ibérique, vivant à l'espagnole et parlant l'espagnol, personnages incroyables que seule pouvait produire dans son brassage racial l'immense creuset américain.

Franco n'a pas seulement obtenu des Américains l'égalité. Il a obtenu la déférence. . . . *

And yet, despite the fact that Spain has never received a single dollar of Marshall Aid from the United States, which has bestowed it on former enemies and on a prosperous neutral, Sweden, which supplied Germany with iron ore and allowed German troops across her territory to impose Nazi domination on Norway—and I write as a genuine lover of Sweden—and offered it to Soviet satellites and even to Communist Russia, and despite the fact also that all of Spain's gold reserve was removed by the 'Republican' leaders, millions going to France (later recovered) and to Mexico, but the bulk of the £50,000,000 going to Moscow where it still lies, Franco, I was reliably informed in Madrid, did not haggle with the American negotiators over the financial aid clauses of the Pacts, nor ask for a single dollar. The figure of two hundred and twenty-six millions of dollars in economic aid for the first year was suggested by the American delegates and he replied, simply: *"Bien—*All right." . . .

I will reveal the length to which an honest, honourable and peace-loving neighbour of Spain was driven to bring her into Europe's strategical defence system in the teeth of the blind and pig-headed hostility of Britain and France. *The germinal idea of the U.S.—Spain Mutual Aid Pacts originated with Portugal,* as a means of bringing Spain into Western defence without the necessity of inviting her to join N.A.T.O. When the instruments were at last signed in Madrid, in the Spanish Foreign Office, British Labour

---

* "Above the four bases which will be constructed (by Spanish workmen) it is the flag of Spain that will fly. Spanish officers will be in command. But Franco has obtained better. The Americans will submit to the customs of the country, pay tax, and not wear uniform in the street. The American Mission of General Kissner consists for the greater part of officers of Spanish origin who bear Iberian-sounding names, who live in the Spanish manner and speak Spanish, incredible people whom only the immense American melting-pot could produce from its racial amalgam.

"Franco has not only obtained from the Americans equality. He has obtained deference. . . ."

and French parliamentary spokesmen had the folly and effrontery to tell the United States that she had no business to conclude them!

The recent British Ambassador to Spain, Sir John Balfour ("I am a Scot, I know nothing about Anglo-Spanish relations", he was reported to have told Spanish journalists when he took up his appointment), hesitated not a moment in acceding to my request for his impressions of the Head of the Spanish State as we sat in the plain if spacious and comfortable ambassadorial study in the Embassy building, repainted a nice green diplomatic tint, in the Street of St. Ferdinand, off the wide and beautiful Castellana avenue (the *"Avenida del Generalísimo Franco"*). "Oh," he started off, with a robust laugh, while I could scarcely get a word in edgeways—"He's a great 'bullfighter': he can play the fiercest *toro*. . . . That he has done great things for this country there is no denying. But I wish he wouldn't go spoiling my last few months in Spain, for which country I have a real affection, and in the Foreign Service,* by plugging this bloody question of Gibraltar, which is as insoluble as a Greek tragedy."

Ten thousand Madrid students had marched up the Castellana a couple of weeks previously, debouched into Fernando el Santo, and surged up to the Embassy, where a brick heaved through a first-floor window narrowly missed the Military Attaché. Indeed, the very next morning after this interview of mine with the British Ambassador an article appeared in the Phalangist daily, *Arriba*, still 'plugging the question', above the strange pseudonym "Macaulay", which I have learned is one of Franco's own pen-names.

"I have received several anonymous letters threatening my life," said Sir John, giving me a sideways look—"I suppose they will bump me off before my time is up."

"Oh, surely not, Your Excellency," I protested. "It will all blow over; the authorities have clamped down on the demonstrators and Franco himself, a knowledgeable Spanish friend informs me, was furious about the whole business. But you should have special protection."

Sir John said he had advised the appropriate Government authority—and went on to speak of the Portuguese claim to the

---

* Sir John Balfour, K.C.M.G., retired from the Diplomatic Service in July, 1954, on reaching the age limit.

Spanish town of Olivença ("look up Clause 105 of the Treaty of Vienna," he counselled as a parting and Parthian shot) and graciously accepted my enthusiastic references to his translation of Góngora's great sonnet on the poet's native Córdoba, where His Excellency had recently delivered a scholarly address in Spanish before the *Alcalde* and all the leading citizens. (See page 244.)

A month previously I had posed the same query on Franco to Britain's first accredited Diplomatic Agent to the Spanish *Caudillo* and the Nationalist Government in 1938 (and yet one still hears the view expressed by fellow-countrymen now veering round to a more objective attitude towards Spain: "Isn't it time we recognised Franco?"), Sir Robert Hodgson, K.C.M.G., K.B.E., whose important treatise, *Spain Resurgent*, had just seen the light. As we sat taking tea in the long library—"the finest lounge in Europe, I'm told," my host remarked—of that holy of holies of London clubs, the Athenæum, in Pall Mall, surrounded by grave and reverend *señores* relaxed in deep armchairs, their white hairs buried in books or post-prandial somnolence, this eighty-year-old ex-diplomat, who had been the first British agent to the Bolshevik Revolutionary Government, summed up his impressions in a Pickwickian monosyllabic monologue: "Get round any corner . . . tough fighting man . . . never daunted by odds . . . get round any corner . . . meet any difficulties."

His Excellency the Spanish Ambassador, the Duke of Primo de Rivera, Marqués de Estella, who had told me with characteristic Andalusian courtesy and hyperbole at a Columbus Day reception at 24, Belgrave Square the previous October that "the Embassy was mine", contented himself with putting forward the modest claim in his pile-carpeted ambassadorial study where I had conversed at different times with three of his predecessors, including the Republican envoy, the novelist Don Ramón Pérez de Ayala, who has returned to Spain and now contributes regularly to *A B C*, that Franco "has proved himself a statesman". Although I did not know it at the time the Ambassador had been at the British Foreign Office the day before to protest about the projected visit to Gibraltar of Her Majesty Queen Elizabeth II at the end of her tour of British Dominions and territories overseas; but I thought His Excellency seemed thoughtful and a shade less genial than at previous meetings. . . .

"Franco?—a charming man, gentle and unassuming", Sir Patrick Hannon, former M.P. for a Birmingham constituency, volunteered in response to my importuning at an Hispanic Council Canning House reception in London—"but that was twenty years ago, mind you, when he was Governor of the Canaries where he received me during a call of the ship on which I was returning from a trip to Tristan da Cunha and the South Atlantic. He had a delightful smile, I recollect."

I approached next a fellow-member of the Authors' Club, Douglas Jerrold, the publisher and historian and former editor of *The English Review*. He was personally and directly concerned, as we shall later see, in the 'plot' to save Spain from what Right-wing elements in both countries believed to be approaching chaos and ruin, and also in the provision of the aeroplane from Croydon piloted by Captain C. E. W. Bebb, and carrying as a 'blind' Major H. E. B. Pollard with a niece and a friend of hers, and Don Luis Bolín, former London correspondent of *A B C*, which, by previous arrangement, 'kidnapped' Franco in early July, 1936, when he was on a visit from Tenerife to Las Palmas—ostensibly for the funeral of the Military Commander of the Islands, General Balmes, mysteriously killed a few days earlier—and landed him first at Casablanca and then at Tetuan, where the military rising against the disintegrating Republic began.

"You met Franco at his Salamanca Headquarters during the Civil War: what did you think of him?" I asked, as we sat facing each other across Jerrold's desk in a book-lined first-floor room of Eyre and Spottiswoode, publishers, of Bedford Street, Strand.

Jerrold, third-generation descendant and namesake of a boon companion of Charles Dickens, whose glance and features remind you of a caged eagle, darted his piercing gaze at me as he slowly remarked: "An impression of power. A man of cool head and long-sightedness—qualities which are far from being essentially Spanish. . . . Of course, many years as ruler may have changed him, but he struck me as a man of great simplicity."

It may not be out of place here to quote the description of the Spanish Leader given by Hitler's official interpreter, Paul Schmidt, at the historic Hendaye encounter:

Short and stout, dark-skinned, with lively black eyes, the Spanish dictator sat in Hitler's coach. In the pictures I had seen of him he had always looked much taller and slimmer. If he were wearing a white burnous he might have been taken for an Arab. . . . His hesitant, tentative way of putting forward his arguments seemed to confirm this impression. It was at once clear to me that Franco, a prudent negotiator, was not to be nailed down.*

The late Duke of Berwick and Alba, wartime Spanish Ambassador in London, made no bones about his conviction after the end of hostilities that Franco should make room "for my King".†

"Why does Spain not get Marshall Aid?"I demanded of His Grace and Excellency one morning in June, 1949, essaying a change of argument as I sat in his fifth-floor study adorned with portraits of the famous, including signed portraits of King George VI and Churchill, and of course of the Spanish Pretender, overlooking his ancestral palace of Liria. This was just then slowly rising from its Civil War ruins ("the Government has given me no penny of compensation," he said). Two floors beneath us was the fabulous Alba private museum with its holograph letters of Charles V, Philip II, and Columbus, and the original lists of the crews of the caravels *Niña*, *Santa María* and *Pinta* with which the discovery of America was accomplished, and of other paladins of Spain's history, not forgetting his illustrious if implacable ancestor who had executed the Flemish patriot, Count Egmont, Fernando Alvarez de Toledo, the 'Great' Duke of Alba. The duke's diplomatic passport, the privilege for life of a Spanish ex-Ambassador, had only just been returned to him after confiscation because of his royalist activities.

"Because the Western Powers," he roundly declared, "will have nothing to do with this man," adding somewhat testily: "He saved Spain in her great crisis; none can deny that . . . now he should step down." I was reminded of a 'middle' I had read by Don Salvador de Madariaga in the London *Spectator* some four years previously, bearing the peremptory title: "Franco must Go!"

"But," I butted in, "he has had Spain declared a Monarchy."

Alba's proud and essentially noble features seemed to light up

---

* *Hitler's Interpreter*, by Dr. Paul Schmidt: Heinemann, 1951 (p. 194).
† Alba, who was fourteen times a Grandee of Spain, had originally agreed to act as Franco's agent in London, and afterwards as Spanish Ambassador, on the understanding that the Monarchy was restored as soon as the national emergency was over.

with some inner conflagration, as he snorted: "A Monarchy—
yes . . . a Monarchy without a king!"

One afternoon in January, 1954, I asked a former war-time
colleague in the European Division of the B.B.C., who had
broadcast weekly in Spanish to Spain between the years 1940 to
1944 on the same theme of Franco making himself scarce and
leaving room for a new democracy, whether he believed that the
Gallego who knew how to wait would go down in Spanish
history as a great patriot. "I am quite sure he won't," my former
colleague, a Lecturer in Spanish at a leading British University,
retorted. "He has been very skilful in playing active and poten-
tially hostile elements in Spain one against the other, and that is
the sole secret of his survival and, from the point of view of
posterity, of his fame. But the long-term results of his rule will, in
my opinion, prove disastrous. . . . You should read Ansaldo's
book, ¿Para Qué? published about ten years ago, I think, in South
America. That will give you the low-down on Franco." The
British Museum Library, however, has no copy of this important
work, and neither has Canning House.*

I knew that my friend had met General Franco when he visited
London in 1936 as representative of the Spanish Army, of which
he was then Chief, at the funeral of King George V—who was
Honorary Colonel of the 8th (Zamora) Regiment, deriving from
Irish Jacobite mercenaries—when he marched in the funeral
cortège behind the Soviet Marshal Tukhachevsky—later 'liquidated' by Stalin with the cheerful advocacy of Vishinsky, then the
Soviet Public Prosecutor (Franco took his meals at the Martinez
Spanish restaurant in Swallow Street, off Piccadilly, and chose to
visit the Zoological Gardens in Regents Park "as children are so
amusing with animals", although he had particularly wished to
visit Woolwich and Sandhurst), and I asked for impressions.

"Just like any other Spanish general," my friend replied. "I met
him at a cocktail party at the Embassy. He seemed to me very
ordinary."

I cannot help regarding this description by my former colleague,
however, as a calculated under-estimate of Franco's impact on
anyone meeting him for the first time. Whatever the Spanish
leader's stature may be—and Napoleon was a little man, and so is

* See Epilogue.

that 'pocket battleship', my eminent friend, the Right Hon.
Leopold S. Amery, c.h.—his is not an ordinary personality, and
he is worlds away from being an ordinary Spaniard. Franco is,
indeed, both an extra-ordinary and an extraordinary Spaniard,
combining charm with Roman severity and Anglo-Saxon
phlegm, and cool-headedness with Iberian obduracy. "Beneath
a mellow, gentle, adipose exterior," a British Press correspondent
reported from Salamanca, "there is an iron firmness. It
is clear that he is adored by his men." The description
might have been written by Goethe after his celebrated meeting
with Napoleon at Weimar—("this pocket general," Ivan Maisky,
Ambassador in Britain of the U.S.S.R., had sneered at the first
meeting in London of the Non-Intervention Committee).

"Franco is devoid of nerves," another Press historian wrote;
"his tireless handling of every kind of problem provided proofs of
ability which marked him out for the supreme leadership of the
Nationalist forces. He has a Napoleonic grasp of military, civil,
and economic affairs." "A clear-headed strategist and organiser,"
wrote yet another correspondent, "an iron disciplinarian, a man
famed for his bravery." Famed for his bravery? Yes, for in
Morocco where he suffered a grave intestinal wound while
leading his Legionarios at the battle of Buit, he was known as
"el más valiente de los valientes"—"the bravest of the brave". . . .
"For three months before the Civil War broke out," the Duchess
of Nájera remarked, as we were returning one afternoon from a
twenty-mile ride on horseback over the immense, boulder-strewn
Avila plains to her country home at Pedrosillo, where I was
fortunate enough to be staying as a guest—"the belief was everywhere expressed among Traditional circles in Spain that General
Franco was the only man who could save the country from ruin
and slavery." An ancestor of her husband had been ducal protector and friend of St. Ignatius of Loyola.

As a boy at El Ferrol, in the north-west corner of Galicia, as a
young cadet at the Military Academy (infantry) in the Alcazar at
Toledo, as the youngest lieutenant in the Spanish Army, he was
known, in the pleasant Spanish way of bestowing on those
considered worthy of it affectionate diminutives, as 'Paco', by
which he is still called by Doña Carmen Polo de Franco, or
'Paquito' —little Francisco— and sometimes to all and sundry as
'Franquito', and when he became the youngest major his sobriquet

was 'el Comandantín'. As a young man he was quiet, serious and studious, possessor of 'a winning smile', yet with a strong character which made itself evident from his earliest years. "A deceptively quiet air," runs a pre-Civil War account; "he is completely devoid of fear, imaginative and resourceful . . . a fine and respected commander of native troops."

A race (perhaps, with the British, the most pertinacious in Europe) which vanquished and expelled after seven centuries of occupation the ubiquitous Arab invader who had saturated every corner of the peninsula, with the exception of some deep caves in mountainous Asturias from where the Visigothic chieftain, Pelayo, sallied forth with a few nobles on the then seemingly hopeless 'Reconquest'; a race which ejected from national soil after even more centuries the powerful and insidiously prosperous Jewish communities which had assisted the Arabs in their invasion of Spain; a race which had smashed the would-be world-conquering Ottoman Power at Lepanto, almost within sight of immortal Salamis, where Cervantes lost his left hand "to the greater glory of his right" in a hand-to-hand engagement to which he ever afterwards referred as the proudest event of his life; a race which, with its bare hands, rose in Madrid and other cities against 'King' Joseph Bonaparte ('Pepe Botella'—'Joe Bottle', as he was derisively called by the irreverent Madrileños) after the death of the patriots Daoiz and Velarde, and vomited forth the Napoleonic armies: such a race, like God—if the comparison may be made without blasphemy—is not mocked. Your Spaniard, Left-, Right-, Middle-, or Monarchist-wing, knows as well as anyone what is what.

The Assyrian god, Ashtar, or Marduck, who symbolised order and resistance to anarchy and chaos, is always depicted in the ancient Assyrian monuments carrying a spear. "This man" Franco, the "narrow-minded tyrant" of Churchill's parliamentary harangues, the "Fascist cut-throat" of Stalin and his 'democratic' satellites, the *bête-noire* and the despair of so many genuine Western lovers of peace and order, is the living embodiment of the Assyrian symbol for his countrymen and countrywomen.

"*Hay orden en el país*—there is order in the country." It is the standard sentiment everywhere in modern Spain, even though that sentiment was decisively qualified by a Spanish fellow-passenger in a train from Santander to San Sebastian in which I happened to be travelling in the summer of 1949 with the broadside: *"Sí, es el orden de un cementerio"*! "He was a *Republicano*," explained the other friendly passengers in my carriage as the man walked up the platform and, for all I know to the contrary, joined others of like opinion in some lonely corner of the Concha beach—"a *Separatista*".

Ashtar, or Marduck—carrying a spear. If Spain were not a Catholic land, *"muy católica"* as my driver emphasised in our conversations as he drove me through Andalusia and the Levante in January, 1953 (he frequently described of his own volition certain activities of the Left-wing elements during the Civil War as *"una infamia"*), the Assyrian God of Order might well be incised on the obverse of the *duro*, the five-peseta piece which bears Franco's now familiar profile and likeness: *"FRANCISCO FRANCO CAUDILLO DE ESPAÑA POR LA G. DE DIOS"*.

Yet in the dangerous years of his early manhood, when he saw death and mutilation in their most horrible guises in the daily sorties against the fierce Riffs in Spanish Morocco, Franco was not always "quiet and studious", although, like Subaltern Churchill in a more peaceful India, he studied history, the lives of great military commanders and the ancient Stoics and philosophers, in his off-duty hours, and works on political science. Photographs of him at North African base camps, as the youngest captain in the Spanish Army, as the youngest major, relaxing in the Prince of Asturias' Regiment in Asturias itself, after recovering from his wounds, show him with alert visage and a lively and attractive smile.

A film of amateur status still survives in Madrid, taken by Don Natalio Rivas, now a hale ninety-five years old, in which Franco makes an occasional energetic and grinning appearance as a handsome young officer-hero from the African wars, in company with some of the leading political and social luminaries of the Madrid of three generations back, and noble ladies of the capital's society who were persuaded to act small 'parts' in this now historic screen 'story'. I learned of it from one who has seen it, Doña Marcela de Juan de López de la Cámara, whose father was a Chinese Mandarin and who speaks five languages fluently and publishes standard Spanish translations of the Chinese classical poets—she approximates in Spain, in fact, to Arthur Waley in England.

Thus, despite his popular reputation outside Spain, Franco was no upstart military adventurer when 'the troubles' started in his country. Springing from good middle-class stock settled for centuries in Galicia, son of a pious Galician mother and a naval paymaster in the naval dockyards at El Ferrol who died in 1942 with the rank of General of Marines, he mixed from early childhood in social circles, was known to the best Madrid homes and cultural elements, and as a brave and competent officer to successive Governments. An avowed Monarchist, he gave, as a soldier who had taken the solemn oath to defend with his life the united Spain won by the fabulous "Catholic Monarchs" Ferdinand and Isabella, honest service to the Republic until lawlessness and anarchy usurped the Government's duty, responsibility and immemorial prerogatives. "Our victory has not been over our brothers," he declared in a speech at Burgos on February 27th, 1939, "but over the world, over international forces, over Communism, over Freemasonry." Indeed, he has something of an obsession about Freemasonry, but it must be remembered that most of the Republican Ministers submitted to the Grand Oriente.

When the Leader of the Right-wing Opposition party in the Cortes (which, because of their majority, should actually have been called to govern the country by the Republican President, Alcalá Zamora), the economist and ex-minister Calvo Sotelo, was abducted from his home in Velasquez Street on the night of July 13th, 1936, by armed Guardias de Asalto in full uniform and his dead body showing bullets through the neck (like the thousands of corpses of slaughtered Polish officers found in the Katyn forest) discovered next morning in an outlying cemetery ("*el orden de un cementerio*".), Franco was already famous in Spain as a brave soldier and a remarkably competent administrator. More than a decade before that, it was to him and not to his superior generals, Cabanellas, Sanjurjo, Mola—all of whom served in Spanish Africa—nor even to the first and now legendary commander of the Spanish Foreign Legion, the often-wounded Millán-Astray, that the Dictator Primo de Rivera turned for expert opinion on the speediest way to resolve the Moroccan dilemma, which was Spain's Indo-China of the time and an exhaustive drain on her best blood and treasure. It was the young Colonel Franco ("the youngest colonel in the

Spanish Army"), the intrepid commander of the *Bandera*,
or First Battalion, of the Legion, who advised against panic
evacuation of Spanish North Africa after the terrible disaster of
Anual, where a whole army perished, which several of the
Ministers in Madrid were proposing; and it was Franco's plan for
a decisive landing in the bay of Alhucemas which Primo de
Rivera adopted and which marked the turning of the tide of
fortune in the long and bloody wars against the Riffs led by the
obdurate and implacable Abd-el-Krim.

("Colonel Franco has the finest strategical brain in Europe,"
had declared the French Marshal, Lyautey—whose fine memorial
monument I passed recently in La Rochelle—after meeting him
in French Morocco).

. . .

Did Francisco Franco, army general, in a vulgar lust for
power and in contempt of the democratically expressed will of
the Spanish nation, rise against the 'Legitimate Government of
Spain' in July, 1936, and, after the bloodiest and most bitterly
fought Civil War in Europe's (but not in America's) history,
impose an iron dictatorship on the country, which not only
the disinterested gentlemen in the Kremlin but also many sincere
Western democrats honestly believe continues up to the
present day? Under the Republican régime Spain had experienced
twenty-eight different governments in fifty months—but then
the administrations of inimitable France come and go with equal
celerity and French generals do not rise up in armed protest. That
the Nationalists won the fighting war in Spain and lost the
propaganda war beyond Spain's frontiers is a platitude, but, like
many platitudes, the co-relative profundity of it has been completely lost in its superficial truth.

An objective analysis of the entire question will be made in
later sections of this work. We are only concerned in these
opening gambits to show the most controversial figure on the
world's stage today as a living, breathing, feeling human being,
and to leave the identification of his right place and significance
in Spanish history, among its 'good' or 'bad' rulers, to the reader's
own judgment after presenting the bare facts of his life, his
known political opinions, his fateful decisions and actions, and
from the record of his speeches, all of which are, of course, on

record—or the large majority—in bound volumes published by the State or individual Spanish publishers, some in good English translations. . . .

II

Franco does not smoke and neither Ministers of his Cabinet nor visitors of any grade are permitted to smoke in his presence in the white, 17th-century ex-royal Palace of El Pardo, some fourteen miles outside Madrid towards the Sierra, which he occupies with his wife on an indefinite 'grace and favour' lease from the State. This veto must be a sore trial for some associates and callers, for the average Spaniard still 'smokes like a chimney' as in Borrow's time. The only place which Franco regards as home—although he has a brand new house, filled with antiques, on a spur of the Guadarrama mountains which an admirer, the late Conde de las Almenas, presented to him but which he seldom uses (his only daughter spent her honeymoon there some years ago) is the Pazo de Meirás, an estate near Corunna given to him by that Galician seaport. This he has enlarged and improved and filled with his own things and favourite knick-knacks.

He is an inveterate talker and has the reputation of being a brilliant conversationalist. He likes to stand all the time, or pace up and down the room, while speaking. "He goes on talking for hours," a Madrid friend of twenty years, not many months back confided to me with a laugh, "and scarcely gives his Ministers any chance to slip away for ordinary necessities, to which he himself appears to be practically impervious." "He must have an iron self-control," said another, remarking on the same rare attribute when describing hunting and fishing expeditions with the *Caudillo* and the subterfuges to which hard-pressed members of his entourage and participating diplomats are put to to avoid discomfort.

Since his campaigning years in Africa, where he was an enigma to the Moors because, I was reliably informed, "he never went with women and at that time did not go to Mass" and where he later won their devoted and lasting respect as a *Beraka*—"heaven-protected"—by riding at the head of his battalion on a white charger in the most perilous positions, seeming to bear a charmed life—since those hard years he "swears like a trooper" on occasion, and is not above telling a 'blue' story when out salmon-fishing in the north or deer-stalking in the south.

If he "never went to Mass" in Africa, he has since followed the national impulse and tradition in identifying himself as a devout Catholic. The well-known journalist, Kees Van Hoek, in an article entitled *Franco Rules Without Fear*, which appeared some two years ago in a British national weekly, wrote that "husband and wife invariably say the Rosary together before retiring at night, ending with Franco's self-composed prayer: 'Lord, Who entrusted Spain to my hands, do not deny me the grace of handing a Spain back to You which is truly Catholic'."

At El Pardo he rises at eight, and plays tennis for an hour before breakfast. He hears Mass in the palace chapel on Sundays and Feast Days at ten. He always keeps on a reading table at the head of his bed the right hand of St. Teresa of Avila, whom some Spaniards think really directs the destinies of modern Spain, and it always accompanies him on a journey. This relic, so precious in the sight of devout Spaniards, who bracket the Saint with Isabella the Catholic as a patriot and with St. John of the Cross as the greatest of Spanish mystics, was originally preserved in the Convent of the Discalzed Carmelites at Lisbon but later found its way to their Reformed house—also founded by the Saint in person during her innumerable peregrinations—at Malagón. Here during the Civil War it was taken off by a captain in the 'Loyalist' army, presumably because of the valuable silver encasement, but recovered by the Nationalist forces which liberated the region, since when it has remained in the personal possession of the Head of the State.*

Such "fanaticism", as this cult of relics seems to the Protestant mind, never comes as a surprise in Catholic Spain where religion is 'hot' news and accorded comparable space and importance in the papers to crime and suicide in the American and French Press and divorce and homosexual cases in the British national dailies; where, indeed, it is no uncommon thing to read (as I read only recently in the leading Madrid daily, *A B C*) such headlines as

---

* "*La mano se conserva en el Palacio de El Pardo, bajo la custodia del Caudillo, que la tuvo durante la Cruzada española iluminando su génio militar.*"—Guía de Avila, por R. Gomez Montero y L. Belmonte Díaz: 1946.

"In Honour of the Archangel St. Gabriel—Patron of the Leather-
workers and the Foreign Service", to turn into a thoroughfare
bearing the comforting but unusual name of "*Calle del Amor de
Dios*—Love of God Street", or to find that such a transcendental
mystic as Santa Teresa is the revered Patron of the Army Service Corps, on the initiative of the late King Alfonso XIII—
perhaps because of her well-known saying, that "God is also
found among the pots and pans."

On the day (a weekday) after my return to Madrid in March,
1954, some *sixteen thousand* people visited the Church of the
Capuchins, in Medinacelli Street, near the Palace Hotel. A long
queue could be seen all day and half the night hugging the walls
of the narrow Calle de Cervantes opposite, in which the immortal
author of *Don Quijote* died, and I had to negotiate my way past a
line of city police keeping order at the church steps before I could
enter to see what all the excitement was about. "There's a bit of
fanaticism there," said a very good friend I shall mention again,
who works in an office in the same street. Her soldier father was
killed at Anual; her mother hails from the Canary Islands, descendant of a Guanche princess. But perhaps such intensity of piety
is better interpreted, in this case of the "cola de Jesús" in the
Capuchin church, as:

> The desire of the moth for the star,
> Of the day for the morrow:
> The devotion to something afar
> From the sphere of our sorrow.

·   ·   ·

"In former years his voice was high-pitched—*ra-ra-ra-ra*!—
just like that!" said a lady who carried out noble works of mercy
in the Civil War, "but it's better now." She told me, what I
had divined already, that Franco places the interests of Spain
before all other considerations and is not bound by any sense of
gratitude for services given or benefits received if events militate
against such recognition. This was proved effectively enough
in his dealings with Hitler and Mussolini, and later in the banish-
ment to the Balearic Islands for Monarchist activities of General
Aranda, who had made an outstanding contribution to the
Nationalist victory by his heroic defence of Oviedo, where
every street and almost every house had to be fought for *cuerpo a*

cuerpo—body to body, after the general had publicly echoed the view of Madariaga and the Duke of Alba that it was time Franco stepped down. And General Queipo de Llano, who held Seville for the Nationalists, once complained of his "monumental ingratitude."

It is perhaps not without significance that the imposing framed portrait of the Spanish Leader in the elegant reception room of the Spanish Embassy in Belgrave Square, London, is inscribed in his own firm hand to "The Spanish Ambassador in London" and not to any particular Envoy by name.

III

Mature consideration of the situation in Spain today leads to one of two conclusions: either that Franco has come to enjoy power so much that he cannot relinquish it, or that he will not be deflected an inch from the course he has set himself, from his conception of his duty which he has publicly stated many times is the lasting "defeat of 19th-century Liberalism" which he avers brought Spain to disaster. "We have liquidated the 19th century," he declared at Valencia as long ago as May, 1939, "which should never have existed"—and the raising of Spain to the status of a Great Power again and an arbiter of weight in the future destiny of Europe.

"He *knows* he is right," the wife of a Spanish friend remarked to me in London. "Spain did not lose a million men, and God knows how many women, with thousands of unoffending people, including priests, monks and nuns, vilely assassinated, for Franco to hand back the country to his enemies who might well plunge us again into a similar catastrophe." These sentiments were exactly echoed to me in Madrid by Señorita Pilar Primo de Rivera, the sister of José Antonio, the founder of the *Falange* shot in the civil prison at Alicante on direct orders from the Popular Front Government in Madrid after he had convinced the Tribunal and all the spectators at his trial that he was guilty of nothing but a fervent patriotism. (You can still see the marks of the bullets on the courtyard walls where he was executed—"passed by the arms" in the Spanish euphemism—after giving comfort and encouragement to four Nationalists who were shot before him). As we conversed in her spacious office in the Calle de

Almagro two assistants entered whose fathers, she told me, were murdered in Madrid by the *chekas*.

Casanova, self-styled 'Sieur de Siengalt', writing his scabrous but highly interesting memoirs in the castle at Dux, Bohemia, where he passed his innocuous old age as librarian, said: "France is sick; in any other country this might be remedied, but I would not wonder if it proved incurable in France." Spain was sick in the middle thirties as I saw for myself, and daily growing 'sicker'. The drastic treatment prescribed by the organisers of the National rising in 1936 and applied *"aunque os pese"*—"come what may: despite everything", a typical Spanish attitude—by the chosen military leader Franco, has made him outside Spain for two decades the most hated and controversial figure in the world. Could a less terrible cure have been found, when, as one contemporary English writer on the Civil War avers, "the whole driving force behind the 'Popular Government' was atheistical Bolshevism aiming at world domination"? In the preface to the second edition of his *Spanish Labyrinth* Gerald Brenan claims that responsibility for governing the country was about to fall anyway into the hands of the Right and that the military rising was both wicked and unnecessary.

The question is of key historical and contemporary importance and the answer to it is to be found not only in the cool and deliberate actions of one man faced with one of the greatest crises in all European history, but in the character of the Spanish race itself. "We would rather die than submit," a Finnish lady said to me one morning in June, 1952, as we shared a table for lunch in the 'water-coach' between Hameenlinna, where Sibelius went to school, and Aulanko (we were discussing Finland's now legendary stand against the Russian invasion). Spain in her Civil War demonstrated, *on both sides*, the same unyielding spirit, by men and women alike: for the dynamic propelling force of the Spanish character is heroism in the face of personal annihilation and a total inability to compromise.

In one of the most penetrating and perceptive studies ever penned on Spain and the Spanish, an essay which appeared in the *Revue de Paris* in June, 1925, that is six years before the fall of the Monarchy and eleven years before the outbreak of the Civil War, the French Academician, Jean Cassou, serving up in essay form a lecture he had first given at the Collège de France and later

3

repeated in the Théâtre du Vieux-Colombier in Paris, has these profound things to say of the Spanish:

Que l'Espagnol, comme le Juif et le Russe, soit porteur d'une mission, cela n'est pas douteux. Il est choisi; il répond à une terre indiscutablement significative et à des souvenirs dont lui seul peut soutenir la charge et comprendre la volonté. . . . L'idée de l'Espagne est dense comme les métaux les plus denses, compacte, résistante et profonde.

("That the Spaniard, like the Jew and the Russian, is the bearer of a mission cannot be doubted. He is chosen; he reacts to a land which is indisputably significant and to memories of which he alone can support the burden and comprehend the impulse. . . . The idea of Spain is dense like the densest metals, compact, resistant and profound.")

On a souvent parlé de l'individualisme espagnol. . . . Mais il faut compléter cette notion de l'individualisme espagnol par celle du phénomène qu'on a appelé l'adamisme espagnol, c'est-à-dire que chaque créature espagnole se trouve dans la position d'Adam, le premier homme. . . . L'Espagne est, de tous les pays, celui qui peut le plus produire des individualités originales, puissantes, libres, prêtes à se développer jusqu'à leurs points extrêmes. . . .

("One has often spoken of Spanish individualism. . . . But one must complete this notion of Spanish individualism with that of the phenomenon which has been called Spanish *Adamism, i.e.* that each Spanish creature is in the position of Adam, the first man. . . . Spain is of all countries the one which can most produce original individualities, powerful, free, and ready to develop to their ultimate limits.")

L'Espagnol, naissant dans la solitude, que nul préjugé ni nulle épreuve n'ont instruit, et qui, s'il sent le désir de s'exprimer, le fera sans règle, sans direction et sans ordre, est l'être le plus libre et le plus absolu. Aucune discipline ne l'attache, aucun vœu, aucune aspiration plus forte que la sienne.

("The Spaniard, born in solitude, whom no prejudice and no test have informed, and who, if he feels the desire to express himself, will do so without rule, without direction, and without order, is the freest and most absolute being. No discipline, no vow, no aspiration stronger than his own binds him.")

And, finally, summing up the whole 'Spanish problem' in one sentence, Cassou roundly declares:

*Le phénomène espagnol nous conduit à mesurer dans toute son immensité
le néant qui nous constitue; mais au bord de cette effrayante considération,
un effort soudain, et le plus puissant qui soit, nous ressaisit et nous rejette
au milieu d'une flambée de vie libre et aventureuse . . . nous devons
être reconnaissants à l'Espagne d'avoir assumé, par les déséquilibres qui la
composent et la déchirent, le visage tragique de l'humanité.*

("The Spanish phenomenon leads us to measure in all its immensity
the nothingness which constitutes us; but beside this frightening consideration, a sudden effort, the most powerful possible, grips us
again and casts us back into the midst of a flame of free and adven-
turous life. . . . We must recognise that Spain has assumed, by the
disequilibriums which constitute and sunder her, the tragic features
of humanity.")

When we other peoples of the West, with our individualism
and primitive characteristics tamed by centuries of civic order and
discipline, and freely elected governments, by the give and take
implicit in the very word "compromise", a word without meaning
for the average Spaniard: when we speak of the need for Spain to
return to a democratic way of life, to democratic institutions and
constitutional government, these profound sentiments on the
Spanish character, published thirty years ago by one of the most
acute minds in France, may well be brought forward for the
serious study of statesmen, politicians and the man-in-the-street.
For they are the facets of the Iberian 'diamond' which make the
Spanish the most intractable people in the world to govern. The
old adage that "a woman and a horse display their best qualities
under a firm hand" needs amplification to include the phrase,
"and the Spaniard".

The terrible crisis which faced Spain in the early summer of
1936 had its exact parallels after the first World War in the
Soviet régimes temporarily imposed on Hungary by Bela Kun
and on Bavaria by Kurt Eisner, and after World War II in
Greece, where, with house to house fighting in the heart of
Athens, the Communists attempted a similar *coup d'état*. Indeed,
I have heard (off the record) from the lips of the Allied Commander-in-Chief in Greece at that time, General Sir Ronald
Scobie, how British sappers discovered in the nick of time stacks
of high explosives which had been planted underground along
the route the British Prime Minister was to take the very next
day from the Piraeus to the British Embassy in Athens to

meet the late Archbishop Damaskinos and the members of the Greek Provisional Government. "I begged Churchill to see them in the British warship in Phaleron Bay on board of which he was to sleep," Sir Ronald confided, "but he insisted on driving up to Athens."

When I gave a talk, by invitation, after a longer address on Spain as an Atlantic and Mediterranean Power, to the members of the N.A.T.O. Defense College in Paris in June, 1953, on the origins of the Civil War I was surprised when the Greek member, a colonel in the Greek Army, rose at the end and remarked that everything I had said about Spain was paralleled in Greek post-war experience. The Greek Premier, Marshal Papagos, said the same thing during his official visit to Spain last October.

At a meeting of homage to the memory of Sir Rabindranath Tagore, at which I was present one evening in the winter of 1944 at the Conway Hall, London (the Dean of Canterbury was on the platform in company with Dr. Negrín, the last 'Republican' Premier of Spain who, according to the *Causa General*, took three hundred million pesetas out of the country), the then Soviet Ambassador, Ivan Maisky, cryptically declared: "Europe is a jungle; none knows who are friends or enemies." Franco at least has been left in no doubt; his enemies have been everywhere vocal, and even stridently vocal, for nearly two decades. If they have persuaded a large part of the world that he took up arms in July, 1936, against the 'Legitimate Government' and murdered the bright hope of Spanish democracy, he himself and a not inconsiderable proportion of the Spanish nation think otherwise. Their sentiments unconsciously echo, in fact, the concluding statement of Churchill's memoirs of World War II: "We gave thanks to God for the noblest of all His blessings, the sense that we had done our duty," his duty to his country being also the characteristic preoccupation of a Spanish patriot.

I V

Would it, in fact, have been so preposterous for Franco to have harboured a similar thought when, after the liberation of Madrid and the broadcast of his last war bulletin: "The war has ended," following in the tradition of the Cid Campeador after the liberation of Toledo, of St. Ferdinand after the wresting of

Seville from the Moors, and the Catholic Sovereigns when 'El Rey Chico' Boabdil rendered up the keys of Granada after seven centuries of Arab occupation, he publicly laid his sword on the high altar of the beautiful church of Santa Bárbara, situated behind the Madrid Courts of Justice?

The instinct of patriotism and love of country—as strong as any of the other instincts natural to man—is not the sole prerogative of the English-speaking race, as we sometimes seem to think, nor even of all peoples with the exception of Spaniards; it is also an ingrained Spanish emotion. When a British business man living at that time in Spain told a visiting Harley Street doctor that "you could get a man shot for five dollars under the Republic" he may have been shooting a democratic line, but the evidence and the statement are against such a supposition.

If the signing of the U.S.—Spanish Mutual Aid Pacts demonstrated anything it was this: that the continuing close alliance and understanding between Washington, Paris and London is not now the only vital factor in the preservation of peace in Europe. American realists have secured an alternative foothold on the European mainland, and now, with the willing and, indeed, inevitable support of Spain and most of Latin-America, could confront from the Iberian peninsula a Russian avalanche even with an England "which never did nor never shall lie at the proud foot of a conqueror" atomised or paralysed by atomic attack. Franco has achieved this outstanding diplomatic victory by 'biding his time' and in the face of the cold determination of French and British (and Soviet) statesmen to block elementary justice or fairplay for Spain, such as a share in Marshall Aid and a voice in international affairs.

During the latter years of his Presidency, Roosevelt (quoting Emerson) admonished Americans that "the only way to have a friend is to be one," an admonition they forgot in their post-war relations with Spain, but which they are now in process of taking to heart. In an article contributed to the London *Daily Telegraph* on February 23rd, 1939, under the banner-heads: "Can Franco Restore Unity and Strength to Spain?—How Britain and France May Aid Him in the Great Task of Peace", Winston Churchill, then of course out of office, made public these pregnant words:

> We seek a united, independent Spain, making the best of itself apart from Europe. . . . The interest of the British Empire is in fact

identical with that of all Spain. Spanish peace, Spanish prosperity, Spanish independence are all that we seek. . . . To Spain we use the invocation of the great Pitt—"Be one People". For the outside world our policy should be "Hands off Spain".

And he went on to say:

I have several times reminded the readers of these columns that Franco was a Republican General who gave full warning to the Spanish Government of the political anarchy into which they were drifting.

He now has the opportunity of becoming a great Spaniard of whom it may be written a hundred years hence: that he united his country and rebuilt its greatness. Apart from this, he reconciled the past with the present, and broadened the life of the working people while preserving the faith and structure of the Spanish nation. Such an achievement would rank in history with the work of Ferdinand and Isabella and the work of Charles V. The strong hand of Britain and France would aid him in his task.*

The extraordinary thing is that "such an achievement"—with the possible exception of "reconciling the past with the present" and proving himself a Spanish Abraham Lincoln, as the late Professor Allison Peers hoped—is, in fact, credited to Franco today even by many of his former opponents; but "the strong hand of Britain and France", far from aiding has, from calculated political aversion and with cold and sustained deliberation, impeded him in his task. Little Portugal, however, never ceased to raise her voice in support of Spain's inclusion firstly within the scope of the Marshall Plan and, immediately after, within that of the North Atlantic Pact. Moreover, it is widely known that she raised the matter of Spain's admission whenever it was possible to cause the other Members to reflect on the absurdity of excluding Spain from an organization embracing the forces of the Western World intended to bar the way to the new communist imperialism. I am in a position to assert that, *on the very morning of the signing of the Pact*, Portugal did not fail to draw attention to the gap which would be left in the Atlantic Pact as the result of the non-inclusion of Spain.

---

* This and other of Churchill's writings and speeches containing references to Franco and Spain have been published in translation in a volume on sale in Madrid.

Is then, "that narrow-minded tyrant" of a Churchillian *arrière-pensée*, that "Fascist cut-throat", of the Moscow daily propaganda diatribes, who is still, after eighteen years, "imposing on Spain his repressive régime against the democratic will of the people," worthy of the friendship, not alone of the powerful United States of America, but of the Western World as a political and defensive unity? Does he "deserve" it?—to call upon a favourite democratic syllogism.

Vamos a ver—Let us (go to) see.

BOOK ONE

'*It is dangerous to believe and to disbelieve; therefore it is far better that the truth should be thoroughly searched, than that a foolish opinion should pervert your judgement.*'

PLATO'S DIALOGUES (PHAEDRUS)

Chapter One

I CROSS NORTHERN SPAIN

As I had been entrusted with the authorship of a portrait from life of the "last of the Dictators" (west of the Iron Curtain) of a "Fascist cut-throat" and "narrow-minded tyrant" under whose "grim oppressive rule" the Spanish nation had for so long been groaning, it seemed advisable that a visit should be paid to the far corner of north-western Spain where such a monster and mountebank was born.

One morning the trunk line between Paris and Madrid buzzed for a few moments, with the result that a car with driver was at Santillana del Mar a week later to convey me along the narrow coastal road through the Cantabrian Range, in the lee of the towering, majestic snow-clad summits of the Picos de Europa, to the chief Spanish naval port of El Ferrol 'del Caudillo'. . . .

The day's journey from Irún to Santander I made in the tri-weekly *autobús* from castled Fuenterrabía, the picturesque and historic Basque frontier town overlooking the Bidasoa and France where I once listened to an impassioned sermon preached to the local fishermen by a young Basque Franciscan who kept on repeating, with apocalyptic fervour, *"Onda-Ravi"*, obviously *"Fuenterrabía"* in Basque. The coach rattled through deserted San Sebastian, elegant Zarauz and historic Guetaria, where Juan Sebastián Elcano, the first man to circumnavigate the globe, lies buried at the door of the church under a tombstone bearing the proud title conferred upon him by Charles V, *Primus circumi-dedisti me*, to Deva.* From Deva a deviation took us inland to Durango and on to Bilbao in time for lunch, thus skirting the age-old Basque capital of Guernica of unhappy memory.

---

* Incidentally, of the 237 men who set out from Spain with Elcano and Magellan in 1519 only 18 survived the perils of the expedition to return three years later to Guetaria from that first world voyage.

Fierce fighting took place through all this northern region in the first year of the Civil War, between the advancing Nationalist troops of General Emilio Mola and the Republican or 'Red' forces reinforced by the Basques of the Separatist persuasion, but little about it is remembered by the world beyond that one name of ill-repute "Guernica". I had once encountered in the London office of *The Yorkshire Post*, whose London editor he then was, an aforetime correspondent in Spain (he lost his life on service in the Far East during the World War through a car accident after a celebration) whose despatches describing the raids on Guernica, later worked up into a book, had touched off the fierce controversy that has raged ever since over whether 'non-military' objectives there were in actual fact obliterated by the bombers of the German Condor Legion, or deliberately set on fire after the raids. A year ago, from this time of writing, I put the question direct to the most knowledgeable person I knew in Spain, of whom none could say that he was a Right-wing partisan for he reported the Civil War from the other side and had his car stolen for his pains by militia in Valencia when embarking in a British warship with his wife for France on the eve of the fall of Madrid.

"Undoubtedly," he said, "Guernica was a legitimate military target. It was a cross-roads similar to that which the Allies bombed so mercilessly in the Falaise pocket during the Normandy invasion, but above and beyond that, there was a big munitions dump there, and I believe, a munition factory. These were the military objectives, and so far as I know only the houses in the immediate vicinity were affected by the actual raids. Who destroyed the rest of the town is anybody's guess." The famed 'tree of Guernica', subject of the Basque patriotic anthem, "*Guernikako Arbola*", under which the elders had deliberated from time immemorial, far from being wiped out of existence, is, I understand from a recent visitor to the newly-constructed town, standing to this day. Moreover it has been clearly proved that an American correspondent named Reynolds, who sent sensational reports about the 'wanton destruction' of Guernica from the air, was, in fact, nowhere near the place at the time.

As if to demonstrate his impartiality my informant then remarked that it was another question where two hundred Separatist Basque officers made prisoner by the advancing Nationalists were concerned.

"Franco had them all shot," he said.

"Good God!" I exclaimed, "I have heard nothing of that—a little Katyn."*

"Well—they were not all shot at once, but executed at different times in batches."

I give the story as I heard it, for obviously it is not one lending itself to easy confirmation. Like many another tale one hears from non-Spanish lips—such, for example, as the statement that there are no 'civil' trials in Spain but that all are military 'courts-martial', the country still being technically under martial law—when repeated to an average intelligent Spaniard it would doubtless be met with the emphatic rejoinder: "*Es mentira*—it's a lie". For whatever criticism and animadversions are made against him by political opponents or supporters, none can attribute to the present Head of the Spanish State that stark admission of a 19th-century Prime Minister, Ramón María Narváez, who, asked by the priest who was administering Extreme Unction as he lay dying whether he forgave all his enemies, cheerfully replied that there were none, "because they have all been shot". In actual fact many of Franco's former political and active opponents and enemies have returned to Spain, which any former opponent is free to do without fear or discrimination provided he is guiltless of crime, where they live today in complete security, or as complete as everyone else enjoys. Many are employed in the Civil Service, so much less well paid than our own. One, returning after ten years' absence, succeeding in obtaining possession of his former home from a Government Minister who was living in it simply

---

* An official enquiry originated in the United States a few years ago in which actual witnesses of the crime testified (with features concealed to avoid identification in satellite Poland) to the circumstances in which 11,000 serving Polish officers were massacred in the forest of Katyn in the early months of World War II. But after the first few reports nothing further was published, perhaps for fear of hurting somebody's feelings. But if ever a crime cried to heaven for verdict and expiation this was it. When working in the war-time Ministry of Information, photographs passed through my hands of the uniformed bodies ranged side by side in long rows. And in September, 1954, I met when voyaging from Tilbury to Vigo a son of one of the victims, who had also when a boy seen from his own home the horrific destruction of the Warsaw ghetto. He declared that Katyn was a Russian affair.

by securing an order from the magistrate. On the other hand, Don Salvador de Madariaga's house, near the Residencia de Estudiantes in Madrid, which I passed the other day, has not been restored to him for he has elected to remain in voluntary exile in England.

Arthur Koestler, who was under sentence of death for several months in a Seville prison, declares in his sensational *Dialogue with Death*, recently reprinted, that after the fall of Malaga to the Nationalist Forces, and up to "Saturday, February 13th, 1937, five thousand men had been shot . . . six hundred from my prison alone" (*i.e.* before his transfer to Seville). *Five thousand!*—and in a town where I had once read the inscription on a fountain: "*No maltrates a los animales; Ellos hacen fácil tu trabajo y te ayudan a ganar el pan*—Don't illtreat the animals; they ease your labour and help you to earn your bread". But he quotes no authority for these startling statistics, and he could not have counted either so many executions or so many corpses himself.

He points out with commendable honesty in the Preface to his *Dialogue* that while reporting the Civil War as a correspondent of the London *News Chronicle* he "felt obliged to conceal three essential facts, that I was a member of the Communist Party; that my previous visit to General Franco's headquarters had been undertaken on behalf of the Cominform, using the *News Chronicle* as a cover; and finally, that at the time I was captured I was also working for the loyalist Government's official news agency." In short he was a spy. He could scarcely complain then of the facts either of his imprisonment or of his sentence.

Once, many years ago during a particularly dry summer on a far Queensland sheep-station of two hundred square miles where I was working for experience as a 'jackeroo', a bush fire started in a distant paddock, probably from the action of the sun's rays shining through a broken bottle and setting alight the tinder-like Mitchell grass. With appalling speed the flames swept over an eleven-thousand acre paddock and came racing across another. Every hand available was employed for the next hour in blazing a wide 'ring' round the woolshed and the station bungalow, which proved effective in halting the conflagration and in saving the key buildings from destruction. The 'bush fire' of a Civil War is an infinitely more terrible thing, but I personally do not consider any justification adequate for 'burning up human beings' as a *cordon sanitaire* to arrest its progress. This, in actual fact, was what was found of vital urgency in some cities, Valladolid, for instance, where, to stem the Leftist 'liquidations', and to save the lives of twelve thousand citizens, several hundred irresponsible elements were shot. The source of my information was the British Embassy in Madrid.

At Verdun Charlemagne is reported to have put to the sword 4,500 Saxon captives in one day—the first 'Christian Emperor of the West'. Alas! his zeal has been far exceeded in our own unhappy age.

The prison experiences and executions Koestler recounts are horrifying, but not so horrifying or appalling as the fully documented descriptions published in the *Causa General—La Dominación Roja en España*. The "General Cause", prepared by the Spanish Minister of Justice in accordance with the provisions of a decree dated June 19th, 1945, is copiously illustrated by photographs left in Republican archives of the hundreds of thousands of civilian victims of torture and assassination, with the addresses and detailed descriptions of the *chekas* which operated in Madrid and Barcelona on the Soviet model, of the anarchist and police terror, of the religious persecution (no Madrid church functioned for over two years with the single exception of the French Embassy chapel) and of the mass assassinations of civilian prisoners both inside and outside the prisons.——

> Oh, cease! must hate and death return?
> Cease! must men kill and die?
> Cease! drain not to its dregs the urn
> of bitter prophecy.
> The world is weary of the past.
> Oh, might it die or rest at last! . . .

one echoes from Shelley.

Between Deva and Durango we met thousands of army conscripts on a route march; the column seemed endless. They all wore khaki shirts with rolled sleeves and khaki trousers, but carried no arms. A fine, upstanding lot they looked, bright-eyed and eager-looking, with fresh, weather-beaten complexions and springy steps.

Rain was falling in Bilbao, centre of the Biscay provinces, greatest of the Basque towns and one of Spain's principal seaports, as the *autobús* drew up outside the central station. Here we had to change into another coach which continued the same afternoon to Santander and beyond. On a previous visit to Bilbao I had found evidence of the 1937 siege in much chipped stone near the central bridge over the Nervión, and in the shell-marks on the main buildings, which recalled to memory the wounds made by the cannon-balls of Napoleon's guns during the French siege of Cairo which may still be seen on the great wall of the Rifai Mosque, below the massive citadel built by Saladin.

The Nationalist general, Mola, who died in an air accident in 1937 near Burgos, had encountered many difficulties in the acute shortage of arms and ammunition experienced in the early stages. Just how critical the situation had been was revealed by Franco himself, with no eye to publicity, during an official banquet given to him a year or two ago by the Municipality of Burgos. The story was recounted to me by the Civil Governor, who was seated at the function near the *Caudillo*.

"During the attack on Bilbao," Franco confided, "I received an urgent telephone call from Mola, who declared he had not got the arms necessary to take the city. 'Do you believe in God, Emilio?' I asked him. Mola paused, then replied: 'Yes, of course— but I have not the guns'. 'But you believe in God, Emilio,' I said, 'and you must do your best with what you've got'. Mola rang off with a grunt.

"That very night our patrol vessels captured a Russian ship sailing without lights and carrying a full cargo of munitions intended for our brothers, the enemy. I rang up Mola at once. 'Do you believe in God, Emilio?' I asked again. 'Well, yes,' he said, 'but I am terribly short of arms of every sort—*sabes*?' 'But, Emilio,' I repeated, 'do you really believe in God?' 'Yes, yes, yes, my General, but—'. 'Mola,' I said to him: 'How many heavy guns do you want?—how many machine-guns?—how many rifles? Good, you shall have them all in the morning. Tomorrow you will have a stronger faith in the Deity'."

North of the Plaza Nueva at Bilbao, beyond the uninteresting 15th-century church of San Nicolás, is situated the station for the pleasant suburb of Neguri. At Neguri I stayed with the mother of my good friend, Juliá. The family had lost their Madrid home with all its contents (in pre-Civil War days I had met there three cousins of José Antonio—they were all killed later) during "the troubles", when Señora de Aguirre had narrowly escaped assassination in the Casa de Campo for displaying a crucifix in her house. When peace came she made a new home in a bright and comfortable flat on the Neguri heights, outside Bilbao.

That evening, while I helped to dry the supper things in the kitchen, she spoke for the first time of her husband who had perished so tragically thirty years before in the Anual catastrophe. "He seemed to have some intuition of disaster on that last day, Colés," she said, and the poignant occasion seemed to take form right before my eyes as she spoke. "A few moments after he had said goodbye at the door of our home in Melilla to join General Silvestre's army at the front, he came hurrying back, calling: 'My rosary, María, my rosary!' Hiding the children away, I brought it from the bedroom and he put it quickly into his pocket as he rode off with a last '*Adiós*, María, *Adiós*'. . . . When the news of the massacre of the entire army reached us the next day we all expected the Moors to enter Melilla and kill everyone in the town as well. But thanks be to God, they never got as far. . . ."

The coach stopped outside a bar in Laredo, a popular summer coastal resort with three miles of sands, opposite a bust of the Emperor Charles who had landed there on first arriving in Spain from the Netherlands, and then continued through Santoña and Solares to Santander, birthplace of the great literary critic, Menéndez Pelayo, whose library, by the provision of his will, is open to readers of all nationalities.

On February 15th, 1941, the entire central part of Santander was destroyed by fire originating with sparks from a chimney spread by a wind of cyclonic force, when 377 buildings were completely destroyed and 1,783 shops, and ten thousand people were rendered homeless, almost at the commencement of the Civil Governorship of my friend, Don Joaquín Reguera Sevilla, who is now Director-General of Labour with offices in Madrid in the old Ministry building in San Bernardo street. He has published a full and detailed account of the conflagration and the means taken to rebuild the city of the Montañeses, an autographed copy of which lies before me as I write.*

Franco, who shares with Napoleon and Churchill the faculty of selecting able associates, was so impressed by the way in which the emergency had been dealt with, and the reconstruction of the city, that he sent for the Civil Governor and gave him the far greater task of developing Spain's labour resources. My friend of twenty years, José Miguel Ruiz Morales, since 1951 Economic Counsellor to the Spanish Embassy in London, was similarly chosen to be Director-General of Commerce in 1950 when Spain's economic fortunes were at their lowest ebb. The present Minister for the Treasury (Hacienda) was a mere Sub-Director in the Department when the Head of State summoned him one day to El Pardo and entrusted him with the Portfolio. "But, Your Excellency," said the awed official, "I am not good enough. It is like asking a man just capable of lifting twenty pounds, to hold aloft a hundred-pound weight!" "Courage," Franco replied: "go to the gymnasium and practice!" Spain's economy steadily improves.

The Santander bus was bound for Comillas, beyond Santillana, where there is a Pontifical University founded by Pope Leo XIII (a young fair-haired Guatemalan student I met there in 1949 spoke flawless English which, he said, he had acquired in a West Kensington boarding-house), and so we pushed on another sixteen miles to Torrelavega, an industrial centre of the province and of various manufactures. Here the manager of the State Parador of Santillana del Mar, whom I knew from a previous visit, met me in the Parador car in which we covered the last lap of the long day's journey to the 'mediæval gem' which the Head of State makes his annual headquarters for salmon-fishing expeditions in the neighbouring Sella and Narcea streams.

---

* *La Reconstrucción de Santander: Problemas de Derecho Público y Privado —El Tratamiento Jurídico de una Catástrofe* (*Universidad Internacional Menéndez Pelayo, Santander:* 1950). The author studied the British system of evacuating and rehabilitating blitzed areas, and of compensation under the War Damage Act.

Chapter Two

BIRTHPLACE

"THE GENERALISSIMO WAS HERE LAST YEAR," said the genial manager of the Parador Gil Blas, "and the year before; but he has not been this year—there are few salmon in the rivers. . . . He had his sleeping quarters on the top floor. This lounge we converted into the dining-room. On Sundays an altar was placed against the end wall, and Franco and his staff heard Mass said by the parish priest from the Collegiate Church." The *Caudillo* was a very abstemious man, the manager added, and drank only a single glass of wine with meals. "Often, he does not return from his long fishing trips until the late evening, but he works far into the night on the State papers, brought from Madrid by courier."

This most historic and picturesque town of Santillana del Mar saw the foundation of fourteen ancient lines of Spanish nobility, including the powerful Mendozas, the Boyas, the Cossíos, and the Herreras. The Abades, or former house of the abbots of Santillana, is today the summer residence of the Archduchess of Austria, Doña Margaret of Hapsburg-Lorraine and Borbón, who is a portraitist of merit, judging by the signed drawings which adorn her spacious studio.

Santillana is a mediæval gem set in the emerald frame of its surrounding hills and fields. There is no anachronistic note. The view has quite a magical effect on the beholder from the high Torreón de Velarde, past the 13th-century church, with its local stone mellowed to a superb orange glow by the centuries, up the cobbled main street, the Calle del Río and its continuation the Calle del Cantón, with the severe frontages of the *casas nobles*, each with massive coats-of-arms. In essentials all is unchanged since the Middle Ages, when the long pilgrim trains wending their way from the farthest confines of Northern Europe halted here on the way to the shrine of St. James the Greater at Compostela, thus avoiding Moorish-held territory. St. Bridget of Sweden passed through Santillana on pilgrimage with her husband, the Prince of Västergotland, and countless other figures whose names have gone to enrich European history.

I used to hear Mass on Sunday seated in the deep shadows of a thick stone pillar in the nave of the Collegiate Church, before the primitive shrine and tomb of the 9th-century martyr St. Juliana, after whom the town was named. The local children provided the choral response to the priest's sonorous invocations, delivered in a fine rich baritone and in the clearest Latin I have heard anywhere in Europe. As he made the ritualistic pauses, these Santillana children let themselves go with a will in a piercing tunefulness!——

The State Parador, named after the celebrated picaresque novel by Le Sage, an early edition of which I read while staying there, stood exactly opposite the 17th-century Town Hall, the most modern building in the town. It perfectly retains its outward and inward aspects of a solid Spanish señorial mansion, with plain 'Roman' facade and original oaken stairs and floors and giant beams. An ideal place in truth for complete repose, for the only sounds to disturb one's train of solitary thought are the laboured rumblings of the great ox-carts carrying their loads of freshly-cut green grass to the storesheds. Much rain falls in Santillana and this has a depressing effect on the spirits of those who have to live there all the year round. "*Muy triste*—very sad in winter here, señor," said a pretty little waitress from Avila, as she brought me one wet day a *copita* of Anís del Mono in the lounge which the *Caudillo* uses as dining-room and chapel ". . . *siempre llueve*—it's always raining."

A fellow-visitor to the Parador at the time of my visit on the way to Ferrol was the Duke of Luna, Don Mariano de Urzáiz y Silva, the Director-General of the State Tourist Department, who is usually accompanied on his duty tours by his two prize alsatians. Proud and famous Aragon is his province. Throughout the second World War he was naval attaché at the Spanish Embassy in London. At dinner one night he told me that General Franco had originally declined the proffered leadership of the Nationalist rising because he was not assured of the support of the navy. As in Russia in the Bolshevik revolution of 1917, so in Spain the navy had been the most thoroughly infected by the Communist bacilli. This became evident at once when the Civil War broke out, for among its first victims were four hundred Spanish naval officers who were cast into the sea by their ships' crews with stones tied round their necks. This happened off Cartagena.

The car for El Ferrol was waiting punctually at nine on the morning arranged, and the long drive began to Franco's birthplace in the far north-western corner of the Peninsula. This journey is among the most exciting of the many exciting road journeys that Spain has to offer, for it leads through that mountain fastness which never submitted to the Moorish yoke and below the veritable peaks of the 'Picos de Europa', the haunt of the elusive chamois and the *capra hispánica*, so named by the crews of the galleons returning from the Spanish Americas because these towering snow-clad summits were the first sight obtained of the home continent. The narrow road winds like a giant serpent down immense slopes on to low mountain ledges, beneath which foam and ripple the swelling mountain streams and the crowded salmon rivers of Asturias; every few yards there is a hairpin bend or a violent turn, inducing road sickness in travellers susceptible to the malady. After negotiating a particularly tortuous stretch of highway, we suddenly came upon Cangas de Onís, once the capital of the tiny northern stronghold which withstood the Arab avalanche, with its famous 12th-century bridge whose central arch—looking like the vertebrae of a dinosaur—rises sixty feet, with a sixty-seven feet span. A further drive through wild mountain scenery, and then a slight detour, and we were in sight of the uniquely situated Covadonga, high and deep in the Cantabrian Range, the cradle and shrine of the Hispanic race.

> Where'er we tread
> 'Tis haunted holy ground——

sang the supreme romanticist Byron, of Greece. A similar impression assails the modern pilgrim to Covadonga, set amid mountain and forest scenery of unexampled splendour, with its modern Basilica and its famous cave still containing the authentic sarcophagus of the instigator and inspirer of the *Reconquista*, the Asturian Visigothic chieftain Pelayo, with ancient inscription recording that his remains repose within.

This inscription on the tomb of Pelayo, in archaic characters which developed into the Castillian eventually adopted as the national language for the whole country, is the exact antithesis in spirit to that which I read in large brass letters on the floor tombstone of a dead Cardinal on my last visit to the vast Cathedral at 'Imperial' Toledo:

HIC JACET
PULVIS
CINIS
NIHIL

so essentially Spanish as that is in the desperate realism of its approach to "just, omnipotent and mighty Death". For from this very cave, which remained ultimately inaccessible to the most daring and enterprising of the Mohammedan invaders, Pelayo and the few nobles and ecclesiastics who had taken refuge with him made their tremendous decision in the early 8th century, in face of apparently hopeless odds, to declare unceasing war against the Moorish hordes and to set forth to regain the totality of the Spanish earth. They could not have known that the Reconquest thus so heroically embarked upon would take nearly eight centuries to achieve fulfilment; their gesture was a forlorn and desperate one, as seemingly forlorn and desperate as was that of the Spanish Nationalists in July, 1936, when, with over two-thirds of Spain in a state of anarchy and chaos they set out on its reconquest in the name of civilisation and Christendom. "*Santiago y cierra España!*"—"Saint James and close the ranks!" is a free translation —had been the war cry of the successors of Pelayo at the battle of Clavijo, over a century later, which marked the first decisive Moorish defeat, and in the following centuries it echoed right through the Peninsula, at Toledo, at Las Navas de Tolosa, where the renewed northern drive of the Almohades was broken by a composite Christian army of all the liberated States, at Valencia, conquered by the septagenarian Cid, at the victorious siege of Granada. The cry was taken up afresh during the critical struggle —critical for all western Europe—for Spain's continued existence as a modern integrated State in embattled Europe.

After gazing at Pelayo's tomb, settled fast in a niche of his immense cave, and attempting to decipher the archaic inscription while nearby streams and waterfalls made liquid music of the day,

I turned to survey the magnificent vista of snow-clad peaks and the vast green forest by which Covadonga is still surrounded. I remembered published descriptions of Moorish stirrups and saddle-guards, of sword handles of exotic workmanship and fragments of bright clothing discovered in recent years in some great neighbouring defile, relics of a desperate fight long ago in the heart of these declivitous northern mountains, and recalled that only a few centuries previously Spanish infantry and cavalry had formed part of the Roman garrison of Wales.

While the heroic Pelayo and his nobles fought to regain their patrimony inch by inch, so that much later the separate kingdom of León and Castille, and the famous city Burgos, came into being, exerting a dynamic impetus on the whole struggle—at this very time Charlemagne was attacking the Emirate of Saragossa and suffering the disastrous rout at Roncesvalles at the hands, not of the infidel enemy, but of the Christian Basques incensed at the destruction of their Pamplona walls by those who came as allies. At Roncesvalles today the actual path followed by the retreating Franks can be traced through the frontier forest, and in the Collegiate church there one finds on display in a glass case in the sacristy a famous relic of the fight, the red slippers of Charlemagne's Bishop Turpin, from 8th-century Reims.

For anyone wishing to understand the Spanish spirit, with its fanatical devotion to its traditional Faith (or equally fanatical hatred by those who have lost it), its violent and instinctive resistance to alien influences threatening the traditional Spanish way of life and thought, a visit to Covadonga is indispensable. It may seem a distortion of history to say that to appreciate the rising of July, 1936, it is necessary to visit the scene of the rising of 718 A.D., but the parallel is not so fantastic as might appear.

There is a direct historical continuity, deny it who may, between the resistance of Pelayo and his embattled nobles besieged in this Asturian mountain fastness by the infidel hordes from the North African deserts, and the struggle for survival and victory over another alien ideology of Colonel, later General, Moscardó and his band of Cadets, Civil Guards and civilians besieged for sixty-seven days in the Alcazar at Toledo—"stormed at with shot and shell", with bombs, dynamite and deadly mines by day and by night. And both Guzmán 'el Bueno' before the 13th-century walls of Tarifa and Moscardó lost hostage-sons killed by the enemy on the refusal of their respective fathers to surrender.

"*Dieron su vida por salvar la de la Patria*", runs the proud inscription round the walls of the ossuary of the Toledo Alcazar, which is the last resting-place of those of that gallant band who gave their lives in the defence of that historic piece of Spanish earth, "*No lloréis su muerte—Envidiadles*—They gave their lives to save that of the Country; weep not for their deaths: Envy them". And the proud quotation from *Childe Harolde* on a marble tablet nearby, placed there by an anonymous group of Britons:

> "—true Glory's stainless victories,
> Won by the unambitious heart and hand
> Of a proud, brotherly and civic band,
> All unbought champions . . ."

From Covadonga it was only a two-hours' run past scattered farms and villages, through Arriondas, Infiesto and Siero, to Oviedo, capital of Asturias, which we reached at lunch-time. Twenty years had gone by since I had last been in the city. Twice in that time it had undergone long and bitter siege—in 1934 during the rebellion of the Communist *dinamiteros*, and during the Civil War when General Aranda and his garrison withstood for a twelvemonth massive attacks which penetrated right into the heart of the Asturian capital, even to the Cathedral itself where the famous Cámara Santa was destroyed with all its precious relics.

In the church of San Juan el Real I read a memorial tablet near the altar-steps recording the marriage there of Franco.

En la conmemoración del XXV aniversario del matrimonial enlace de S. E. el Jefe del Estado Caudillo de España y Generalísimo de los Ejércitos Don Francisco Franco Bahamonde con la Excma. Sra. Dña. Carmen Polo de Franco, cuyo fausto acontecimiento tuvo lugar en este templo parroquial de San Juan el Real de la ciudad de Oviedo, el día 22 de Octubre de 1923, —Oviedo, 22 Octubre, 1948.*

---

* "In commemoration of the 25th anniversary of the marriage of H.E. the Chief of State Leader of Spain and Generalissimo of the Armed Forces Don Francisco Franco Bahamonde with the Most Excellent Lady Carmen Polo de Franco, which happy event took place in this church of St. John the Royal, of the city of Oviedo, the 22nd October, 1923."

In the Sacristy a priest solemnly engaged in totting up a spidery column of figures rose from his chair and brought me the open Parish register . . ."*D. Francisco Franco Baamonde* [I read] *y Da. María del Carmen Polo Martínez Valdés, por palabras de assente mutuo . . . soltero el Teniente Coronel y Jefe del Tercio de Regulares de Africa . . . treinta años, natural del Ferrol residente en Ceuta . . . padrinos SS. MM. los Reyes D. Alfonso XIII y Da. Victoria Eugenia. . . ."*

We were now through the Cantabrian mountain chain, with the famed Picos de Europa left far behind, and flat green landscapes unfolded on our left as we drove on along the coastal road through Luarca. From Ribadeo the road again ascended into the high Galician range, where we seemed to be soaring into the clouds on the way to Villalba, along a high and winding mountain road from which fantastic views could be obtained over half the province.

As we entered Villalba dusk was falling. It was eight o'clock, and we had been on the move since nine that morning. But the township bore an uninviting aspect, and in the most likely-looking hotel no rooms were available. So we drove on in the gathering darkness, ascending again into the mountains beyond the wretched village of Cabreiros.

Suddenly a cluster of lights appeared below, in the near distance. A steep and winding descent brought us to a tram terminus, and at ten that night precisely, by the strokes of the luminous clock in the tower of the brand new Town Hall, we drew up outside a hotel in the main square of El Ferrol del Caudillo, in far Galicia.

Chapter Three

THE EARLY YEARS

THE CELEBRATED RÍAS, OR FIRTHS, OF GALICIA approximate to the *viks*, or deep inlets or bays, on the west coast of Sweden, from where the sombre and cruel Vikings sallied forth each spring in their long, serpent-prowed open ships in the latter Middle Ages to prey and slay up and down the undefended shores of Europe. They must certainly have felt themselves at home in this far north-western angle of the Iberian peninsula, for the *ría* on which El Ferrol del Caudillo lies extends inland like a Norwegian or Swedish *fjiord* for eleven miles (we drove along it), and the harbour is, with those of Vigo and Cartagena, among the largest in Spain, and, after Sydney, one of the most spacious in the world.

The town itself, situated at the very confluence of the Cantabrian Sea and the Atlantic Ocean, is hidden from the harbour by green hills which also overlook the big naval shipbuilding yards and the submarine base of La Graña. El Ferrol is the Portsmouth and Southsea of Spain combined, for besides functioning as Spain's most important naval base, a distinction it has held for two centuries, it is a favourite residential place for naval families. Like Portsmouth, again, in its close relationship with the Royal Navy, any disaster which overtakes any unit of the Spanish fleet has immediate repercussions in the sailors' homes of El Ferrol which was converted into a city of mourning when the Nationalist cruiser *Baleares* was sunk with the loss of all hands in the Civil War.

In character, in civic planning and in the architectural design of its houses, Ferrol strongly resembles the neighbouring seaport of La Coruña, from which it is separated by only a few hours of open sea. This often provides as stormy a crossing in the high-powered El Ferrol—La Coruña ferry steamers as does that open stretch of the Kattegat between Frederik-shavn and Gothenburg for the high-powered Swedish ferry vessels.* For the most part the houses are of three stories, the upper two of which each have *miradores*, balconies enclosed like those of Corunna by glazed windows for protection of the dwellers against the blusterous Atlantic gales.

In one of these houses, number 136 in the curiously named Calle de Frutos Saavedra, a turning off the main *plaza*, Franco was born into a typical Spanish middle-class home at one hour after midnight on December 4th, 1892, the son of a naval pay-master, Don Nicolás Franco y Salgado Araujo, who as a younger man had made two voyages to the Philippines on a warship sailing from El Ferrol. Antecedents on both sides were connected with the sea for generations. His paternal grandfather had been a Superintendent-General of the Spanish Navy and a writer of naval text-books, his paternal great-grandfather was a reviewing officer of the naval administration. On his mother's side, too, there were family links with the navy, for the father of Pilar Baamonde y Pardo, whom Nicolás Franco married in 1890, was himself a naval commandant, scion of a landed family of the El Ferrol region.

"She was small, home-loving, and possessed of a plenitude of spirit so needed then, when one realises the vicissitudes of the era", Joaquín Arrarás wrote of Franco's mother in his study *Francisco Franco*, of which an English edition was published in 1938 to which I am indebted for some of the biographical information imparted in these pages:

> "Pilar Baamonde" (he writes) "had that delicate, transparent beauty that is the pride, almost the inheritance of Galician women. An oval, symmetrical face, and pensive melancholy eyes. . . . A mistress always of herself, her moral courage, strengthened by the intensive life of her spirit, she faced life's problems with a serenity and a fortitude that might be called stoical were they not more aptly described as Christian."

---

* A Spanish proverb celebrating the roughness of this short ferry voyage, says:

> Quien pasó la Marola
> pasó la mar toda

"Who passes the Marola (as this open stretch of the Atlantic sea is locally known) passes the entire ocean." Yet the ferry-steamers on this service are not the size of those plying between Sydney and Manley.

("All the men," writes a Spanish historian, "who in the broad historic scene have achieved glorious things for Spain were sons of energetic and exemplary mothers—St. Ferdinand, the Cid, Alfonso X 'the Wise', Philip II, Pizarro, Cisneros, Cortés, Gonzalo de Córdoba, el Gran Capitán, the 'great' Duke of Alba.")

She died on February 28th, 1934, at the age of sixty-eight, while spending a few days in Madrid intent on making a pilgrimage to Rome, the mecca of all devout Spaniards and their mothers and wives. Thus Franco enjoyed the advantage of his mother's understanding, loving encouragement and womanly wisdom for the first four decades of his life, up to the time when he had become the youngest Spanish General and had reluctantly been called in by a Republican régime which had no love for the army to deal with a grave Communist revolt in Asturias and a Separatist outbreak in Catalonia. His father, who had been given the rank of a General of Marines on retirement, died in Madrid during the Second World War, on February 23rd, 1942, at the age of 88.

Someone in Spain whose identity I have been unable to discover took the trouble to cast Franco's horoscope at the time of his birth, and I give it here for those—I am not of their company—for whom such things bear significance. "No planet was at the zenith," runs the translation, "five planets were above the horizon. Mars was in the sign of the Fish, symbol of Christianity, indicating championship of religion. Sun in Sagittarius, the governing sign of Spain, foretelling national significance of career. Chief planetary hurdles were Neptune and Saturn, which are responsible for most of Europe's social unrest. Mars showed a favourable aspect, and Venus promised 'abundant aid.' . . ."

Within a fortnight of his birth, Franco was baptized, on December 17th, in the large and handsome Church of San Francisco, situated alongside the harbour, with the dockyards a short distance away and the Naval School in the town above, being given the names of Francisco Paulino Hermenegildo Teódulo (the last two with a definite 'Visigothic' ring about them). The spacious interior, brilliantly illumined when I visited the church by glorious morning sunshine, has many memorials to noted Spanish naval officers, and a large oval bronze plaque beside the high altar containing the names of the officers and ship's crews who went down with the ill-fated *Baleares*. . . .

The 'delicate, transparent beauty' of Galician women is certainly in full evidence today in El Ferrol ("*del Caudillo*—of the Leader" was added to the town's name after the elevation of Franco as Head of State), where a visitor is constantly brought up with a sharp consciousness of their refined good looks and innate gracefulness, even as we are told by classical writers were visitors from the Greek mainland to the island of Cos by the grace and loveliness of the Coan women. Indeed, it is a matter for some pondering that local inhabitants do not adopt a practice similar to that in some Danish towns and seaside resorts, particularly on the island of Funen, of affixing at a suitable angle on their window-sills small mirrors from which an oblique unobtrusive view is obtained of passers-by (they could be excused, being Spanish and non-pagan, the parallel Danish custom of displaying in most front-room windows supple terracotta nudes.)

But if the womenfolk of El Ferrol are often 'easy on the eye', as the familiar saying goes, so that visitors inclined to such things instinctively pause in their tracks to enjoy the passing scene—the El Ferrol bread is far from 'easy on the tongue', for the leather-like brand served up in the town's hotels and restaurants is, without exception, the toughest and the most indigestible I have come across anywhere in Spain, where the rolls are again white, after ten years and more, and generally quite edible. Ferrol bread is even more unpalatable, in truth, than the 'chemicalised sawdust' served up today for white bread in the region of my home.*

The unpretentious house in which Franco was born, and where he spent the formative years of his childhood and boyhood, stands in a long street of houses of identical design and only a stone's throw from the city centre, the main square now known as the

---

* "Dr. Charles Hill, Parliamentary Secretary, Ministry of Food, moved the second reading of the Food and Drugs Amendment Bill. He said that now that chemical substances of one kind or another were added to food it was not easy, and in many cases it was impossible, to determine in advance what might be the long-term effect of a regular consumption of small quantities of new chemicals."—*The Times* (Cleaner Food Bill), 24th July, 1954. *Verb sap!* . . . "Shelley Winters, the American film actress, who is in London to film 'I Am a Camera', was taken ill on the set at Shepperton yesterday. A spokesman for Romulus Films said: 'We believe food poisoning is responsible'."—*The Daily Telegraph*, 13th November, 1954.

"Plaza del Generalísimo". It is distinguished from its neighbours
by a striking bronze plaque, affixed several years before the Civil
War, which commemorates the exploits of Ramón Franco in
first traversing by air the South Atlantic, and of his elder brother
Francisco when Lieut.-Colonel commanding the Spanish *Tercio* in
Africa. The old name for the street is Calle del Sol, "Sun-street".

Here, then, in this modest dwelling—*"muy humilde"* remarked
my chauffeur—were born the five children of Nicolás and Pilar
Franco: Nicolás, Spanish Ambassador to Portugal since the end
of the Civil War; Francisco, nicknamed *"Paquito*—little Francis"
because of his leanness and smallness; Pilar, who now lives in
Madrid, Ramón, the future aviator, who perished in a forced
descent in the Mediterranean in 1938, and a second daughter
Pacita ("little Peace") who died when five years old.

Descended on both paternal and maternal sides from families of
sailors, it was in the natural order of things that Nicolás should
enter the Naval College as a cadet and that his younger brother
Francisco should seek also to enter the College in the same category
with a view to following the navy as a career. But as the long-
term effect of the disastrous Spanish-American war and the
consequent heavy losses of naval tonnage, the Treasury in Madrid
suddenly 'cracked down' on naval recruitment, and further
preparations for entry into the Naval College were suspended
in 1907, the precise year when Francisco, having secured his
bachelor's degree, passed the stiff entrance examination. Nothing
daunted, he took straight away the examination for entry as
a cadet into the Infantry Academy at Toledo which he passed
easily, being admitted to the Alcazar military establishment on
August 29th of the same year, at the age of fourteen.

An early studio portrait taken in El Ferrol at this time with
Nicolás shows both boys proudly wearing their respective cadets'
uniforms, the elder seated and smiling the complacent self-
congratulatory smile which has remained with him right into
late adult life, the younger standing by his shoulder and looking
lean as a dart, small-boned, dark-eyed, bearing a compelling
expression of youthful eagerness and acceptance of life on his
small, bird-like face—"a slender youth of delicate features and
large shining curious eyes . . . with a restless, merry, lively
disposition that led him to take part in all the pranks and adventures
that were a part of those colourful years."

Like most Spanish boys then and today, the future Head of State had received his early education at a Catholic educational foundation, a private school in Ferrol, conducted by religious where, like Henry Vaughan in his "angel-infancy", Franco too may have

> . . . felt through all this fleshly dress
> Bright shoots of everlastingness.

He later described to me some of those early "pranks and adventures" in the famous seaport where he was born—how he used to play 'bush' *fútbol* on the open spaces above the harbour and the high dome of San Francisco; how he used to go fishing with his school cronies with home-made rods and lines, and of how they would play at pirates by purloining the gangplanks of the harbour ferry-steamers when no one was about and push them out into the open water ("I was always falling in," he told me, with his attractive smile). It was, perhaps, during these unlawful expeditions of his boyhood that he developed the capacity for playing a fish patiently, a quality that he was to introduce with so much success in after years in all his dealings with international problems and international ill-wishers; although Max Borrell confided to me during the chat in his Madrid headquarters to which reference was made in the Prologue that the Generalissimo was not a particularly good rod with salmon until Borrell took him in hand, when he showed himself to be a remarkably apt pupil. No summer in Spain now would seem complete to the Madrileños without some new Franco fishing story.

This one, probably apocryphal, was causing a good deal of amusement in the salons and cafés of the capital in the autumn of 1949. The Head of State, who was cruising in August in his yacht *Azor*, was said to have been playing a big fish off San Sebastian when a sudden, unexpected jerk on the line threw him off his balance into a choppy sea. A local youth fishing from a boat some distance away, who witnessed the mishap, plied his oars with a will until he reached the *Caudillo*'s side, when he dived into the water without more ado and held up the Leader until the arrival of members of the yacht's crew who thereupon hauled both unceremoniously aboard.

The youth was invited to the *Azor* where he was effusively

thanked by Franco and his staff and handed a medal and a gift of money. When, however, he returned home to the old fishermen's quarters of San Sebastian (where, incidentally, Wellington's entry in the Peninsular War is commemorated by a sculptural group outside the Church of San Vicente, with a tolerable aquiline likeness) and proudly recounted the day's adventure to the assembled members of his family, his father, a secret Basque Separatist, waxed very wrathful and fumed: "You young jackass! —why didn't you leave him to drown? Heaven will never send us such a chance again! . . ."

Franco, the tale has been recounted to me, suffered the pangs of his first romance in these last days of his boyhood in El Ferrol, where he became enamoured of a dark charmer who lived in a neighbouring street. There he would stand seemingly transfixed to the pavement after study hours gazing long at the windows of the first-floor flat where she resided with her parents. In Spain, too, however, the course of true love is often tortuous, and the eager, swarthy youth was never allowed to remain until his lady-love became aware of his devout vigil, for the ground-floor *portera* would come bustling out into the porch in front of which he was standing with a large broom and proceed to sweep away into the road the dust and rubbish, and the quietly adoring future Head of the Spanish State as well.

A few days before the official invitation reached me to visit El Pardo, Franco received a deputation from his native province which had come to Madrid to present him with an album of etchings of Galicia by the artist Castro Gil, and to bestow upon him the title of President of Honour of the Federation of the Galician Clubs ("Centros") of Spain—more 'homage'! In expressing his thanks to the deputation for the gift and the honour, the *Caudillo* gave an enlightening word-picture of the character of the Gallegos in these terms (my translation):

"Our region has ever been prodigal of sacrifice, modesty and good manners. From Galicia have come men and the means to supply the national Armed Forces. Galicia is ever modest, but marvellously efficient. All the Gallegos scattered throughout the world are fully sensible of the pride of their origin which they cherish equally, with their pride in being Spaniards."

If the speaker of this regional panegyric falls short in the eyes of many of his critics of being a paragon of Galician modesty ("I am not accustomed to be influenced by events; I am accustomed to dominate them"), he passes muster in the other qualities adumbrated by him as those characterising a good Gallego, to wit efficiency and integrity (*"buena manera de ser"*).

"The man is a gentleman," has been the verdict of not a few of those who have interviewed him, British correspondents among them.

---

* "The man is a gentleman," wrote a military correspondent in a Letter to the Editor published on March 17th, 1953, in one of the British National dailies; "power has consequently not given him a rush of blood to the head, or love of display, or made a tyrant of him." British parliamentary critics kindly note.

Chapter Four

I AM RECEIVED AT EL PARDO

WHEN THE FIRST OPPORTUNITY CAME to see General-issimo Franco at his official residence at the Pardo Palace, situated some fourteen miles outside the capital, I was staying at the new Hotel Mercator, in the Calle de Atocha, the famous old street, above the Mediodía station and the line for Toledo, where Part One of *Don Quijote* first saw the light in 1605 from the printing press of Juan de la Cuesta (an arresting bronze plaque showing the Doleful Knight and his immortal Squire 'on the road' adorns the present building). The letter, hailing from the *"Casa Civil de S. E. el Jefe del Estado y Generalísimo de los Ejércitos"* and signed by the Marqués de Huetor de Santillán, head of the Civil Household, and ending with the traditional wish *"Dios guarde a Ud. muchos años*—God keep you many years", came as a surprise, for I had been given to understand by the Spanish Foreign Office that the Head of State might not be able to receive me until later in the summer, after the seasonal migration of the Government to San Sebastian. Sixty foreign applicants, I learned later, were at that time awaiting interviews with him, some of them ready to fly to Madrid at an hour's notice from far corners of the world.

What was I to wear? I had brought no morning dress to Spain, and the invitation said *"Chaqué o uniforme."* After a good deal of enquiry and telephoning I managed to raise a pair of striped morning trousers, a fawn waistcoat and a dark 'American' jacket.

"But you can't go like that," said my good friends Leopoldo García-Durán y Parages and his high-born wife Carmen, "it wouldn't be correct—it would not be a compliment to Spain." I appreciated their point. But the audience was for the following morning, June 3rd: how and where could I obtain the necessary *Chaqué* in time? I could not very well ask Sir John Balfour for the loan of his, and the First Counsellor at the British

Embassy, my good friend Bernard Malley, with whom Ramón Serrano Suñer was on close terms of friendship, was not of my build.

"Wait," said Carmen, and suddenly left the luncheon table to return with a morning tail coat and dark waistcoat which her father, she said, had worn at all his audiences with King Alfonso. "A good fit," she remarked as I tried on the garments. And thus it was that I went to my first meeting with the Spanish *Caudillo* wearing the morning dress of a former Royalist War Minister, the late Vizconde de Eza, who had actually founded the Spanish Foreign Legion in which Franco first won fame and which he eventually commanded, and accompanied by a Secretary of Embassy, Don Aurelio Valls, who had once taken the chair at a talk I had given on Spain at the Allied Circle when he was serving with the Spanish Diplomatic Mission in London.

The Foreign Office car threaded its way through the congested central thoroughfares of Madrid in the direction of Argüelles, but slowed down as we neared the Puerta de Hierro and the impressive Faculty buildings of University City, one of the most bitterly contested of the capital's suburbs during the War of Liberation, but now almost entirely reconstructed in impressive red brick, with the sole exception of the Casa de Velázquez the rebuilding of which is to be put in hand by the French Government.*

Soon we were proceeding along the tree-lined drive of the 17th-century Pardo palace, built on the site of a former hunting lodge used by Philip II and later by the Hapsburg Philip IV, whose bosky environs may be recognised in canvases by Velasquez and del Mazo of royal hunting scenes. The car stopped at the low white main entrance, where two Moorish sentries saluted as we alighted.

A flight of steps led to the first floor, where a tall footman in traditional dress preceded us through a thickly carpeted room hung with tapestries and furnished with ornaments of gilt and buhl and ormolu into an adjacent waiting-room, where were assembled the Liberian Minister to Spain, a tall, dark-skinned, dignified figure, and various Missions, including delegates to a

---

* In November, during a walk from the Residencia de Relaciones Culturales, I noticed that reconstruction was not yet started.

current Agricultural Congress and another comprising all the Cistercian abbots of Spain, looking very imposing and mediæval in their long white habits. Groups stood about conversing quietly, while some Phalanx official in dark shirt and white jacket behung with medals and decorations slowly paced up and down looking as though he longed for an early lunch. A richly-coloured carpet which almost covered the considerable floor expanse bore the date "1824" and the name of the Royal factory at the time. On the walls hung four superb Goya tapestries, reproducing scenes from the familiar Prado paintings. "Note the colours", remarked Valls in his soft-toned English, "fresh as if new, *verdad?*" Over two hundred tapestries in fine condition are preserved at El Pardo.

An hour passed. The white-jacketed official now sat silent and pensive on a tapestried settee looking more than ever in need of an early lunch. The respective missions were given their audiences and in due time I found myself in the ante-room to the Head of the State's capacious '*despacho*', alone save for a military aide who informed me that he was one of the four attached for duty at the palace. It transpired later in conversation that he had been present at Tetuan when Franco alighted on July 19th, 1936, from the Croydon-hired aeroplane which had brought him from Las Palmas to take over the direction of the national rising after the murder of Calvo Sotelo.

"Are you a general?" I enquired.

"*Teniente Coronel*," the aide replied smilingly, turning a khaki cuff round to display the respective stars.

"*Ud. habla español muy bien*," he complimented with a grin, and I thanked him for the agreeable lie. I spoke of the clear pronunciation of the Burgos folk, and told him of a girl from that region who, upon my enquiring for some mineral water in the Albergue at La Bañeza, had made vocal music of her reply— "*Mon-da-rith, señor*." The aide thereupon mentioned that the Galician people spoke "very sweetly", with a soft and charming accent.

Franco, said the aide, was fond of the countryside and preferred the tranquillity of El Pardo to the bustle and noise of the capital. "For exercises he takes an occasional walk to the palace farm, or plays golf on the course here; he plays tennis but has given up riding now. He paints, and the walls of one of the rooms upstairs are hung with his pictures."* Those he considers the best among his paintings, however, including certain fine copies of Old Master 'still-lifes', adorn some of the rooms of his Galician summer home at El Pazo de Meirás, which, with its grey stone walls and towers standing on a gentle, green, English-looking slope above Corunna, strongly resembles a transplanted Tudor castle.

"Are they good?" I asked.

"Not at all bad," he replied, adding that the man who for nearly two decades has controlled Spain's destinies also liked to occupy part of his small leisure in writing film scenarios.

The aide referred to Franco's capacity for work, remarking that often he did not lunch until four in the afternoon and sometimes not till six o'clock in the evening—"and he has taken nothing since his customary breakfast of fruit and a single cup of coffee."

Recollecting the several thick volumes of the Spanish Leader's speeches, I now enquired if Franco enlisted any expert help in their preparation, for some are of considerable length and display much learning, such as the one he delivered at Barcelona on Balmes, the Spanish Christian philosopher famous for his defence of Catholicism.

"He prepares them all himself," was the answer, "either by

---

* "Following the example of Sir Winston Churchill and President Eisenhower, General Franco has started 'painting for pleasure'. News of his new hobby leaked out recently when *Arriba* published a three-column picture showing the *Caudillo*, wearing a wide-brimmed sombrero and a pin-stripe suit, working at his easel in the grounds of El Pardo, his official residence fourteen miles north of Madrid.

"Working in full sunlight, with his palette firmly hooked over his left thumb, the Generalissimo was shown screwing up his eyes as he gazed appraisingly at the mountain background of his half-finished painting.

"The Palace of El Pardo, one of Spain's smaller and more attractive royal residences, is built on a wide loop of the Manzanares River, and its grounds slope gently to the water's edge. Forming a solid back-drop are the impressively broad shoulders of the Guadarrama Mountains— misty green in the early morning, bleached to a dull khaki by the blistering midday sun, and theatrically but briefly mauve and crimson at sundown.

"In between is a vast expanse of dust-coloured scrubland strewn with blue-grey rock and smudged with low bushes and stunted trees." . . . *Sunday Times*, July 25th, 1954 ("Atticus").

writing a draft in his own hand, or dictating notes to a steno-grapher." General Franco, I knew, had taken some English lessons when Captain-General of the Canaries—his teacher there is in fact today one of the four official translators in the Foreign Ministry—so I asked if he spoke it. The aide replied, "No, I believe not: but he is studying it by ear now from records."

Franco on occasion still drives, sometimes on hunting forays, in the big black Mercedes-Benz car given him by Hitler (whose own I had once seen parked near the majestic 'filigree' tower of Ulm Cathedral with its 528-ft. spire, the highest in the world). On all ceremonial occasions he uses one of the two bullet-proof Rolls-Royce models, costing £10,000 apiece, supplied to him from Britain. The Governor of Gibraltar, when inviting all Spaniards who wished to do so to visit the Rock and witness the arrival at the end of her world voyage of Queen Elizabeth II—an indis-cretion which brought him a hurried recall by air to London and a rap over the knuckles from the competent authorities—made a pointed reference to the fact that Britain's sovereigns moved about freely among their loyal subjects "without any special precautions being taken for their safety". He thus showed himself prone to our common English failing of regarding a foreign people of a totally different temperament and tradition as if they too were English.

The Governor, moreover, was obviously unfamiliar with recent Spanish history, or he would have known that three *Democratic* Prime Ministers, Cánovas, Canalejas and Eduardo Dato, had all fallen victims to assassins' bullets in the streets of the capital.

Only the original tapestried swing-doors, imperfectly joined, separated the ante-room in which we were waiting from Franco's study, and from time to time there emerged through them a good deal of noise and shouting, as though a heated argument, or some sort of fight was in progress. Mr. Roy Howard, President of the Scripps-Howard Group of nineteen American evening news-papers, was closeted with the *Caudillo* and—as I learned later—not speaking Castillian was emphasising his points, and his pointed questions, with Valls as interpreter, by verbally firing them at Franco alternately like missiles from a trench mortar or a sub-machine gun, and Franco's replies, sometimes interrupted by a robust laugh, were being directed back with equal ebullience.

By this time the aide had seated himself alongside me on one of the decorative palace chairs, in a gesture of friendly familiarity which Spaniards can so easily adopt with strangers, and I asked him where the Cabinet held its meetings. He rose and silently beckoned me to the door opposite the study, and we entered a long room, thickly carpeted, with a low ceiling and one big table with rows of facing chairs, and, at the head of it, a larger chair with ornamental armrests.

"*Aquí!*" he said, "sometimes the Ministers are in conference the whole morning, usually returning after lunch for another session lasting often until evening and sometimes far into the night."

Indeed, in this conference room some of the most fateful wartime sessions of the Spanish Government had taken place. Here the critical questions of Spain's precise relations with the Axis and the Allied Powers, each complaining of "unethical conduct", of her precarious existence on the margin of the world conflict, were thrashed out between the Government Ministers and "Paco", who is a brilliant conversationalist and likes to talk for hours pacing up and down the carpeted floor.

"Originally this was the dining-room," the aide explained, "but as you see it makes a very good conference room."

When we returned to the ante-room the swing-doors suddenly opened, and Mr. Howard, followed by Señor Valls, appeared with a sheaf of notes and expressed regret for taking so long. There was no time for response for the aide was holding the door open and I walked straight up to a large square table over which a stocky, khaki-clad figure was inclining. The room, I observed at once, was not so spacious as the ill-fated Mussolini's former sanctum in the Palazzo Venezia at Rome, but bigger than Hitler's had been in the now demolished Brown House in Munich where, when I visited it in 1936, his desk had stood opposite an oil painting of the first World War showing German infantry clambering out of their trenches to meet a British attack in the sector where Lance-Corporal Shickelgrüber himself had become a casualty.

As I approached Franco turned and advanced a step, and a moment later I was exchanging a handshake with the 'despot' whom half the world condemns, and whose purpose and motives are repeatedly arraigned by the other half. His dark luminous eyes stared at me with that "long enquiring look" which other visitors have remarked upon.

Valls returned and the *Caudillo* beckoned us to two chairs placed immediately opposite his own, beside the celebrated Empire table which I momentarily observed was tidily stacked with piles of typed documents and publications of all descriptions.

On the wall an ivory crucifix was suspended, with another full-length tapestry as ample backcloth.

Chapter Five

FACE TO FACE

"**E**SE HOMBRE" WAS ATTIRED IN the service uniform of a full General of the Spanish Army, less the red sash with pendant tassels only worn on ceremonial occasions, and with a single decoration pinned to his left breast, the Medal Laureada de San Fernando, Spain's highest military decoration, in rubies. When I talked once at Claridge's with Field Marshal Viscount Montgomery, K.G., his left breast was 'rainbowed' with five banked rows of ribbons; but the tunic of the Generalissimo of all Spain's Armed Forces, and the Leader of the Nation, was innocent of one. Sometimes, as Chief of the Phalanx, Franco wears the ruby-set Order of the Yoke and Arrows, but he was not doing so on this occasion. One hears occasionally that his personal relationship to the *F.E.T.* is that of a *mariage de convenance* and not of affection.

He certainly seemed in very fit condition; his dark eyes shone warm and brightly and he had a rubicund complexion, as of one who lives much in the open air. His sparse and greying hair was brushed straight back from a broad forehead on which no wrinkles were perceptible. Sitting very straight in his high-backed chair he shuffled his feet once or twice, but I could not testify whether this was due to nervousness of myself or because they did not quite reach the ground.

At the age of 61, and after a ferocious internal war and nearly two decades of power, the Head of State bore the appearance of a man quite unbowed by his arduous responsibilities or by the national tensions and international storms that have raged about his head for most of the time. As a matter of sober fact, his countenance in repose is almost as cherubic as Churchill's and this cast of his features was, if anything, enhanced by his tan. A simple man? It could be, but patently a man of power and character, of strong will and a penetrating intelligence. . . .

"I have been charged, Your Excellency, with the task of

73

writing a biographical study of you." Thus I began in a Castillian which would sometimes in the past cause Spanish friends to screw up their faces in an anguished desire to apprehend my meaning. Franco nodded encouragingly, with his steady gaze and without uttering a word.

"I was at El Ferrol recently and saw the house in which you were born. I was surprised to find that, although there is a plaque outside identifying it as the birthplace of Your Excellency and your brother Ramón* the house is preserved neither as a museum nor as a national monument."

Franco, who had understood me, turned to Aurelio Valls and remarked quietly that the house was, in fact, still family property; that the *Ayuntamiento*, or Municipal Council, had approached him with the object of preserving it as a permanent memorial, but that he was permitting the families of "tres marineros"—three sailors—to continue to live there as he did not wish to put them to the inconvenience of seeking alternative accommodation in Spain's largest naval port and dockyard. He spoke with a gentle lilt of the voice and in the soft Galician accent to which the aide referred, and, what was certainly for me quite unexpected, with a slight lisp, less sibilant than Sir Winston Churchill's but nevertheless just as marked.

"I was not able to discover very much about your childhood," I resumed—and Valls repeated the word "niñeza" as Franco glanced round enquiringly.

The *Caudillo*'s features now relaxed in a pleasant smile as he replied: "I didn't have much; I was a cadet at fourteen and then no longer a boy, but a man. I wanted to enter the Spanish navy,

---

* The late Commander Ramón Franco, pilot of the first aircraft, the *Plus Ultra*, to fly the South Atlantic, with Ruiz de Alda as navigator and two others. In 1929 he attempted a second more difficult crossing in the *Numancia*, which came down in mid-Atlantic. He and his companions were rescued by the British aircraft-carrier H.M.S. *Eagle* to which the Spaniards later sent a trophy, a piece of sculpture, as an expression of gratitude. The Spanish Naval Attaché in London, Captain Fontán, who was for many years Naval A.D.C. at El Pardo, saw the trophy in the captain's quarters of the *Eagle* when the aircraft-carrier paid a courtesy visit to Vigo in 1953.

Ramón Franco lost his life when his plane fell into the Mediterranean in 1938.

but there were no vacancies at the Naval College in my year and so I went to the Infantry Academy at Toledo instead." He smiled again, recalling his early years: "I played 'fútbol', which was just becoming known in Spain then; I fished in the harbour with other boys of my age, and sometimes we took the planks used as gangways by the ferry steamers and played at pirates in the bay. I was always falling into the water I remember," and he smiled broadly at the memory.

In questions hastily prepared I had included one based on private information that he "did not like England much". I intended asking why he was not more tactful in public pronouncements about Britain, why he did not sometimes say something pleasant about my own people. "The remembrance still rankles," I had rehearsed, "of that war-time sneer, made to placate Hitler, perhaps, about America 'exchanging fifty old destroyers for some bits of a disintegrating Empire'."

But Franco forestalled me by making some reference which I did not quite follow about thinking not of "moro o rubio" Englishmen, "of fair or dark" Germans, but simply of the inhabitants of a country in their totality, and then of his own accord introduced the subject of the famous Hendaye meeting, of which a photograph exists showing him greeting Hitler with a beaming smile.*

"I told Hitler that he would never defeat England, either in the air or on the sea. I asked him why, therefore, he did not stop fighting her and pointed out that it was lunacy thus to weaken Western bulwarks against Communism. He disagreed—he thought he was a god" (Franco here used the portmanteau term "endiosado—engoddened") "and was not disposed to listen to reason."

"Did he demand access to Gibraltar?"

"He wanted German units to pass through Spain," commented the *Caudillo*, "but he did not press the matter unduly at Hendaye.

---

* "Germany and Italy realised the crucial nature of our Civil War struggle as a struggle for our existence as a nation," a Spanish diplomat remarked to me, in particular reference to this picture, "and so naturally the *Caudillo* met him with a smile and not with a grimace." In any case, a smile comes much more readily to a Spaniard than almost to any other National—and doubtless it misled the megalomaniac Hitler in that first round.

That came later. I said Gibraltar was our business, that it was a Spanish affair, and that we could never allow it to be taken for us."

It is clear from the published testimony of Schmidt and Ciano, and from captured German documents, that what Hitler was really after at that interview was the naming of a fixed date for Spain's entry into the war on the side of the Axis. He did not get it from Franco, although he all but got it later from Serrano Suñer during the visit of the then Spanish Foreign Minister ("that crafty Jesuit", Hitler and Goering called him) to Berlin. Subsequently, in a mood of bright anticipation, the German war-time Ambassador to Spain, von Stohrer, made the journey to El Pardo to thank the Head of the State for fixing the date at last, quoting a secret despatch from Ribbentrop. He met with an icy reception and the retort: "I must remind you, my dear Ambassador, that you are in Spain. There is only room for one man to govern this country, not two. That function still belongs to me." Shortly afterwards von Stohrer, who, when I lived in Egypt, was once rescued by R.A.F. aircraft after a foolhardy car expedition alone into the Libyan desert, was recalled to Germany.

Recollecting the reputation Franco had enjoyed with his *Regulares* in Africa as "el más valiente de los valientes", and the popular tale that he liked leading his men into action mounted on a white charger, I now asked if he was without fear, or had he ever been conscious of it? He replied logically enough that he thought fear innate in man, and continued:

"I have known fear but as I have always regarded my life as a gift ('regalo') from Providence I have never worried overmuch about personal safety. Since I became responsible for the welfare of the Spanish people I have at times experienced it in a more intense form. There is a moral and spiritual anguish in taking some decisions in a position of authority which is worse, much worse, than any purely physical fear." He went on to speak of Cabrera, nicknamed "the tiger of the Maestrazgo", a famous guerrilla leader in the Carlist wars who had spent some years in exile in England, after carrying out ruthless reprisals in revenge for the execution of his aged mother. He married an Englishwoman and settled down at Virginia Water.

"Cabrera went in for fox-hunting," Franco remarked, "but it was noticed by the other riders that he always avoided taking gates or hedges and would lead his mount away in search of easier exits. One day a hard-riding Englishwoman asked him if he was afraid to jump the natural obstacles at a hunt ; Cabrera replied (I give Franco's own quotation): '*Señora, tengo miedo solamente de una cosa, morir sin gloria*—Lady, I fear only one thing, to die without glory'—to die a foolish death."

"A very Spanish attitude," Valls suggested with a smile, and the *Caudillo* nodded his head.

Again I mentioned Ciano's Diaries and the memoirs of Paul Schmidt, Hitler's interpreter, whom I tracked down to his flat in Reitmorstrasse in Munich some months later to seek his personal impressions of the Hendaye interview only to find him away on holiday. Franco said that such personal accounts were rarely reliable as source-books, because of the vanity of their authors who "always wish to stand well with posterity. To obtain an objective view of Napoleon," he added, "it is necessary to read the accounts of his conversations with his generals and his letters to Josephine, in which he gives a far from flattering picture of himself."

"Napoleon gives an even less flattering self-portrait," Franco went on, "in the marginal notes he made in the copy of Machiavelli's *Prince* which he carried about with him on his campaigns." This actual copy of a celebrated essay, originally written with Ferdinand of Aragon as model, marked with Napoleon's own annotations, was, I learned later, published in facsimile in Republican territory during the Civil War and Franco obtained a copy of the special edition by sending a courier to secure one through the fighting lines. . . .

At the time of my first interview with the Head of the Spanish State France was in the throes of a dangerous political and national crisis following the unexpectedly sudden fall of Dien Bien Phu, the 'Verdun redoubt' of Indo-China, and I asked him what he thought Napoleon's attitude would be to France were he to return to life at that particular juncture. Franco replied that General de Castries and his men had fought well, but said the high strategists had been in error in joining decisive battle with the Viet-Minh forces where they did.

Suddenly he rose from his high-backed chair and beckoned me with an easy gesture to his working table where, from the mass of documents and publications piled upon it, he extracted in a moment a recent copy of *The Illustrated London News*, which he opened at a double spread of pictures of the French positions and trenches at Dien Bien Phu, with, in the lower left-hand corner, a field sketch-map showing also the surrounding outposts of Gabrielle, Dominique, Eliane, Huguette, Claudine and Isabelle.

The frontispiece illustration, which must have been pure gall to the patriot Franco, I discovered some time later in London, when I looked up the files at Ingram House in the Strand, was of the Queen, accompanied by the royal children, being handed the keys of Gibraltar on disembarking after her triumphal Commonwealth tour. The issue also contained a page-review by Sir John Squire of a translation of the full-length historical biography of Antonio Pérez, Secretary to Philip II, by the Madrid medical specialist and eminent Spaniard, Don Gregorio Marañón, who used to be an ardent and active Republican but is today reconciled to the régime.

Franco, with whom I was now standing shoulder to shoulder, placed a forefinger squarely on the map and ran it round the sketch of the Dien Bien Phu redoubt to the shaded triangles representing the surrounding hills.

"The position was strategically quite untenable," he repeated; "regard these hills, each with Viet-Minh observation posts and batteries from which precise gunfire could be ranged on every part of the defences. Look at the airstrip—in full view and range of the enemy forces and thus quickly and easily rendered unusable. The French were guilty of a strategical blunder to make in such a place their decisive stand."* As I had myself once been in action with my battery in just such an exposed position, and had, in fact, been knocked out by enemy fire from just such a range of hills, I was all attention.

Franco seemed quite absorbed by his calculations as he stood looking at the map before us, darting his finger from one corner of it to another. He was perhaps recalling some critical phases of the Civil War, for the Nationalist forces, and even he himself, on more than one occasion, had been so surrounded, despite his own

---

* This was precisely the complaint of Colonel Langeland, the second in command at Dien Bien Phu, at the secret enquiry held at Hanoi after the armistice.

pet system of using every available coign of observation. Whenever a Nationalist commander had reported that his troops were encircled and that he was unable to manoeuvre them he was invariably told: "Well, you must fight your way out then." . . . For, from beginning to end of the Civil war, not one unit on either side ever surrendered.

Recollecting a remark of the aide that the Generalissimo often read far into the night, I asked before taking my leave if he read English authors in the original and if so which were his favourites. He replied that there were excellent Spanish translations of the best European writers, and left it at that.

"I hope, Your Excellency," I said, "that I may write a worthwhile book about you, but I intend to make it as objective as I can." Franco inclined his head, as if to say, "So be it," gave a parting smile and a handshake. A moment later I was back in the ante-room listening to Mr. Roy Howard estimating just how long it had taken him to make the deferential aide understand the particular corner of the palace he was at that juncture most desirous of identifying.

Chapter Six

OBLIQUE VIEW

THE PRESIDENT OF THE SCRIPPS-HOWARD American Newspaper Group recounted, while we were waiting to leave, an interview he had obtained as a visiting American reporter with David Lloyd George, then Minister for Home Affairs in an Asquith Government, simply by sending up to his Whitehall sanctum a visiting card by a reluctant and sceptical commissionaire, and of his several visits to Russia and interviews, one of nearly four hours' duration, with Stalin whom, he added, he had always found to be a very genial person fond of a good joke (and so was the wolf in Red Riding Hood).

"But this man Franco," he exclaimed, with a quick smile, "has the quickest and most lucid brain and the most realistic approach to international problems, of any of the many rulers of nations I have interviewed during the past forty years."

We descended the staircase together and entered the waiting car, as the Moorish sentries came again smartly to the salute. Presently we were gliding along the tree-lined highway back to the capital. It was then that he announced that he wished his interview to be cleared for cabling that night. This involved, first the writing up of the interview and then translation in the Palacio de Santa Cruz of the entire text into Spanish and the rushing by urgent messenger of the article to El Pardo for Franco's perusal when he could spare the time, and its return immediately to the Castellana Hilton Hotel, opposite the stately equestrian statue of Isabella, on the Paseo de la Castellana, where Howard was staying—all in the matter of a few hours.

"Well, we got the interview through in time," said Valls the next day in his flat beyond Retiro Park, where he had kindly invited me to lunch with him and Señora de Valls and their year-old baby. The following afternoon the Howard interview with the Head of the Spanish State was tea-time reading—for those of them who take afternoon tea—for some three and a half million inhabitants of the great Western Continent first discovered and temporarily

The typical middle-class Galician house situated off the main square of El Ferrol, north-western Spain, where Francisco Paulino Hermenegildo Teodulo Franco was born at 4.30 a.m. on December 4, 1892. A Municipal plaque jointly memorialises his service in Africa and the exploits of his brother Ramon, first to fly the South Atlantic   (*Courtesy of Instituto de Cultura Hispánica*)

Aged 17. The youthful 2nd Lieutenant. A signed portrait for home, on passing out from the Military Academy at Toledo and posting to the 8th Zamora Regiment, of which H.M. the late King George V was Honorary

Aged 14. 'A slender youth of delicate features and large shining curious eyes,—in military cadet's uniform, with his naval cadet brother Nicolás, since 1937 Spain's Ambassador to Portugal   (*State Archives*)

settled by the Norwegian Viking Lief Ericsson in the tenth century (as the Norse sagas say) and later sighted, after a lapse of five centuries, during his first voyage from Palos, by the Genoese *converso* and cantankerous visionary, Cristobal Colón. (In Madrid I had been introduced to a direct descendant of Columbus, a daughter-in-law of the Duchess of Nájera. Her brother, the Duke of Veragua, a commander in the Spanish Navy, bears an extraordinary resemblance to authentic contemporary portraits of his famous ancestor, as does Lord de L'Isle and Dudley, v.c., to his famous forebear, Sir Philip Sidney, whose godfather was Philip II after whom he was named.)

In due time the full text of Mr. Howard's interview came into my hands, and as it reveals Franco from a different angle on that very June morning of my own first meeting with him it may be of interest to readers of this biographical investigation if I reproduce it *in extenso!*, with the kind sanction of the interviewer in his capacity as Editor for the *New York World-Telegram*:—

Madrid, June 3rd.—A sweeping reorganization of the tactics employed by the nations aligned against international Communism was advocated today by Generalissimo Francisco Franco in a private conversation with this writer. The Spanish Chief of State, the only soldier credited with an unchallengeable victory over a Communist-directed army, believes that the cold war tactics of the anti-Communist coalition are failing because they are not concentrating on Russia's greatest weakness—lack of non-strategic imports from the non-Communist world.

General Franco believes that every anti-Communist nation interested in halting the spread of the Red menace, should immediately embargo trade of every kind with Russia and her satellites. By such action the free world would be striking at the Achilles heel of communism.

General Franco developed the basis for his beliefs in the course of an unhurried and wholly informal discussion of the world situation at El Pardo, his suburban headquarters, in what was formally a royal hunting lodge. During the talk the Generalissimo evidenced a very real admiration for President Eisenhower and in many expressions relative to the new Hispano-American relationship, reflected the warm feeling toward America which is so much in evidence throughout Spain and which is in such striking contrast to the attitude in many other European travel spots.

He explained the reasoning back of his call for a reorganization of the free world's alignment against Communism with the force and clarity of a soldier, despite the fact that his plans call for at least temporary subordination of military activities in favour of the civilian effort.

6

it was in response to a request for an appraisal of the effectiveness of the anti-Communist coalition that America's newest military ally stated his opinion with candor and a refreshing absence of diplomatic double-talk.

"The success of the Western coalition has been considerable," said the Generalissimo, "but it could be greater with better organization. The West has a staff united for effective work on the military side. It is not equally well-organized for political action. The coalition needs a united civilian staff co-ordinated with the military but empowered to deal directly with all political and economic matters of mutual concern. Unity of action on political problems is as necessary in cold war as is unity on military problems in a hot war.

"Russia's military strength is very real but it is not sufficiently dominant to cause Moscow to put it to the test now. As a result, the economic problems of the cold war today are of at least equal importance with the military problems. If the anti-Communist nations of the West will unite with those of the Far East on a joint economic programme, they can win the cold war on all fronts. If they win the cold war, they may avoid a hot one. Unfortunately at the present time they are not winning the cold war. They will not win it until they put the desire for peace above the desire for profit through trade with Russia.

"Perhaps Americans do not realize the intensity of the need of Great Britain and other industrial nations of Western Europe for a restoration of their prosperity. The desire is as natural as it is dangerous, though in some instances it motivates a willingness to betray the future for the sake of the present. However, if the coalition nations can be assembled around a conference table, it can be demonstrated why an embargo of all trade with Russia is necessary and why even some of the most innocent-appearing commodities have strategic value once they have passed through the Iron Curtain."

He developed in detail his arguments for an air-tight embargo against all exports to Communist areas and pointed out the length and bitterness of the austerity programme under which the Russian people have existed since 1917 and to which they have been held by the iron fist of the Russian Terror. Following World War II and the aggressions in Eastern Europe, the people of Russia proper benefited slightly and temporarily through the drainage from the satellite states of their resources. However, the people of the satellite states having been bled white are now proving difficult to control. There has been continual grumbling and mounting discontent in the newly communized areas, as was revealed by the recent uprising in East Germany.

Franco believes it is through imports that Russia hopes for a solution of this problem of restlessness and discontent. Her momentary concern is not for strategic imports for war purposes but for imports to promote peace, in

General Franco's opinion. If she can insure this peace among the captive satellites for the next few years, Moscow knows she can crush the last vestiges of conflicting nationalism there while a new generation develops, completely indoctrinated in Communist ideology and Red fanaticism.

"It is self-deception to believe that embargoing strategic materials alone is any insurance against Russian aggression," Franco said. "Moscow knows that extensive commodity trade with the free world will ease tensions inside the Iron Curtain, and increase them outside when the scramble for business starts. Germany, which once profited so greatly from its Russian trade, is counted on to contribute heavily to the dissension.

"Apparently Americans find it difficult to realize the extent of the disaster suffered by the industrial nations of Western Europe through the loss of their former markets, now inside the Iron Curtain. It is unrealistic to ascribe their desire for a resumption of trade to mere greed. In many instances actual survival is at stake, and will continue to be until an alternate economic outlet is developed.

"In the face of these conditions, the only alternative to a mad scramble for trade inside the Communist area is development of new world markets outside the Red orbit. It is this necessity for new markets that makes mandatory the immediate creation by the anti-Communist coalition of a joint political and economic council to co-ordinate with and serve as a counterpart of the joint supreme military authority.

"Such a political body could organize and mastermind a trade embargo enforced against all Communist countries. It would assure identical treatment for all participating nations. Even more important, this civilian council would organize and direct the new economy of the free world, which must be created to compensate for the lost Communist markets. This task would demand the best efforts of the free world's greatest economic planners. It would require extensive surveys to locate new and potential markets and to revive old and under-developed ones.

"Extensive commercial and governmental financing would be necessary. But all this should be done on the basis of long-time self-liquidating loans. Because the new economy must be designed for permanency, it should operate on a strictly business basis, divorced from any giveaway policies.

"No temporary or makeshift organization will suffice. Communist tactics change from day to day, but Communist strategy is long-range and undeviating. The strategy of the anti-Communist world must be equally so.

"I repeat and re-emphasize that to meet this situation a united supreme civilian authority has become an immediate necessity," Generalissimo Franco concluded.

What is the outstanding viewpoint that this statement reveals? It reveals, in my opinion, unequivocal confrontation with the

inescapable fact of the 'cold war'—the realistic recognition that
the hostility of the Communist *bloc* to the Christian West is
unchanged and fixed. When, a few weeks after the publication of
Mr. Roy Howard's article, the question of the admission of
Communist China to the United Nations' organisation became
a burning topic in the world Press, and accounts appeared of an
approaching visit to Peking as the guests of Mao-Tse-Tung of
Mr. Attlee, Mr. Bevan and other British Labour luminaries, the
Australian Prime Minister, the forthright Mr. Menzies, announced: "I do not discuss recognition of my enemy while I am
in the field with him."

Life had published horrifying photographs of murdered
American prisoners-of-war in Korea, and of hundreds of poor
South Korean soldiers brutally clubbed to death by their Chinese
and North Korean Communist captors in disused caves; while
Judge Waris Ameer Ali wrote in the London *Daily Telegraph*
that it had been reported on good authority that after their
surrender to the outnumbering forces of Mao, National Chinese
officers "suffered death by being flayed alive in the presence of the
men they had commanded." Judge Ameer Ali added, with some
bitterness: "It will be interesting if, when visiting Peking, Mr.
Attlee and his companions learn anything of the subsequent fate
of the rank and file."

Franco, at least, is logical in his undeviating attitude towards the
world-wide Communist conspiracy and its implications:

> I know where I'm going,
> And I know who's going with me;*
> I know where I'm going,
> But the Lord knows who I'll marry. . . .

---

* Namely, the Spanish people, for (Franco has said) "if ever Russian
Communist forces reached Spain every man, woman and child would
fight to the death against them."

Chapter Seven

'CAUDILLO' — OR KING?

LET US INVESTIGATE, AT THIS STAGE, the explosive question of Franco's attitude to the restoration of a Spanish king; for, as we know, he has obtained by a huge majority a decisive and truly democratic vote from the entire Spanish nation (barring exiles) in declaring Spain to be again a Monarchy* The man himself *is* a monarchist—by training, by tradition, and by conviction. In 1916, when he was recovered from wounds and during one of his rare spells of home service from his fifteen years' front-line campaigning in Spanish Morocco, he was attached to the regiment of which the late Prince of Asturias, despite tragic physical handicaps, was Honorary Colonel-in-Chief, and a field photograph taken at that time shows a lean, dapper and smiling Franco assembled with fellow-officers about an equally dapper and happy-looking young prince. In 1923 the late King Alfonso XIII was best man by proxy (the Captain-General of the Region taking his place) at his wedding in the homely, attractive church of San Juan el Real at Oviedo, capital of the northern province of Asturias, to the beautiful seventeen-year-old Carmen Polo y Martínez-Valdés, daughter of an Oviedo business-man resident in the main square. Five years later Franco was appointed to his first big military assignment outside Africa, the Directorship of the Military Academy at Saragossa, by General Primo de Rivera, with Don Alfonso's active and enthusiastic support.

Even when giving effective service to the Second Spanish Republic he made no secret of his monarchist sympathies, and since he assumed leadership of the country he has repeatedly promised that another king will be installed on the vacant throne in due time, adding only the cryptic qualification that the royal candidate must be "different" to former Spanish kings and that

---

* The actual figures of the referendum were: In favour 12,628,983. Against 643,501; with 295,208 blank returns and 25,669 spoiled ones.

such installation would take place "only when I choose". Certainly, this able and astute man shows himself in no hurry at all to honour his pledges; in fact a statement by him is on record that while he lives he will remain Generalissimo of the Armed Forces and *Caudillo* of his people ("I dedicate what remains of my life to the service of Spain") perhaps a dangerous statement and attitude, for he might become homicidally mad, like Ivan the Terrible, or Hitler, or otherwise *non compos mentis*.

What is little enough known beyond the frontiers of that tawny wine-skin land is that the 'rock' on which split any possibility of the early post-war restoration of a king was the flat and reiterated refusal of the Pretender, Don Juan de Borbón y Battenberg, Count of Barcelona, to reign over a Spain governed on the lines of a Syndicalist State according to the twenty-six points of the Phalangist *credo*, the programme drawn up by the founder of the *Falange* and its chief 'martyr', José Antonio Primo de Rivera, who was by profession and vocation a barrister-at-law. In a declaration published in the *Journal de Genève* on November 11th, 1942, the third son of King Alfonso and Queen Victoria Eugenia, whom the king had formally recognised before his death in Rome as his heir, said: "I will do my best to guarantee Spain's spiritual unity and her historical continuity, to alleviate with a father's affectionate authority the recent happenings, and to give a real satisfaction to the longings of the great mass of Spaniards who hope for a juster and better life."

It was understandable, of course, and perfectly obvious that the new heir to the Spanish crown had fully absorbed the tenets of Anglo-American democratic processes, with some help no doubt from his own and British advisers, and that, after his five years' impregnation with the British system as cadet and commissioned officer in the Royal Navy, "very happy years", as he has said, he would in his own way restore democratic government to the Spains, allowing every party voice and vote in free elections—including, presumably, the Communists and Anarchists who had brought the country to near ruin and alien slavery when the Civil War broke out.

Franco, however, would have none of this. For him the whole Republican experiment, followed by the Civil War, the Crusade, the War of Liberation, had discredited for good and all the Western democratic system so far as Spain was concerned;

for him 19th-century Liberalism was a dead letter, that Liberalism ushered in by the disastrous French Revolution, the tragic if long-delayed consequence of the equally disastrous Reformation which had sundered Europe's spiritual unity. "Man was born free and is everywhere in chains." The Reformation and the French Revolution had finally resulted in the atheistical Bolshevik creed, in militant international Communism, a thirst for world domination, the worship of the State and the subversion of the mind, the personality and the soul of man. ("England is separated from us by the Reformation. . . . European civilisation stands or falls with the Church," a noted Spaniard has said).

"What I cannot and never will do," Franco told Don Juan in one of the severest rebukes that can ever have been sent by a Commoner-ruler of a country to the legitimate aspirant to its throne, "is to betray the spirit of those who fought beside me, convert Spain into a lowly and unchivalrous nation, or anything but what my conscience and duty demand I should do in the best interests of Spain."

It is worth while reproducing this historic correspondence *in extenso*, for it illumines unequivocally and without reserve the implacable stand of one of the two men and the hesitant, would-be-amenable attitude of the other.

In March, 1943, while he was living in Lausanne and three years before he moved with his family and entourage to Lisbon, Don Juan affirmed in a letter to Franco: "My acquiescence in this (*i.e.* endorsement of the Phalangist programme) would imply a patent denial of the very essence of the Monarchist virtue, profoundly averse to the fostering of party divisions. . . ." But the reintroduction into the Spanish political scene of the extreme Left-wing parties would foster party divisions infinitely more and risk plunging the country into another fratricidal struggle, as any counsellor with the minimum of political acumen could have advised his monarch. But Don Juan, a descendant of 'the Great White Queen' Victoria, wished to reign 'democratically', like his distant kinsman, King George VI in Britain, and after all, was not the entire Western democratic world (and, of course, Soviet Russia), then still in the throes of mortal conflict with Nazi Germany and militarist Japan, determined that "Franco Must Go" as soon as peace was restored? Even the Spanish Section of the

European Division of the B.B.C. repeatedly said so in rude broadcasts to Spain, which caused the British Ambassador, then Sir Samuel Hoare, some uneasiness.

So on January 25th, 1944, the Pretender addressed another communication to the 'usurper' of the royal prerogatives, in which, it is of some interest to note, no word of recognition, let alone of gratitude, escapes for anything Franco may have done during the Civil War to rescue the country of both of them from the abyss:

> Your Excellency [the letter runs] is one of the very few Spaniards who believe in the stability of the National Syndicalist régime. You are one of the few who believe that our nation, still irreconcilably divided, will have sufficient strength at the end of theWorld War to resist the attacks of extremists. You are one of the few who believe that you can succeed, through mollification and concession, in gaining the respect of those foreign nations which have noted with disgust your policy towards them. . . . I am convinced that Your Excellency and the régime which you direct cannot survive the end of the war. . . .
>
> I have always refused to accede to Your Excellency's written requests to me to identify myself with the Falangist State, because I have believed it to be incompatible with the very essence of the character of the Monarchy. . . .

But both the Excellency and his régime survived the end of the war—as our friends the Americans say, "And how"—despite every conceivable pressure and international calumny.

Some days after Britain and the United States had announced, in 1944, an embargo on petroleum shipments to Spain, Don Juan, perhaps in the absence of advisers at this time, made a surprising *volte face* and *did* identify himself with the Nationalist ideals, as completely as when he crossed the French frontier as plain Juan López at the beginning of the Civil War to ask for permission to fight with them for "the new Spain". On February 3rd of that year he sent this telegram to Franco:

> In a letter addressed to Your Excellency on the 25th last and in recent statements to Press anticipating international complications which I had predicted for some time, I have adopted this attitude solely for patriotic purposes of preventing situation developing in which only two political solutions open to Spain would be

maintenance at all costs of Your Excellency's régime or that which those vanquished in our Civil War are trying and will try to impose with foreign aid.

I am confident that Your Excellency interpreted my attitude in this way. I appeal with all my heart to your well-proved patriotism that, forgetting divergences of opinion, we may reach agreement permitting restoration of the Monarchy within brief time, thus escaping present difficulties and saving Spain from danger of new Civil War.

By acting in this manner we would still be in position to defend the principles which led us to rise up against the Popular Front. Tomorrow perhaps it will be too late. I am sure that Your Excellency conscious of the grave dangers which threaten Spain and anxious to overcome present difficulties, will not refuse to consider this one solution which the interest of our country so urgently demands. Long live Spain.—*Juan, Count of Barcelona.*

What was to be the *Caudillo's* reaction to this ingenuous and ingenious personal effort on the part of a thwarted Pretender, who, naturally and understandably, wanted so much to be king of his people, but whose instinct and vision of the tremendous spiritual and international issues involved in any restoration were so patently inadequate? The Count of Barcelona was not left long in doubt, and the reply telegram was not long delayed:

I reply to your telegram of the 3rd [wired the temporary occupant of the royal palace of El Pardo]. Your statements, made with an eye to appealing to foreigners, have created a very bad impression in Spain even among persons most closely attached to the Monarchy. They strike a discordant note in the face of the unity which all Spaniards who are not reds, both within and outside the country, have respected.

Recent developments in Spain's foreign relations are due only to our active defence of our rights and of our sovereignty. Spain is not willing to lose the fruits of our victorious crusade because of the world war now being fought, and it will defend its sovereignty with all means, not counting days or years, to the last man and the last Catholic.

The restoration of the Monarchy towards which we are heading firmly is not assisted by the dissidence and conflicts provoked by Monarchist groups nor by public expressions of disunity and hostility towards the régime born of our crusade and freely recognised by all nations.

I have tried at all times in my letters to overcome your obstinacy and I truly regret the disagreements caused by obvious errors which you are unwilling to disavow.What I cannot and never will do is to betray the spirit of those who fought beside me, convert Spain into a lowly and unchivalrous nation, or anything but what my conscience and duty demand I should do in the best interests of Spain.— *Francisco Franco.*

What was Don Juan's reaction to this clear, outspoken and decidedly disrespectful rap over the knuckles, which, whatever its subtlety, bespeaks the attitude of a *man*? He swung right back to his original position, hostility to the régime and a peremptory demand that it should be brought to an end forthwith and that this pertinacious little Gallego who knew how to wait should find another home.

On March 19th, 1945, the Infante issued his famous Manifesto, at the same time calling upon all Spanish Ambassadors to resign their functions, a demand only obeyed in the event by that great monarchist and faithful friend of the unhappy Spanish royal family, the Duke of Berwick and Alba, distant kinsman of James II and Sir Winston Churchill, who, shortly after he had announced his resignation to representatives of the British Press at a sherry party at Claridge's rasped out as we sat tête-à-tête in the pile-carpeted reception room of the London Embassy: "Franco must go: the Monarchy and the Catholic Faith are the only factors which hold Spaniards together."

As the Manifesto, abortive as it proved to be, is of historical importance, it is reproduced here, as much for its intrinsic documentary value as for the fierce light it throws on the fallibility of kings-in-waiting and their faithful advisers:

Today, six years having passed since the Civil War ended, the régime implanted by General Franco, inspired from the beginning by the totalitarian systems of the Axis Powers, so contradictory to the character and the tradition of our people, is fundamentally incompatible with the circumstances which the present war is producing in the world. The foreign policy followed by the present régime also compromises the future of the nation.

Spain runs the risk of finding herself dragged into another fratricidal conflict and of seeing herself totally isolated from the world. The present régime, whatever may be its efforts to adapt itself to the new situation, provokes this double peril; and a new

Republic, however moderate it be in its beginnings and intentions would not be long in drifting toward one of two political extremes, inducing the other extreme again to take recourse in another civil war.

Only the Monarchy can be an instrument of peace and of concord to reconcile Spaniards; only it can command respect in the foreign field, through an effective state of law and achieving a harmonious synthesis of order and freedom based upon the Christian concept of the State.

For these reasons . . . I raise my voice and solemnly ask of General Franco that, recognising the failure of his totalitarian concept of the State, he abandon power and open the way for the restoration of the traditional régime of Spain, the only one capable of guaranteeing Religion, Order and Liberty.

Under the Monarchy—just, tolerant, and healing—there must enter a number of reforms vital to the interest of the nation. The primary task will be: immediate approval by popular vote of a political constitution, recognition of all international rights, of the rights inherent in the human person, and guarantee of the corresponding political liberties; establishment of a legislative assembly elected by the nation; recognition of the diversity of the regions of Spain; full political amnesty; a more just distribution of wealth and the suppression of unjust social differences. . . .

Strong in my faith in God and in my imprescriptible rights and duties, I wait for the moment when my greatest longing may be realised; the peace and concord of all Spaniards. Long live Spain.

This also bespoke a manly attitude, hypothetically admirable if practically very unpractical.

As far back as July, 1940, Franco had declared in Seville: "If Spain has a king again he must come with the character of a peacemaker and not that of a conqueror . . . the new Monarchy will be very different from that which fell in 1931." Two years later he said that Don Juan "could not expect to become king of Spain because he did not sympathise with and did not understand the reforms in the past three years", to which forthright admonition the Pretender retorted in a statement published in the now suppressed Argentine national organ, *La Prensa*: "I could not lend myself to any action which would make restoration of the Monarchy appear as the crowning ornament of the structure created by the present régime."

On January 23rd, 1945, addressing 35,000 railwaymen, Franco

revealed in a sentence the foundation-stone of his régime: "Politically we represent unity, neither Right nor Left." "Unity" is indeed the keynote, the *Leitmotiv* of his entire message as Leader and First Administrator of the nation, a re-affirmation and re-creation of that unity that had been achieved for Spain in the 15th century through the vision and heroic energy of Isabella, the half-sister of Henry of Trastamara, born at Madrigal de las Altas Torres on April 22nd, 1451, with very poor prospects: the national unity which had cracked under the Bourbons and split altogether under the Republican democratic system. "I am the instrument of Providence", once claimed 'this man', this pertinacious Gallego—as Churchill himself had claimed during his war leadership—"to maintain the unity and integrity of our country."

Spain, Franco said in a speech at the end of World War II, had discovered the existence of modern political problems, such as the conflict between social and national virtues, several years before they had begun to beset other countries. While (he told the Phalanx National Council in December, 1942) the interests of the country might some day demand the return of the traditional régime "which has given us days of glory in history", even then he revealed his terms for such a restoration by stating that the throne "must be subordinate to the régime". "Before our eyes," he added, as if in vindication of the stand he had taken on the question, "lies a world which is the victim of the cancer of its own mistakes." Spain would create a new life, but it would be "a Spanish life".

Later he told the National Council, in a statement which revealed as by a magnesium flash what was at the back of his mind, that "restoration (*i.e.* of a king) can never serve as an excuse for foreign machinations intent on stimulating appetites incompatible in the present historical times." And this was followed by the blunt Cæsarian boast: "I am not one who lets himself be easily influenced by events—*I am accustomed to dominate them.*"* Certainly, the Generalissimo and *Caudillo* has *something* of Hitler's and Mussolini's insufferable self-pride and arrogance, even though he is saved from their bull-frog megalomania by the profession and practice of Spain's traditional Faith. . . . "I am

---

* My italics.

accustomed to dominate them"—or was this the proud boast of a confident man rejoicing in his own God-given strength?

Some years ago in London, in a corner house in Eaton Square where the Spanish Institute had been installed in accordance with the reciprocal arrangement whereby the British Council was permitted to open a British Institute in Madrid, a Spanish-born Provincial Visitor to English Benedictine Communities said to me after a lecture by the late Professor Allison Peers: "It was the Bourbons who ruined Spain." Indeed, the Bourbons, of French and Austrian blood, hardly became characteristically and by temperament Spanish until the 19th century nor ever understood the true genius of the Spanish race. They had in point of fact, proved a disintegrating and demoralising influence, a fact clearly revealed, and of 'malice afterthought', by Goya in his devastating full-length painting now in the Prado (in the Goya room, where I returned to see it again only yesterday) of Charles IV and his Queen, María Luisa of Parma, with their royal litter, and in the starkly frank portrait of their son, Ferdinand VII, the '*Afrancesado*', *i.e.* a Spanish collaborationist during the Peninsular War of Independence.

Yet, whenever the danger of disintegration threatened, the immemorial tradition-loving element in the Spanish character had asserted itself, even at the eleventh hour, and saved the country from the ultimate catastrophe. "Larra lamented over half Spain as dead," writes the greatest living Spanish scholar, the octogenarian Menéndez Pidal, in *The Spaniards in Their History,** "yet the deceased rose from the tomb to continue the mortal struggle. A hundred years later, when Azaña proclaimed the death of Catholic Spain, the latter rose and it was Republican Spain that fell. This was the fated destiny of the two sons of Oedipus, who would not consent to reign together and mortally wounded each other. . . ."

That national and political disintegration, which seemed likely to prove mortal for Spain's independence and unity in 1936, menaces, as I write, the fair land of France. "We have too much freedom here," a young schoolmaster remarked to me in his home in the rue Fléchier at Le Havre one Spring day last year: "the

---

* The English translation by Dr. Walter Starkie, C.M.G., C.B.E., D.LITT., published by Hollis & Carter, Ltd., London, 1951.

Mayor and municipality of this town are unable to carry out their duties and functions because of obstructive tactics by the Communist councillors, who refuse to pass the mayoral budget. Consequently we have neither mayor nor municipal council: both have resigned." Until the ensuing municipal elections, then some eight weeks ahead, not only Le Havre, but Cherbourg, Brest, and other big French ports were similarly paralysed in municipal affairs. At Caen, at the house of the Deputy-Mayor situated in the short rue Lebailly and opposite the majestic Norman abbey-church of St. Etienne in which William the Conqueror is buried ("We are sure there is still a bone of him left," a citizen assured me), and where the population sheltered from the American pre-invasion air bombings, I was told that the local Communist councillors ask permission to telephone party headquarters in Paris "at public expense" before voting on the simplest municipal issue. "In turn," said my host, "party headquarters in Paris is controlled from Moscow."

The invitation in the early summer of 1954 to the Comédie Française company to visit Moscow, where their performances were demonstratively attended by the Kremlin leaders, and the return visit to Paris of the Ballet from the Bolshoi Theatre (which misfired), were—as I read in more than one article in the French Press at the time—coldly calculated by the Cominform to blind the French public to the true significance of the crisis in Indo-China. Paris papers also reported at this time that the apostle of Existentialism, Jean-Paul Sartre, who has done more, perhaps, than any other living French author, including Henri de Montherlant, to demoralise and spiritually disintegrate the youth of France, was in Moscow as guest of the Soviet Cultural Relations Department.

France, where democracy has run to seed and liberty has lost its head, found herself confronted by the same dire crisis as confronted Spain in July, 1936, and Russia was exerting enormous pressure after the fall of Dien Bien Phu, both open and concealed, as I saw for myself, to bring about the overthrow of the Fourth Republic and the ushering in of a 'Popular' Government controlled by the Extreme Left.

> El comunismo actúa de mil formas, se viste con mil disfraces, si bien la piel de oveja es siempre la que predomina. . . . Su tendencia es siempre destruir valores positivos donde quiera que se hallen: religiosos, morales, artísticos, históricos, sociales, económicos . . . y, cuando no puede des-

truirlos, se contenta con paralizar o neutralizar a quienes puedan defenderlos.
Por eso es preciso que vivamos siempre alerta. . . .
(From an Editorial in *El Diario Montañés*, Santander, 14.5.54)*

By chance at this date (when travelling and writing in Spain)
I happened upon a *Daily Mail* leader for May 10th, 1954, com-
menting on the tragic reverse suffered by the French forces in
Indo-China which seems to sum up unconsciously the position
taken up by Franco *vis-à-vis* the restoration of a king who has
pledged himself to restore full democratic liberties to his people
and a 'democratic' Cortes:

> In all that has been written about the fall of Dien Bien Phu [it
> said], one episode stands out for coldbloodedness. When a tribute of
> respect and grief was paid in the French National Assembly to the
> defenders of the fortress, all the deputies stood—except the Com-
> munists and their allies. It was a contemptible exhibition which
> shamed those who remained seated. Any Frenchman with a spark of
> feeling would have joined in the Assembly's homage. Those who
> fought at Dien Bien Phu . . . were soldiers doing their duty—
> soldiers sent out to fight and die. They were the ordinary men whom
> the Communists are supposed to love and serve. But once again the
> Reds have shown exactly how little the human soul and the brother-
> hood of man mean to them. . . .

And the editorial went on to point out that the presence of
Communists in the Assemblies of countries which are "fighting
Communism in the field is as irrational as though Nazis had
been allowed to sit in Parliament (*i.e.* the British Parliament)
during the last war. Yet we have all become accustomed to the
paradox. . . ."

One finds today in the homes of many of the Spanish aristo-
cracy, displayed in handsome silver frames conspicuously placed
to attract a visitor's notice, a portrait of a good-looking, dark-
haired, clean-shaven young man standing beside a chair in which

---

* "Communism operates in a thousand ways, its appearance wears a
thousand disguises, if, usually, the lambskin covering is the predominant
feature. . . . Its tendency is always to destroy positive values wherever
they may be: religious, moral, artistic, historic, social, economic . . .
and, when they cannot be destroyed, it is content with paralysing or
neutralising whoever is defending them. Because of this it is necessary
that we live always on the alert. . . ."

sits a striking-looking woman, of regal appearance, carrying a mass of raven hair above unmistakable Bourbon features. Usually the portrait bears an inscription in heavy angular handwriting: "*Para Jimmy*", or "*Paco*", or "*José y Carmen*", followed by the flowing signatures "*Juan de Borbón*" and "*Mercedes*". The photograph is of the legitimate king and queen of Spain who, with one word from the present ruler of their country, could be installed overnight with their charming children in the Palacio de Oriente, restored at last to the throne of their ancestors, for Don Juan's wife, a grand-daughter of the Carlist Pretender who caused an earlier civil war in Spain, is directly descended from the Spanish Bourbon monarchs too.

That word is not given, and while "*Su Alteza Real*" the young Prince Juan Carlos de Borbón, whom many think will be the next king of Spain—but not before he is twenty-five—was allowed to pursue his studies with tutors at San Sebastian, taking his examinations at the Madrid Instituto de San Isidro, and is now in residence in the Duke of Montellano's palace in Madrid prior to entering the Military Academy at Saragossa, his father continues to eat the bitter fruit of exile in his villa Belden at Estoril, in Portugal.

Meanwhile the unfortunate and saddened Queen Victoria Eugenia, or Queen Ena, fulminates against Franco and all his works in private to leading members of Spanish society who call on her at Ouchy or Lisbon, against "that terrible man" who keeps her beloved son from his rightful place among the few reigning European kings. Yet, if surviving indications in Spain itself are a reliable guide, she herself contributed less than she might have done towards the consolidation of the monarchy and the winning of lasting respect and affection for it from the Spanish people during the years she shared the dangerous and hazardous reign of Don Alfonso.

Twenty years have passed since I visited the great square 18th-century palace in Madrid overlooking the meagre Manzanares river and the towering Guadarrama mountains beyond, which Velasquez painted in as background to his famous portraits, and handled some of the books the Royal Family had left on the shelves in their respective libraries on that tragic day when the Queen departed with her sons and daughters on her melancholy journey into exile. The English novels and the books of travel

Aged 24. 'The little major'. 'Commandantin' Franco in field uniform disembarking with his regiment on the coast of Spanish Morocco, where he served for 15 years, during one of the major actions against the Riffs (*State Archives*)

Aged 30. 'The youngest colonel in the Spanish Army'. An historic photograph of Franco taken in 1923, when C.-in-C. of the Spanish Foreign Legion, with the late General Millán-Astray, its first, oft-wounded commander

(*Courtesy of Instituto de Cultura Hispánica*)

and exploration had, I then noticed, evidently been popular reading with both royal mother and children, but in the Queen's own small library the pages of none of the works in Spanish, or of Spanish origin, were so much as cut.

Her temperament had been too reserved, too cold and aloof, too unsmiling for her warm-blooded subjects. Her Majesty might have done worse than to emulate the geniality, graciousness and approachability of Alfonso's mother, the beloved Queen María Cristina—for the Spanish are the most responsive people in the world, who instinctively interpret Christ's admonition: "Give and ye shall receive back, and receive abundantly." "She was a woman of little intelligence," the great savant, poet and writer, and renowned professor of Greek, the late Don Miguel de Unamuno, who wanted never to die but to live for ever even in this imperfect world, declared to me years ago, and, like myself, he had no desire to be unchivalrous. Had Queen Ena been another María Cristina the history of Spain in the past quarter of a century might well have been different. Indeed a king might be on the Spanish throne today.*

Comparisons are always invidious and not infrequently odious, and nothing is farther from my wish than to advance them in anything written here, particularly in respect of the tragic figure of an exiled and unhappy Queen. But evidence by hearsay or report is one thing; first-hand observation is another.

Not long ago I was the chance witness of a spontaneous reception given by a typical working-class Madrid crowd to the wife of the Head of the Spanish State. I was walking under the colonnades of the spacious Plaza Mayor, in the old quarter of Madrid, looking in the windows of the watchsmiths, the toy shops and the fascinating men's hat shops, with their scarlet-lined

---

* A friend and colleague for whose views I hold great respect, comments on these paragraphs: "You seem a little hard on Queen Ena. She came to Spain at the tender age of eighteen. Her uncle Edward VII (who did not approve the match) had drilled into her the importance of taking no part whatsoever in the politics of her new country. 'Don't ever come back to me if you lose your throne,' he is reported to have told her." And, of course, it must not be forgotten that on the very day of her wedding in San Jerónimo el Real, Madrid, she and Don Alfonso were welcomed in the Calle Mayor with an anarchist bomb which killed four horses in the procession and their postillion outriders.

7

boinas and tasselled *torero's* caps, on the afternoon of the
arrival in the Spanish capital on an official visit of President (or,
rather, ex-President) Trujillo, of the Dominican Republic.
Presently I continued my promenade towards the massive red-
brick and iron *reja*-ed façade of the Palacio de Santa Cruz, once
a prison for noblemen and today the Ministerio de Asuntos
Exteriores, or Spanish Foreign Office, whose wide and thickly
carpeted stairs I had climbed on various occasions to talk with
Don Emilio de Navasqüés, the youthful Under-Secretary of State
for Foreign Affairs, and the very friendly and helpful Technical
Chief of the Office of Diplomatic Information in charge of press
matters in the Foreign Office, Don Luis María de Lojendio.

Turning down narrow Calle de Zaragoza I soon found further
progress held up by a hundred or more people surrounding a car
drawn up outside a jeweller's, a modest shop far removed from
the fashionable establishments in the Avenida de José Antonio or
the Alcalá and their central environs. I asked a waiting Spaniard
what was afoot, and he replied that the wife of the *Caudillo* was
making a purchase inside the shop. So I waited with the crowd,
standing exactly opposite the shop, observing its orderly behaviour
and the fact that the only guards in sight were two ordinary un-
armed local city police standing nonchalantly on the pavement.
In the car itself was merely the driver. Over the shop was the
name, "Pérez Fernández".

After a minute or so the shop door opened, from which I could
observe other patrons within inspecting goods and making
purchases. In a moment a tall, smiling, hatless, dark-haired woman
emerged and walked easily through the waiting groups to the
car, the door of which was now held open for her by the chauffeur.
On her appearance the entire crowd, no member of which could
have had previous advice of the visit, broke into a spontaneous
clapping of hands which continued until the car moved off down
the narrow turning with the hatless occupant within smiling
brightly and even affectionately and waving a white-gloved hand
to right and left. It would have been simple enough for anyone in
that crowd to have uttered hostile cries, or even to have offered
violence, and to have got clean away in the confusion.

Had I hated the woman (whom I once heard described in
London, and by a servant of the régime at that, as "the most
bigoted woman in Spain") I could not have denied that on this

occasion she radiated happiness, and that the large gathering of Madrileños parting to allow passage for the automobile reflected in an unmistakable way the confident ease and natural joyousness of the occupant. It was the sort of spontaneous reception one would not expect to find in "a police State".

Yet when the Infante Don Juan Carlos visited El Pardo, on first arriving in Spain to enter a Madrid school, to meet the man who keeps his father from occupying the vacant throne, it was the wife of the *Caudillo*, who today seems to have won by sheer goodwill and personality the place of "uncrowned Queen of Spain", who welcomed him at the palace gates with a deep curtsey. On the occasion of the coming out last autumn of the Infante's eldest sister, a cordial message of congratulation was sent her by Franco from El Pardo; while plans have been settled for the Infante to serve for a spell in the Spanish Army.

In the present condition of Europe, with Soviet pressure implacably increasing on all frontiers, and 'fifth columns' ready and prepared to betray their respective countries at a word from the Kremlin, it seems in the highest degree unlikely that Franco will summon Don Juan *père* now to wear the crown of the Spains, or that there will be any increased agitation or activity by Spanish monarchist circles and sympathisers to persuade him to do so. "Better the devil we know than the devil we don't know."

Is "the Gallego" displaying thus the Fascist propensities of a narrow-minded tyrant with a base lust for power, in keeping the Pretender out of his rights *sine die*? "Spain," he pointed out in a New Year broadcast in 1950, "whether one likes it or not, is destined by nature to be the key and life of the West. Our political system is not a transitory régime . . . every enterprise needs a captain and, as such, I am thoroughly conversant with Spain's needs." Nine months later he repeated the claim: "Spain is the Keeper of the European castle; she is at the hub of the most important sea-air routes. In the ideological field her attitude is one of great reserve towards social and political ideas which the Western world defends—her foreign policy is ahead by several years." "I have chosen the forward post of duty in defence of Spain," he declared on another occasion, "and I would never desert you."

Franco's considered opinion is, I imagine, that traditional Spain could not survive under a democratic king. "Only the anarchists want Don Juan," he has been heard to say, "they know that they could get rid of him more easily than me. . . ."

"They will kill us all the next time they get the power," the Duke of Alba remarked when I last saw him in Madrid, only a few months before his sudden death at Lausanne, referring to the Left-wing elements of the people; but were he alive today he would not allow that the establishment of Don Juan on the throne would bring nearer such a horrible eventuality.

Yet assassination has been raised to high policy by the extreme Left-wing leaders in other continental countries besides pre-Franco Spain. "After the war," Sir Charles Petrie, the historian, revealed to me apropos of nothing in particular at a reception a few years ago at the Spanish Tourist Office in Jermyn Street, London, "the French *Maquis*, or Communists hiding under its cloak, liquidated fifty thousand members of the French Right."

". . . More!" exclaimed Dr. Lacroix, the Mayor of the strangely-named Paris suburb of Kremlin-Bicêtre—"a Socialist island in a Communist sea"—when I mentioned the figure at his last birthday anniversary dinner, to which he and his wife kindly invited me, "it was more. And not only of the Right. There were many Socialist victims, for the Communists fear us more than the others. My Socialist predecessor in the mayoral chair here was shot dead in his office by a 'Resistance' man. . . ."

The times are dangerous, too dangerous for the present Head of the Spanish State voluntarily to change places in midstream with an inexperienced prince of no proved sagacity. Or so he thinks . . . The battle is not against men but against principalities and powers, against the powers of darkness and wickedness in high places. Spain may yet be destined to keep alight a second time the torch of civilisation and Christendom through another Dark Age. . . .

With his naturally wavy fair hair, almond skin, firm yet rounded features and modest charming smile, the Prince Don Iuan Carlos, now fast growing into a young man, possesses such features, grace and bearing as qualify him in Spain for the description, "*guapo—guapísimo*", a handsome fellow, "extremely good-looking." In the State Albergue at La Bañeza, situated in the centre of the vast plateau or *meseta* of Old Castile (*"adusto como el mar, heroico como el semblante de los antiguos héroes*—austere like the sea, heroic as the appearance of the old-time heroes," to quote Ricardo León), I was looking through an old copy of a Madrid society magazine at a photograph of him and his younger brother, the Infante Don Alfonso, taken after he had gained his *bachillerato* at the Madrid Institute of San Isidro. At that moment the driver of the car in which I was returning to the capital caught sight of it and exclaimed, "That's our King!"

In such a land of paradox and the unexpected as Spain no prophecy, unless quickly fulfilled, is of much enduring validity: but the signs and portents at present certainly favour handsome young Juan Carlos more than they seem to do his tall, well-meaning and frustrated father who has now waited over twenty years for a call to the throne.

As our car passed through the ancient plaza of La Bañeza and onwards into the immense *campo*, across which the ribbon of white road disappeared in the far, encarnadined distance, over-arched by the great blue vault of sky, this impression was more than ever confirmed by a quotation from some speech copied in deep blue lettering on a crumbling outpost-wall, which said:

EL SERVICIO DE ESPAÑA ES NUESTRA LEY, Y LO QUE DAÑE O AMENACE SU UNIDAD, SU LIBERTAD O SU GRANDEZA, ES NUESTRO ENEMIGO—FRANCO.*

The fact needs to be realised, of course, especially by his critics in the Western world, that Franco could easily have had himself proclaimed king of Spain at any time since the end of World War II—*"El Rey Don Francisco Primero, por la Gracia de Dios"*. He was urged to do so by many leading supporters of the régime, particularly among the generals, as a means of resolving or immunising the many conflicting political elements in the country, and of placating the undoubtedly deep monarchical sympathies of a considerable part of the population.

It is no secret inside the country that he has in the past given serious consideration to the idea. Nor would such a step have been incompatible with the national spirit, for Spain has had

---

* "The service of Spain is our law, and whatever endangers or threatens her unity, her liberty or her grandeur is our enemy."

many warrior-kings in her history, from the Hispano-Goth
Asturian Pelayo, who initiated the Reconquest (it took seven
hundred years!) in the 8th century, down through Alfonso VI,
the liberator of Toledo with the Cid Campeador, and St. Ferdin-
and, conqueror of Seville, to the great Isabella herself, first
unifier of "the Spains" and the immortal conqueror of Granada,
with her consort King Ferdinand of Aragon, the model for
Machiavelli's *Prince*.

Nor would it have been incompatible with the broader history
of Europe, for the commoner Gustavus Vasa, ancestor of Gustavus
Adolphus, Charles XII, and Queen Christina of Sweden, became
king of the Swedes and Wends in the 16th century, after his
brilliant and successful resistance to Danish encroachment:
and was not Henry VIII of England the grandson of a Welsh
chieftain, and Napoleon I, the Emperor of France, a soldier by
profession of humble island origin?

Had Franco been the all-powerful megalomaniac which some
of his bitterest critics and opponents aver he could scarcely have
countered such a temptation to personal aggrandisement, even
though he wields today more power as a Commoner-ruler than
any Spanish king since Philip II. But his Galician balance and
sound sense, his detached attitude towards himself as an instrument of Providence entrusted with the direction of Spain's
destinies at a critical moment in Europe's fate, together with his
obviously sincere faith as a practising Catholic: these elements in
his nature, and the fact that he has no son and heir upon whom the
crown could devolve, and that his daughter, the dazzling Marquesa de Villaverde, shows no political aptitude and does not
want to, except perhaps at home, have together persuaded
Franco to continue in service as the benevolent authoritarian
soldier-ruler of the Spanish nation.

This was made evident at the meeting between Franco and the
Pretender near Caceres on December 29th, 1954. Later he declared
in *Arriba*: "No human institution exists able to guarantee the
future; only the patriotism and virility of a people can assure
that . . . . the successor to our National Movement is the same
National Movement". The decree authorising his infant grandson
to bear the name "Francisco Franco", with his father's patronymic
Martínez-Bordin afterwards, can have no significance other
than a frustrated natural longing for an heir.

Chapter Eight

JEWRY IN SPAIN

THE HISTORICAL FACT seems to be beyond dispute that during the Visigothic epoch Spanish Jews attained to such riches, power and influence that the Visigothic monarchs introduced discriminatory measures against them, whereupon Jewish leaders in Toledo, Seville and elsewhere entered into a secret understanding with the Arabs in North Africa promising aid and collaboration in the event of an invasion of the Peninsula. This induced the Berber chieftain Tarik to cross the Straits in 711 A.D. with a force of seven thousand men (some accounts say twelve thousand) and to begin the great Islamic drive into Europe and seven centuries of occupation in Spain.

A hundred years before, in 614 A.D., King Sisebut had instituted a *Fuero Juzgo* making compulsory the conversion of all Jews residing in the Visigothic kingdom. " Thus was begun," comments Hugh J. Schonfeld in his *History of Jewish Christianity*, "that pernicious policy which peopled Spain and Portugal, except for intervals of Moorish rule, with crypto-Jews down to the present day."

After the expulsion by Ferdinand and Isabella in 1492 the Christianised Jews who remained in both countries had grown so numerous that they formed a distinct class by themselves. *"Copiosos frutos de conversión"*, they became known as "New Christians" or, more particularly, as *Marranos*, and in Mallorca as *Chuetas*. As the conversions during this period, whether compulsory or real, were numerous, it came about that in the principal Jewish centres few of the patrician families could say that they had no Jewish blood in their veins, and Schonfeld gives an entertaining illustration of this with the following story.

When King Joseph I of Portugal thought of publishing an edict compelling all who were of Jewish descent "to wear a yellow cap" his Minister, the Marqués de Pombal, presented himself before the monarch with three yellow caps.

"What are these for?" asked the king.

"One for Your Majesty," replied the Minister, "one for the Grand Inquisitor, and one for myself."

It was, in fact, the suspicion that many of the "New Christians" secretly practised Jewish rites while outwardly conforming to the ordinances of the Church, a suspicion which Schonfeld considers fully justified in many cases, that led the Spanish clergy to call in the aid of the Inquisition. When the Jewish moneylenders of the time were asked to advance money to back the enterprise of Christopher Columbus they unanimously refused, but the money was immediately forthcoming when Isabella offered her jewels as security. The Jews had become troublesome and arrogant with prosperity long before the Catholic Kings decreed the Expulsion, and when Columbus at last set out on his transatlantic venture (with Jewish Christians actually among his crew) there were boatloads of Jewish refugees in the river at Palos de Moguer awaiting transportation to those Mediterranean shores where their descendants, the Sephardim, speak to this day the Spanish current in the 15th century.

As early as the 13th century accusations were levelled against Jewish communities in Spain of being the authors of such improbable crimes as "poisoning wells" and secretly "killing Christian children"; in fact, one of the most celebrated trials of the time concerns some Avila Jews denounced as being responsible for the killing of the "Niño de la Guardia", about which books have been written. From time to time the fanatical cry of "Hep! Hep!" ("*Hierosolyma est perdita*"—"Jerusalem is lost") would ring through the land, bringing riots and pogroms.

"The race is half-Arab and half-Jew," remarked the late, French-born, Marquesa del Ter to me at one of her celebrated 'At Homes' at Almagro 25 in pre-Civil War Madrid. Her husband, whose mother was Welsh, was third descendant of the famous Carlist guerrilla leader Cabrera, "el tigre", about whom Franco had spoken during my first meeting with him at El Pardo. . . .

One morning when I was carrying out research in connection with this book, a writer friend met me on the steps of the British Museum with the news: "You know, there is a Spaniard here who has been carrying out research in the Reading Room for months to prove that Franco is a Jew; and there is an ex-diplomat engaged on other research to prove that he isn't." I was later introduced to the Spanish investigator, a brilliant scholar who was just then completing a study of the *converso* Luis Vives, who was Spanish tutor to Mary Tudor. He stated that my friend was labouring under a misapprehension. "It could never be a question',' he said, "of Franco being a Jew. At most he could only be a *Marrano*, and even this seems very improbable, although he manifests some characteristics which have been evident in other European *Marranos*."

It happened, however, one day that the Spaniard had on his desk a volume of the *Jewish Encyclopedia* lying open at a biographical notice of one Jacob Frank, or Frankl, the founder of the "Frankists", a semi-Christian religious body which came into being among the Jews of Poland in the middle of the 18th century, and on the page was a reproduction from a contemporary portrait sketch. Concealing with one hand Frankl's headgear and with the other his neckerchief, the Spaniard enquired of a countryman recently arrived from Spain of whom the portrait reminded him. "Franco," was the immediate reply. And indeed, as I saw for myself, the resemblance was certainly striking.

It is a fact that the name, or variations of it, has been borne by Jews of distinction in many parts of Europe for centuries. Thus, the president of the Portuguese Jewish community in 1684 was a Mendez Mordecai Franco, while Moses Franco was a Jewish historian and schoolmaster in Constance last century. The Talmudist and Chief Rabbi of Hebron, in Palestine, in the latter half of the 19th century, was one Rahamin Franco, and Samuel Franco was a Turkish cabalist and chief rabbi of Salonika in the very year of the Spanish expulsion. "Francolm", "Fränkel", "Frank" and "Frankau" are other variants of the name, which may possibly have originated in the Middle Ages in the Judengasse of Frankfort-am-Main. "Frank", in any case, seems to have been a name given by Eastern Jews to any European Jew.*

---

* "His own passionate hobby is the tracing of his lineage back to the obscure days when his forefathers apparently were hounded from Spain by the Inquisition. His theory is that his name grew out of the marriage of a Mendès and a Franco in Spain or Portugal before the 14th century."—From an article on Pierre Mendès-France, late French Premier, in *Life*, 20th September, 1954.

Kees van Hoek, in his excellent article, "Franco Rules Without Fear" which appeared in the British weekly *Everybody's* some two years ago, speaks of Franco as having "the prominent nose of his race" (though I, personally, consider the feature not so prominent as all that) and other writers of equal or different merit have insinuated a Jewish origin for the Head of the Spanish State, and it is an interesting point that "Baamonde", the name of the Galician township from which Franco's mother took her name—which I passed through by train recently—is derived from a Jewish word meaning "monte alegre".

Even if the belief were true there would, of course, be no discredit attached to it. All to the contrary. Benjamin Disraeli, Viscount Beaconsfield, a full-blooded Jew whose grandfather had been a Hebrew merchant in Syria, is counted as among the greatest Prime Ministers and patriots in all Britain's long history. In George Borrow's time the Spanish Prime Minister, Mendizábal, was a Jew. But for the final word on the matter, the testimony of a brilliant Spanish scholar must be accepted, namely that Franco could not be a Jew, and it is very improbable that he is of Jewish descent.

What, however, is beyond cavil is that Spain has, and has had for many years, no Jewish problem at all, and there is no consciousness in the country of any anti-Semitism or discrimination. All the other way. During the war the Sephardic Jews were offered Spanish citizenship in their thousands to save them from the Nazi extermination camps and since the war Jews have met with especial kindness and consideration within the Spanish State. Writing in the *Jewish Forum*, published in Baltimore, on March 17th, 1944, a Professor Levi reported the "stupor" of a Jerusalem rabbi named Neuman, "taking temporary refuge in this pestilential zone which Spain is represented to be by some ignorant intellectuals", at finding an Institute of Hebraic Studies in full activity and responsible for the issue of a monthly review. "For the first time in my life," the rabbi is reported to have declared, "I was received with an extraordinary cordial and friendly welcome, precisely because I was a Jew, and this occurred in the Spain of today which many believe to be anti-Semitic."

According to World Jewry statistics there are no more than three thousand pure Jews living in Spain today.

Chapter Nine

SPANISH AFRICA

S PAIN, AS HER MILLION ODD TOURISTS and visitors each year inevitably discover and as inevitably bruit abroad when returning to their native lands, is a country of extremes and often of appalling contrasts—extremes of climate and human conditions, of wealth and poverty, poor and rich, and of paradoxical variations in temperament, of heroism and sanctity encountered side by side with spasmodic manifestations of baseness and savagery. But perhaps no aspect of life there so moves and disturbs visitors and residents alike as the sight of riches and luxury flaunting themselves beside extreme poverty— the aristocrat, the business magnate, the big manufacturer rolling in their new-model American cars along the main roads, on either side of which builders' mates and agricultural labourers work from sun-up to sun-down for a pittance of some thirty pesetas daily.

"The Spanish live in worse conditions than the tribes of the Atlas," declared M. Georges Duhamel, the eminent French novelist and *homme de lettres*, lecturing in France last year. His remark stung the Paris correspondent of the Madrid *A B C* into a reminder, spread over two columns of the paper, that Monsieur Duhamel had been the object of much hospitality, some of it expensive, during his extensive tour of Spain.

There are many contributory factors to the low standard of living and the conditions of extreme poverty which prevail in most of the villages of Spain and even in the outskirts of many of the cities. These include the conservatism of the people and their suspicion of modern methods either on the land or in their homes, the acrid harshness of the soil, a devastating Civil War which ruined the national economy, immediately followed by a World War which prevented the country from securing essential imports, prolonged droughts and phenomenal frosts, such as the one that ruined the Valencian orange crop in February of 1954, and the

deliberate denial of all post-war economic aid by the Western
Powers until the signing of the Spanish-American Mutual Aid
Pacts.

"Spain is a poor country," a First Secretary of the Spanish
Embassy in Paris remarked to me in his office in the Embassy
building, a stone's throw from the Arc de Triomphe—"how poor
one only realises when flying over the immense agricultural
richness of France." As a young undergraduate at the University
of Granada he had known the ill-fated Andalusian poet, Federico
García Lorca (I am acquainted with three other Spaniards who
knew him intimately).

Although, as I was several times informed in Spain, the wages
of workers have been doubled and the living conditions of the
working classes are steadily improving throughout the length
and breadth of the land, the plaint is still heard rising to heaven
far and wide of sordidness, poverty and extreme want among the
Spanish peasantry. But little or nothing is heard or said of the
sordid living conditions and extremes of poverty existing cheek
by jowl with riches in the homelands of the complainants, yea,
even in the great, rich and powerful United States of America.
Thomas Merton's 'apologia pro vita sua', *Elected Silence*, published
in America under the title of *The Seven-Tiered Mountain*, has many
pages of description of the overcrowded slums of Harlem and
New York's East Side. Speaking of the United Kingdom in the
British House of Commons in 1945, Labour's 'heavy-weight'
M.P., Mrs. Bessie Braddock, Member for the Exchange Division
of Liverpool, made herself responsible for this forthright, if
inelegant, outburst: "Throughout the country, and particularly
in industrial areas, people are living in flea-ridden, bug-ridden,
rat-ridden, lousy hell-holes!"*

Hamish Fraser, a former Scots Communist fighter with the
International Brigade in Spain, has something pertinent to say in

---

* A report by Professor Sir James Spence, issued by the Nuffield
Foundation in July, 1954, stated that in the Durham and Newcastle
areas "one room in seven was unfit for human habitation" and "one
family in three was overcrowded" necessitating "great parental
devotion and high domestic skill in caring for children." Yet the
finger of scorn is pointed at 'Franco Spain' for the poverty of the
lower classes, and even at those fortunates who live in spacious
whitewashed caves in the genial South!

his booklet *Spain and the West* on the perennial question of the poverty of the Spanish peasant. "During the war there was Lease-lend to Britain, and after it an American loan followed by Marshall Aid. . . . Alone, Spain has had to bear the entire cost of a total war that Europe might remain free. That is why Spain suffers needless poverty."

I remember once in a bookshop in Cadiz, in the narrow Calle de los Reyes Católicos where the Andalusian poet, playwright and Academician, José María Pemán was born, making a passing reference to the poverty in the South of Spain by quoting in my own Spanish translation the time-worn Anglo-Saxon maxim—"It's always jam tomorrow, but never jam today". A señorita wearing black mantilla and the high Andalusian tor-toiseshell comb favoured by Cadiz women, who were the favourite dancers of Imperial Rome, was glancing at the time through some second-hand volumes in the shop with the *patrón*, and oh! how she laughed.

Pemán, whose fine play in verse about the great Navarrese missionary, St. Francis Xavier, *El Divino Impaciente*, I saw on its first production in Madrid in 1932, is in my opinion one of the most gifted and lyrical of modern Spanish authors, 'every rift loaded with ore'. During the North American Cultural Week organised in the Spanish capital in the spring of 1954 and opened in the Ateneo by the United States Ambassador, Mr. Dunn, Pemán, who was President of the Spanish Academy, spoke of *Hispanidad*, 'the essence of things Spanish', which, as I have mentioned, forms one of the main planks of Spain's foreign policy. He said: "According to the dictionary, Hispanity means not merely the physical tract of land that belonged to Spain. It is also the 'Hispanic status'. Hispanity is the statue of Fray Junípero Serra in the Washington Capitol; Hispanity is the possession of names like New Mexico, Florida, Colorado, Nevada, Texas, California, Arizona and other States which were in the Hispanic zone until the mid-19th century; Hispanity is the *auto de los pastores* which is represented in Texas, and its torrential flood of cattle descended from five hundred bulls, and the rollicking Carnival of Tampa."

"Hispanic," he went on, "in brilliant anticipation was that effort of Charles III which saved the Pacific coast for the West, calling a halt to the Russians who had crossed the Bering Straits and settled in Alaska. Hispanic, because sprung from Salamancan and Sevillian roots, is the rancher of the West, a more representative and universal type than the Wall Street banker or the Hollywood actress. When a little boy, in the mists of Stockholm or under the sun of Naples, plays at being a virile adventurer of the West, America puts one of his spurs on him, but Spain puts on the other. . . ."

In a restaurant near the Hauptbahnhof in Munich in the summer of 1954, a lively and smiling waitress who hailed from Berlin told me that her hours were "from nine in the morning until midnight, Sundays included". In Upper Bavaria, in the lovely little village of Lenggries, which I have known since 1936, a waitress in the central Gasthof Post revealed to my wife and myself during a Bavarian evening '*Heimatfest*' that she had been at work since six that morning and on duty the previous twenty-four hours "from six a.m. until two the following morning". "It is the only way I can keep myself and my child," she said.

'Franco's Spain' is not the only country in Western Europe where workers labour long for bare subsistence. If it comes to that, I myself, as an independent writer work like a dray-horse for less than a civilised subsistence.

Is the Spanish *Caudillo* aware then, of the deep indignation felt today by other peoples at the continuing plight of the Spanish poorer classes and their meagre wages? Undoubtedly he is, and many of the measures introduced into the Cortes since the war have as their express object its amelioration. But with the present Head of the Spanish State it is a question of "Patience, and shuffle the cards". Rome was not built in a day, and he knows that an all-round improvement in living conditions for the peasants and workers, and the raising of the general standard of living in Spain, cannot be the work of one generation or even of two, but these desirable ends must represent a long-term plan.

"Yes," commented a knowledgeable friend, a foreign correspondent in Madrid, "but if only they wouldn't *boast* so much about their achievements in Social Welfare, as if no other country is able to rival them." He himself has occupied for forty years with his wife a comfortable flat off the fashionable Almagro street for which they still pay the pre-war rental of 300 pesetas a

month—roughly, under three pounds in the sterling equivalent.*
"And this daily adulation and homage; it is nauseating. One
would think that Franco would get sick of it." But royalty, the
British Royal Family at any rate, get just as much of it, both in
the daily newspapers and in the illustrated weeklies which will
not let them alone for a single week or day; while the doings of
ex-kings and would-be royalties frittering away their time on
both sides of the Atlantic, the colour-schemes of their new houses
in Paris, Estoril or New York, the thrice-told tale of their love
romances and voluntary or forced abdications, are served up
month by month and year by year by the 'popular press' until
such normally important events in human life seem to have lost
all original validity.

Franco gave an example of his monumental, his almost
'Chinese' patience when a noted Madrid painter, Salaverría
(now dead), asked for several sittings at El Pardo in order to
paint a portrait of the *Caudillo* which had been commissioned by
an important national body.

"How many sittings would you require?" Franco enquired;
to which the artist replied:

"Three of one hour each, your Excellency, or two of an hour
and a half each."

"Can you not do the study in one sitting of three hours?"

"But it would tire Your Excellency," to which the answer
was immediately forthcoming: "Oh no, that's nothing!"

And so, for three hours one day while his head was being
sketched and painted, Franco sat motionless like Patience on a
monument, gazing out of a window into the pleasant gardens
and bosques of El Pardo, no doubt thinking up some long-term
project for defeating Spain's periodical ruinous droughts by the
provision of more dams, or another deep scheme to outwit his
international foes. ("He has time for everything," remarked one

---

* Last November a Basque lady in whose *pensión* in Calle de Ferraz I
had occasionally stayed showed me over her fourth-floor flat in the
ultra-fashionable Alfonso XII street, facing the Retiro park and containing two bedrooms, living room, kitchen and bathroom, for which
she told me that she was paying still the pre-Civil War rental of 200
pesetas monthly (roughly 36s.). And no questions asked as to her
political views.

day some Madrid friends who have their summer home only a few miles from the Pazo de Meirás, Franco's Galician 'castle'.)

Some months later he received in his more spacious study-cum-working room a delegation from Spanish Morocco comprising the Grand Vizier and Khalifan officials in their flowing white *burnous* and hoods. Led by the Spanish High Commissioner at Tetuan, Lieut.-General García Valiño, they had journeyed from North Africa to assure the Head of the Spanish Realm of their loyalty and support, and that of the indigenous inhabitants of the Zone, in the Spanish stand taken against recognition of the Sultan newly appointed by the French Resident in Morocco.

Replying extempore to the Grand Vizier's address on this occasion, Franco said:

> I can assure you that Spain will continue to be true to the treaties and loyal to her Moroccan brothers. She will inflexibly defend the unity of Morocco and the letter and spirit of the agreement, not accepting situations and facts which are contrary to our way of thinking, and also to international morality and signed treaties. We are sure that the force of reason will in the end triumph over the unreason of force. Until that time comes, the Moroccan Zone entrusted to our keeping will continue under the sovereignty of His Imperial Highness Prince Mouley el-Hassan ben el-Mehdi, assisted by our High Commissioner (my translation).

Rarely does "this man" display any emotion, but on that particular occasion he was obviously moved by the presence of his old enemies, and swallowed to restrain tears as he crossed the carpeted room to shake each delegate warmly by the hand and to give each also a cordial *abrazo*. Once before his calmness had deserted him, when visiting the warship *Canarias* in the harbour at Barcelona and speaking with members of the crew hailing from the islands who had actually been serving in the ship at the time that he flew out from Las Palmas to head the rising in Spanish Morocco. The journalists on board reported then that he wept . . . ("as well he might" his convinced opponents would cynically add).

It is a revealing sidelight on the entirely new relations existing between Spain and Spanish Africa to discover, as I discovered during an autumn sojourn in Galicia, that the popular Captain-General of the Region which contains one of the most revered shrines in all Christendom, the tomb of St. James the Apostle at Santiago de Compostela, is a pure-blooded Arab and a devout Moslem. He is Ceuta-born, Lieut.-General of the Spanish Army Sidi Mohammed Ben Mezian Bel Kaseni, with his headquarters in Corunna, where, at a party given by Spanish friends, I met his wife whose complexion is as fair as the average European's. His daughter, a noted beauty, was married while I was in Galicia to a tall and handsome sheik from French Morocco.

"*Por el Imperio hacia Dios*". Today, any ambition towards imperialism in Spain, which once boasted an Empire "on which the sun never set", has perforce to be content with her North African Possessions, comprising the Protectorates of Spanish Northern Morocco (facing Gibraltar) and Spanish Southern Morocco (on the Atlantic, south of French Morocco), Ifni, south of Agadir, which enjoys Spanish sovereignty, Spanish Guinea, and the Spanish Sahara (of a total area of 266,000 square miles) all desert, as is evidenced by the fact that the Camel Corps for the entire region has only three officers of captain's rank.

One of them is brother of my long-term friend, Julia de Aguirre, of the Dirección General de Turismo in the Calle de Medinaceli, and I ate my 1950 Christmas Eve dinner as a guest of the family seated between Captain de Aguirre, in his light tropical beribboned drill uniform with blue facings, who had flown into Barajas airport only a few short hours before, straight from the open Sahara, and their mother, a native of the Canary Islands and widow of one of the senior officer victims of the massacre of Anual. During the Civil War she had been dragged from her Madrid home on the accusation of displaying a crucifix and placed before a firing squad in the Casa de Campo, but a friend and a Republican passing nearby at the time recognised her and held the militia-men's fire, and she was imprisoned for the remainder of the war instead of being shot outright.

Two days before, 800 miles away in the Great Erg, the captain had been bitten in the hand while turning to shout an order to his native troopers as his mount stood up. The Madrid doctor who had examined the injury when he called in a lounge suit on the morning of Christmas Eve enquired, puzzled: "What bit you—a large dog?" and glanced up wide-eyed when the reply came back: "No, doctor, my camel."

In Spanish Northern Morocco five places enjoy Spanish

8

sovereignty and count as Spanish territory, Alhucemas, the scene of the brilliant landing in 1926 planned by Colonel Franco, Ceuta, which has many of the characteristics of a Spanish provincial town, Chafarinas, Melilla and Peñón de Vélez. In the entire zone of the Spanish Moroccos a single Khalifa normally exercises powers delegated to him by the Sultan at Rabat. But when a new Ruling Sultan, Moulay Mohammed Ben Atafa, was enthroned by the French authorities without previous consultation with Spain, his authority was challenged by the Spanish zones. On January 21st, 1954, a declaration repudiating the choice and demanding that the Khalifa of Spanish Morocco should assume sovereign powers was signed by 430 pashas, caids and reigning nobles and presented to the High Commissioner by the Grand Vizier in the presence of thirty thousand people at Tetuan, where:

> Sharp-teethed, ferocious mountains
> Snarl at the opaque Moorish *pueblo*,
> Closed and silent no more . . .

and

> Long-exiled Jews, in black gowns and caftans,
> With sadness shading their short, stubbly beards,
> Trail the world's tragedy through the narrow white lanes,
> And learnéd Moors
> Whose liquid, impersonal eyes
> Gaze down upon you from a moon of white whiskers
> And velvet-ivory skin,
> Sail proudly past the Arab quarter,
> Their wide gowns flapping
> In the African wind——.

Franco is not disposed to tolerate Communist-inspired bloodshed and unrest at the boundaries of Spain's African territories (in the French Zones, as I read for myself in the Paris papers, no less than five hundred Europeans were murdered that spring, many of them in broad daylight), without taking resolute steps to ensure that peace and order are safeguarded among the peoples for whose safety and welfare he is responsible. Spaniards have a long memory where North Africa is concerned; it was from there, encouraged and welcomed by the prosperous Jewish communities under the Visigothic dispensation, that, led by El Tarik, from whose patronymic the Rock is named, the avalanche of Arab Islam surged across the Straits to Gibraltar in 711 A.D. Engulfing all Spain with the exception of a few deep caverns in mountainous Asturias they penetrated into France as far as Soissons and Poitiers, where they were defeated by Charles Martel. Southern Spain, from which the invaders were not finally ejected for seven more centuries, is impregnated today with Moorish culture and customs and the Spanish language is as salted with the Arabic influence as the English language is with French.

The fateful battle on the Guadalete, the historic river which waters the plains of Jerez, home of the famed Spanish sherries, and the Tarshish of the Old Testament (it is thought) where the flower of the Visigothic youth and nobility, less their King Roderick, was annihilated, has been nobly celebrated by the French poet Emile Deschamps in *Rodrigue pendant la bataille*:

> C'est la huitième journée
> De la bataille donnée
> Aux bords du Guadalété:
> Maures et chrétiens succombent,
> Comme les cédrats qui tombent
> Sous les flèches de l'été. . . .

> Enfin le sort se décide,
> Et la Victoire homicide
> Dit: 'Assez pour aujourdhui !'
> Soudain l'armée espagnole
> Devant l'Arabe qui vole
> Fuit . . . Les Espagnols ont fui ! . . .

> * * *

> Mort au dernier roi des Goths !

> (It is the eighth day
> Of the battle joined
> On the banks of the Guadalete;
> Moors and Christians fall
> Like the leaves which drop
> Under the arrows of summer. . . .

At last the outcome is clear,
And the homicidal Victor
Cries: 'Enough for today!'
Suddenly the Spanish Army
Before the pursuing Arab
Flees . . . The Spaniards have fled! . . .

*   *   *

Death to the last King of the Goths!)

As early as the 13th century individual Spaniards sought to return the compliment by 'invading' the North African coast. Thus we find that Blessed Ramón Lull, the monk-scientist-mystic of Mallorca, whose sloping wall tomb surmounted by his bearded effigy is to be seen in one of the side-chapels of the beautiful cloisters of the Franciscan monastery at Palma, from which Fray Junípero Serra sallied forth one day for the eventual evangelisation of far California, actually expired in his eighty-second year through being stoned to death off Bougie, in Tunisia, while making one of his missionary incursions into the lands of the infidel.

But the big Spanish 'come-back' occurred three centuries later, during the reign of the Emperor Charles V who undertook a big expedition to Tunisia in which took prominent part the 'Great' Duke of Alba, Don Fernando Alvarez de Toledo, whose proud aristocratic features were somewhat similar to his modern inheritor, the late Duke of Berwick and Alba. Some of the finest and best-preserved tapestries in the Peninsula record the story of this African campaign in a series of vivid life-like scenes —embarkation at Barcelona, disembarkation on the Tunisian shore, and battle. They are preserved today in the Moorish-built Hall of Ambassadors in the Alcazar at Seville. In these the figures of Charles V, and his nobles and commanders and leaders of the expedition may all be picked out and identified without difficulty.

On the low sandy shore of the remote island of Djerba, Homer's 'Isle of the Lotus-Eaters' in the Gulf of Gabès, with whose enchantments the reading of the Odyssey makes us unforgettably familiar, still stands the fort built by an army of the invading Spaniards during the African campaign, together with a gruesome reminder of their end in an inscribed marble column near the capital, Houmt Souk, marking the site where the skulls of the slaughtered Spaniards were built into a huge pyramid-trophy by the Arab defenders. The tidal wave of Islam was, indeed, as great and immediate a threat to Western Christendom in the 16th century as is Soviet expansion in Europe and the world in the 20th. One evidence was this great *desastre de les Gelves* where Don García de Toledo succumbed (1510),

Until the Dictator, General Primo de Rivera, brought to a victorious conclusion the long drawn-out war against Abd-el-Krim and his fanatical followers, Morocco had been the field of glory and promise for the Spanish army officer ever since the tribes had revolted against French and Spanish over-rule in 1909. And Franco chose it for his own early career when a second lieutenant as the surest theatre where glory and rapid promotion might both be won. "I don't want decorations," he said to his superior officers, who sent recommendation after recommendation to the War Office in Madrid in recognition of his conspicuous valour in action, "I would like promotion." By then he had met during a leave the beautiful black-haired fifteen-year-old school-girl of Oviedo, Carmen Polo Martínez-Valdés, and had to better his prospects in order to wear down the obstinate resistance of her parents to his suit. ("I will come back as a colonel," he had told them after failing to obtain their consent as a lieutenant, "and ask you again.")

Thus, two years after leaving the Infantry Academy at Toledo as second lieutenant he had reached captain's rank, and four years later, when recovered from severe wounds sustained in the fierce campaigns of 1916, he was promoted major. Seven years afterwards he was appointed Commander-in-Chief of the crack Spanish Foreign Legion, and in 1925, at the age of 32, he became the youngest general in the Spanish Army, and indeed in Europe. This fighting life in Africa he has described in direct and work-manlike prose in his one book, *Marruecos: Diario de una Bandera* ('Diary of a Battalion'), published in Madrid in 1922 and long out of print.

After decades of warfare and turmoil due to mismanagement, corruption and indifference among powerful circles in the Madrid of those years, all Spanish Morocco now enjoys conditions of complete tranquillity, conditions in striking contrast to the alarming events taking place almost daily in the neighbouring zones. "*Hay orden en el país.*" Franco, who has enjoyed for nearly forty years unique prestige among its proud and fierce inhabitants, continues to enjoy it today in similar or even greater measure as Head of the Spanish State and Chief of the Armed Forces. On appropriate occasions in the Spanish capital he sallies forth accompanied by a mounted Moorish 'blue and red' bodyguard as impressive and colour-filled in its way as any sovereign's escort from the royal palaces of London, Stockholm, Copenhagen or Brussels.

Even when I was in Northern Spanish Morocco before the Civil War one could stroll unaccompanied in the narrow streets and *souks* of Tetuan in perfect safety. The British Vice-Consul upon whom I called one day was, in fact, brutally murdered later, but not in Spanish Morocco; he was struck down by an assassin's dagger in the British Consulate of a Middle Eastern country to which he had been transferred in the normal course of duty. . . .

In Tetuan live many of the Sephardic Jews whose ancestors were expelled from Spain by *los Reyes Católicos.* They shuffle about its narrow alleyways, under the high sun-awnings in the tawny African sunlight, wearing their long black gowns and 'pill-box' headgear, speaking a Spanish current in the 15th century. Such an archaic Spanish is spoken too by their scattered compatriots at Salonika, Smyrna and all round the shores of the "tideless, dolorous, inland sea". During World War II Franco revived for all of them Spanish citizenship, thus saving tens of thousands from Hitler's gas chambers and death camps. They had only to present themselves before a Spanish Consul and claim the citizenship by making a formal declaration. Scant appreciation of this gesture of mercy was, however, evinced by the State of Israel after the war at the United Nations where the Palestinian delegate voted against Spain's admission to U.N.O. and in favour of the withdrawal of Ambassadors from Madrid.

I am a devoted reader of the Old Testament, and love its living poetry. But how unjust that a brand new State, only brought into being through the dispossession of the Arab inhabitants of land on which they had been settled for a millenium and more and over which they were promised sovereignty by Lawrence of Arabia in the name of the Allied Powers in return for the invaluable services they rendered towards victory in the first World War, how unjust, I say, that this State should be enabled to cast a vote against membership of the "United Nations" of a key European people of twenty-nine millions the foremost of all in the defence of that Western Christendom for which they had suffered and bled, of a race settled on Iberian earth since the fall of Babylon! How unjust indeed that a State that had turned a blind eye to the pirate-hanging by the Stern gang of unoffending British soldiers in deserted olive groves and to the assassination in its chosen capital of a special Delegate of that same United Nations, the almost saintly Count Folke Bernadotte, which allowed his murderers to escape scot-free and refused any Swedish investigation—how unjust, how tragic and how farcical that such a State should have the power to vote against Spain!

"U.N.O. is an abortion," Franco declared in his forthright way to the late Christopher Buckley, the war correspondent, in an interview granted at El Pardo in January, 1949. Perhaps he had the anti-Spain votes of Israel in mind at the time, although his attitude may undergo some modification now that, on the initiative of the United States, Spain has been invited to send an "observer" to the United Nations.

Chapter Ten

SOLDIER BY SECOND CHOICE

AMONG THE EXHIBITS TO BE SEEN in the small museum installed off the great central courtyard of the Alcazar at Toledo are two old motor-cycles of British make whose engines were run to grind what corn there was in the citadel for making the rough and tough bread on which the defenders mostly sustained life during the sixty-nine days of the siege. There is also a primitive press on which was printed the garrison's daily bulletin, surviving copies of which reveal the grim humour as well as the heroic fortitude of the defenders under their gruelling ordeal; and in glass wall-cases may be seen two bound volumes of old copies of *The Illustrated London News*, each pierced and torn by shrapnel splinters, but with the undamaged portions easily decipherable (they are open at pages dated January 24th, 1914, and February 3rd, 1912, respectively).

These and other volumes of Europe's first illustrated weekly without doubt provided mental fare and recreation for the young cadet during his three years at the Toledo Infantry Academy which, as has already been mentioned, he entered on August 29th, 1907, and from which he graduated with a second lieutenant's commission on July 13th, 1910. For even though Franco's knowledge of English may have been rudimentary or even non-existent—although it is hard to credit that anyone of his intelligence could have remained wholly ignorant in those formative years of the tongue which shares with Spanish the distinction of being one of the two most widely spoken in the whole world—the copious photographic and line illustrations would have provided a perpetual fount of interest to the budding soldier, and it may well have been of inspiration too, particularly the vivid action sketches contributed by R. Caton Woodville and other early artists of scenes of battle and siege from the South African war. These may have given Franco a partiality not only for the famous periodical on which I myself once served as sub-editor for three years—for he still sees it regularly—but a taste also for service in the field in Spain's African zone of influence.

At Toledo, moreover, with its unique situation and age-old legends of the Cid Campeador and other Spanish paladins, and its precious architectural monuments, a young and keen mind would be daily confronted by ever-present reminders of the centuries of struggle against the Moors, as well as of the later no less dramatic era of Spain's historical civilising mission in North Africa. I have come upon little information in Spain of these early years of Franco's military career beyond evidence that they were years of unremitting study and hard discipline, but the course of it proves that they forged his character and shaped his historic, realistic outlook, as undoubtedly did the landmarks of the fine old imperial city where generations of warriors, prelates, poets, sages and artists have left a palimpsest of the indomitable Spanish genius.

He was ever afterwards to remain powerfully conscious of the sharp and tragic contrast of the days of Spain's might and glory, as signified by Toledo's massive Cathedral, the late Gothic gem of San Juan de los Reyes, once intended by the Catholic Monarchs to be their last resting-place and with the chains struck from Christian slaves released by them from the Moorish dungeons still hanging from its walls, the masterpieces of El Greco and his home, the former house of the Jewish treasurer of Pedro the Cruel—and the 'green-sea fruit' of 19th-century Colonial losses and political humiliations, and assassinations.

"We have a bad recollection of the times when foreign armies have passed," Franco once remarked; "the simple passing of the French Army of Napoleon to war against Portugal cost us the devastation of Spain, the loss of our American empire, our unity and our economic power." "By the ineptitude of a French admiral," he said on another occasion, "Spain's naval power was crushed at Trafalgar."

Nobly, nobly Cape Saint Vincent to the north-west died away;
Sunset ran, one glorious blood-red, reeking into Cadiz bay;
Bluish grew the burning water, full in face Trafalgar lay;
In the dimming north-east distance, dawned Gibraltar grand and
   gay.

"Here and here did England help me,—how can I help England?"
say,
Whoso turns, as I, this evening, turn to God to praise and pray,
While Jove's planet rises yonder, silent over Africa.*

"Cape Saint Vincent"—"Cadiz"—"Trafalgar"—"Gibraltar"
—"England"—"Africa". Significant names for Spain too, and for
a young Spanish cadet in historic Toledo.

Small wonder then if the Alcazar, with such time-worn
memorials surrounding it, contained during the epic siege—in the
memorable phrase of *"El Tebib Arrumi"* (the late Víctor Ruiz
Albéniz) "a nest of eagles", however broad the sneer at their
incredible resistance in Koestler's *Spanish Testament.* Small
wonder, too, if the budding patriot Francisco Franco grew
restless under the enforced inactivity of his first commissioned
posting, namely to the 8th Zamora Regiment (of which His late
Majesty King George V was Honorary Colonel), partially
descending from the Irish Jacobite mercenaries "the Wild
Geese", even though it meant a sojourn near his home and family
at El Ferrol.

". . . *silent over Africa.*"
In the Spanish Zone of Morocco, just then permanently
established by a new treaty with France, the warlike tribes were
rising in revolt against European domination, and Spain was
entering a dire period of all-out war with the rebellious Riffs
which was to cost her dear in blood and treasure for the ensuing
fifteen years. Spanish Morocco was the Indo-China of the time
for Spanish arms and resources, with a parallel story of strategical
blunders and ministerial corruption, but Spain was fortunate in
finding soldiers of the calibre of Franco and a leader of the calibre
of General Primo de Rivera to bring the seemingly fruitless and
unending struggle to a final triumphant conclusion. ("Spain has
only one man in Africa," Lyautey once said, "Franco.")
In the very year of Franco's spell of home garrison duty
Morocco became a burning question of the day in European
politics, a growing crisis brought to a head by sudden troop
concentrations in the French Zone and by the appearance of German military detachments at Agadir by the Kaiser's orders from

* Robert Browning.

the gunboat *Panther*, ostensibly to protect his subjects in the Protectorate. Service conditions were as unattractive there to Spaniards as they could well be. The Riffs were known to torture and mutilate with cruel ruthlessness prisoners; sixty-five per cent of the Spanish troops "of all ranks, from generals to privates", were victims of malaria, and the advance battalions were continuously in action in critical and dangerous positions: while even at the base at Melilla a curfew was imposed because of fierce Riff attacks after sunset.

It was at Melilla that a nineteen-year-old infantry lieutenant, a volunteer at seventeen "for glory and for death", stepped ashore in February of 1912 at the commencement of what was to prove the most remarkable career in modern Spanish military history and one of the most meteoric, in fact, in the history of war. General Berenguer was at that time reorganising the *Regulares*, the name given to the crack Spanish Moroccan regiments, and the late Vizconde de Eza, upon whose tomb in the splendid 11th-century Romanesque church of Santo Domingo in Soria a prayer lamp perpetually burns by special permission of the Pope, had founded as Minister of War the Foreign Legion, to which he designated Millán-Astray as the first commanding-officer. Within a year Franco was entrusted with the command of a company and given the substantive rank of captain (at the age of twenty) in recognition of outstanding qualities of leadership and valour displayed in constant action with the enemy. "During this period of his career," writes Arthur F. Loveday, O.B.E., in his valuable source-book, *Spain, 1923-1948*, "as in fact throughout his life, he was noted as a constant and untiring student of strategy and military history." In fact he modelled his military career on the lives of his own historical heroes.

Only three years after receiving his captaincy, Franco won the distinction of being promoted to commandant, thus becoming the youngest major in the Spanish Army. He was also awarded the Military Medal, which he was to win again in a later critical sortie against the enemy, when he had a reputation for his " cold-blooded and cool " demeanour.

In 1947 Franco threw some light on what these early years in Africa had done to him in an interview accorded to an American journalist, Constantine Brown. "I am a man," he then remarked, "who has never harboured ambitions for power and command.

Ever since my youth life has subjected me to hard tests. I have had to fulfil posts of command and responsibility much beyond the capacity of my years and experience. But I am a man with a strong sense of responsibility and duty, and duty is something bound up with the conscience of every man." (He told Brown, incidentally, that if he believed it was imperative in the interests of Spain that he should resign his position he would do so "immediately and joyously" since for him the position of command was "always a duty and a sacrifice".)

In 1916, in the merciless battle of Buit, he sustained severe intestinal wounds which, after hospital and long convalescence, brought about a second home posting for two years to the Príncipe Regiment stationed in Asturias, of which the Crown Prince of Spain was then Honorary Colonel. He had "hovered between life and death," runs a contemporary account, "but his youth pulled him through".

Of the arduous and perilous years which he spent in Africa with the tough and hard-fighting Legionaries, Franco wrote, as mentioned, his own soldierly account in his one book, *Marruecos: Diario de una Bandera*, published in Madrid in 1922 by the Editorial Pueyo and now long out of print. It is, perhaps, some indication of a balanced character that, despite the power and prestige which he has enjoyed for nearly two decades, he has never used his position to influence a re-issue of this work, which might well have been made compulsory reading for every Spanish Army officer.

In a somewhat effusive and hyperbolical Foreword his superior officer at that time, Lieut.-Colonel (later General) Millán-Astray, wrote: "Major Franco is known in Spain *and in the entire world* (my italics) for his own merits and for those characteristics which distinguish all good soldiers, namely: valour, intelligence, military spirit, enthusiasm, devotion to duty, spirit of sacrifice, and a virtuous life, which make up the whole man (*'las reúne por completo'*). . . ." So close indeed were the two men, both by military association and by temperament, that a correspondent of *Paris-Match* wrote at the time of Millán-Astray's imposing funeral in Madrid in 1953, that with the interment of his old chief and battle comrade the Head of the Spanish State was "burying his own youth".

'*Comandantín*' Franco informed his readers in an Author's Note that they would not find in the book a literary work, but only "a concise and true account of the history of a battalion, whose destiny it was to bear the honour of repeatedly shedding its blood for Spain". Here is a typical passage—a proud and straightforward account of an inspection of the Legionaries in Melilla by a visiting British general, "a veteran of Europe's battlefields":

> *Las unidades esperan formadas en orden de parada; un cornetín señala con sus notas agudas la llegada del visitante, suenan la Marcha Real inglesa y española y los legionarios firmes, inmóviles, como estatuas, se presentan en su primera revista. La música interpreta el Tiperary y con la alegre marcha inglesa revista la fuerza seguido por nuestro Teniente Coronel, el veterano general de los campos de Europa. . . . La felicitación del general inglés fué el más alto honor para nosotros . . . recientes están aún sus palabras en la prensa inglesa en defensa de la Legión Extranjera española, que conoció en sus albores.* (pp. 22-23).

In his book the author outlined, four full years before General Primo de Rivera was to put the plan into execution, the master strategical stroke destined to bring to an end many disastrous and costly years of bloody conflict in Spanish Morocco. "Alhucemas," wrote Franco, with finality, "is the focus of the anti-Spanish rebellion, it is the road to Fez, the short cut to the Mediterranean, and there is found the key of a great deal of propaganda which will end on the day that we set our foot on that coast" (p. 278—my translation).

This landing, effected at the cost of "one dead and five wounded", by twelve thousand troops on an enemy coast defended by sixty thousand embittered and embattled Moors, has become a classic in military annals; it was possibly closely studied by General Eisenhower and his American and British invasion experts before the Normandy landings in World War II. The vanguard of the landing forces was under the command of "Coronel Francisco Franco".

His first biographer, Joaquín Arrarás, has written an eloquent summing up of Franco's career in Africa.

> After fourteen long years [he says under the chapter-heading "Unscathed and Unbowed"] of active military life almost uninterrupted Franco returned to the Peninsula. He had participated in

the operations of Beni-Arás, the reconquest of Melilla, the retreat from Xauen, and the landing at Alhucemas, always in the vanguard as leader of forces in battle. The records of the war are full of references to his bravery. Bullets seemed to revere him as they did the prophets of Moorish legend who had miraculous powers and turned bullets into rose petals. Through the course of the African campaigns the path was covered with graves, and many commanders and officers had fallen.

Millán-Astray was wounded while speaking to Franco, who had seen two of his own aides-de-camp and his standard bearer fall dead at his feet. . . . Of the officers of the First Battalion, which Franco commanded, not ten per cent. survived. He had bullet-riddled caps and cloaks, various horses he was riding had been wounded, and at Alhucemas the explosion of a shell buried him. . . . The only time that Millán-Astray admonished him was for the fearlessness with which he defied gunfire in the advances. Sanjurjo jokingly threatened to club him if he should find him again on his white horse in the thick of the firing line. . . ."

Franco had seen death at his side "many a time" but thanks to his good fortune "it has not known me". He had learned the art of war, the "know-how" of fighting and surviving and this secret he did not hide but proudly revealed. He had always regarded his life, he told me at El Pardo, as "un regalo—a gift", and this gift Providence had permitted him to retain while the dark angel of Death was robbing it of all around him.

If Franco's prescience and mental and military aptitude so strikingly bore the fruit of permanent peace, good administration and the tranquillisation of the fiercest tribes in North Africa, could he have been so very much out when he announced in a manifesto in August, 1936, that the Spanish Army was to be compared at that moment "with a surgeon who is operating to save Spain"? If, in the same pronouncement, he also roundly declared that "Spain is Republican and will remain so; neither régime nor flag will be altered", he is not the first leader nor the first surgeon to change his mind about the right remedy for a nation or a patient's ills. "Do I contradict myself?—very well then, I contradict myself. . . . I am large; I contain multitudes."*

And his basic claim was amply fulfilled—that "crime would be

---

* Walt Whitman.

replaced by order and acts of banditry by acts of progressive work".

More than a century and a half earlier Spain's soul sickness was diagnosed by no less, and no more, a person than the reprobate Casanova, who has this revealing passage in his astounding memoirs, which the detached and humanistically minded Havelock Ellis nevertheless found comparable to those of St. Augustine. (Book VIII: *Valencia*):

> Poor Spaniards! this beauty and fertility of your land are the cause of your ignorance, as the mines of Cerro Potosí have brought about that foolish pride and all the prejudices which degrade you. Spaniards! when will the impulse come? when will you shake off that fatal lethargy? Now you are truly useless to yourselves and the rest of the world: what is it you need? A furious revolution, a terrible shock; a conquest of regeneration: your case is past gentle methods, it needs the cautery and the fire.

In short, a surgical operation!

The "cautery and the fire" was also Franco's portion in Africa during the same number of years (exactly) that the "Lion of the North", Charles XII of Sweden, was absent from Sweden a a generation before Casanova's own lifetime, fighting his country's battles in Poland, Russia and Turkey.

The long and complex annals of the Riffian war are today condensed into a few pithy sentences in works of reference, or provide a minatory chapter or two in military handbooks on strategy, and there is no need to recount here the details of its progress or retrogression from the first skirmishes on the gravelly banks of the river Kert to the final triumphant disembarkation in the bay of Alhucemas.

The war made Franco and prepared him for the greater destiny of saving—or ruining, according to belief and taste—his country, and the best surviving commanders who brought the Moroccan 'incident' to a final successful end all later became leaders in the Nationalist rising against the threatened sovietisation of the Peninsula: the bearded white-haired Cabanellas, whom I used to pass sometimes in 1932 on the south side of Madrid's Gran Vía; Sanjurjo, the "Lion of the Riff," whose escape from the death sentence at his trial for the August, 1932, Monarchist revolt in

Seville I reported from the High Courts of Justice (I can still see the wispy brown curls on his ample neck, for my seat was not far behind his chair); Goded, who was captured and shot by the Republicans; the cautious, bespectacled Mola who lost his life in an air crash in 1937; Queipo de Llano whom Koestler writes of as an 'epileptic sadist' and whose tomb I found in 1950 in the Chapel of the venerated Virgen de la Macarena, inside the Roman walls of Seville; Aranda, who later turned against Franco: and *'el gran mutilado'* Millán-Astray.

One African engagement only need be mentioned in passing, the appalling massacre of Anual which has passed into Spain's history in the same sinister remembrance that the massacre of the legions of Varius in the Teutoburg forest passed into Roman and then into Europe's history. For in this one battle, *eleven thousand* Spanish soldiers perished and their general, Fernández Silvestre, expiated the ambush next day, it is believed, by taking his own life. In any case, he was never heard of again.

A man who had held responsible command in the forward areas at such an experience of "cautery and fire" had already faced the worst, and must have experienced in heart and mind and spirit the most poignant pangs of a true patriot. He could have no base fear, so far as his own safety was concerned, or the validity of any honest decision he might make in a crisis, of anything that might later befall. . . .

At the conclusion of the Moroccan War Franco was promoted, at the age of thirty-two, to Brigadier-General's rank, awarded again the Military Medal for gallantry in the face of the enemy, was made a Knight Commander of the French Legion of Honour and granted by France additionally the Badge of Military and Naval Merit. It had taken the "little Gallego", the lean cadet with the lustrous dark eyes and keen, bird-like face, from the modest middle-class home in "Sun-street," the modern Calle de "Frutos Saavedra" in far Ferrol, sixteen years to achieve the height of his ambition.

Chapter Eleven

THE PATRIOT

"THERE, BELOW ME," wrote the late Hilaire Belloc, that inveterate traveller and master-stylist, in his book *Many Cities*, which for historical pith and condensation one would seek far to equal: "—lay Aragon. . . . The name alone is enough to fill a man with delight and to magnify him with the story of twelve hundred years. It was up the torrent of Aragon that the swarm of Mohammedans rode when they swept into Gaul. It was down from that first beckoning of water that the first of the counter-attacks began, forcing its way down, march by march, generation by generation, till, a thousand years ago, the Christians held Jaca and Huesca.

"A lifetime later," runs his word-picture, "that thunderous little torrent of Aragon spread its name greatly outwards till Saragossa was taken, then the dark awful range above the Castle of Job beyond; till, in battle after battle, after advances and retreats innumerable, alliance and counter-alliance between the Christian lords of rough keeps and the Moorish chiefs of the valleys, the tide came to an end on the heights of the sources of the Tagus, and the whole kingdom was formed."

More than Castille, more than León, adds Belloc with that historical insight which was part of his paternal inheritance, does that advance of Aragon stand as the type of reconquest, and as the beginning of those ceaseless adventures "which are now the secret of the Spanish blood".

To famed Aragon, to its two-thousand-year-old capital of Saragossa (Zaragoza—"*Tharagotha*"—directly deriving from the Roman name for the city, "Caesar-Augusta"), came now in early 1928 the youngest general in the Spanish Army, the youngest general in all Europe, after his fifteen years as a serving field officer in the thick of the Moroccan war—chosen before all his superiors by General Primo de Rivera, under whose eyes he had boldly led the vanguard in the decisive Alhucemas landing, to be the first Director of the re-formed General Military Academy there. The Academy tradition descended from the first Spanish Military Academy established at Seville only a year or two before the Napoleonic invasion, and from the second and third, dating back to 1824 and 1882 respectively. Its principal function was to provide two years' preparatory studies for cadets destined for the infantry, cavalry, artillery, engineers and commissariat, but above all to develop friendly inter-service liaison and "a real intimate solidarity among all the branches of the army".

On October 5th, 1928, when the Academy opened—or re-opened—its doors after many months of preparation, which included not only the drafting of the curriculum but also the building of living quarters and class-rooms, Franco set the pace and tone of the new College in his first address to the 494 students assembled in the courtyard—a speech fully reported in the Spanish Press at the time:

> To the experience of those (he said, in one significant passage) who, aged in the profession of arms, have dedicated their lives to work and study, will be united that of those others whom the fortune of war has enabled to vindicate their skill and enthusiasm, and who today cover their breasts with the most esteemed military decorations.

The passage might have come from a speech of eighteen centuries ago to pensioned legionaries at Itálica, the Roman settlement outside Seville for old soldiers and their families, an important section of which still awaits excavation to this day the ancient theatre being the only part fully cleared.

The very city in which the Academy was situated, a city of early Christian martyrs, a city particularly venerated by devout Spaniards for the column of porphyry preserved below the high altar in the famous Basilica of El Pilar on which the Virgin Mary is said to have appeared to St. James the Greater, the patron saint of Spain; the heroic city which, on the Santa María Gate, still bears the scars from the legendary resistance it offered to the troops of Marshal Lannes in the Peninsular War, Franco cited to his cadets as an inspiration in their studies, even as the famed and immortal city of Toledo had inspired his own.

> I am sure [he said] that you will emulate the history of those loyal soldiers who for over a century wrote the most brilliant pages in the

history of our nation . . . the nobility of those hidalgoes* which again dwells in our hearts, *and the unconquered and heroic city of Zaragoza which set the scene,* offering to you in its stones and monuments the first and most solid lesson of heroic sacrifices.

The military life, the Director pointed out, was not a road "to pleasure and delight" but carried with it "great sufferings, hardships and sacrifices". "Glory, also," he added, with a rhetorical flourish, "but, like the rose, it comes forth among thorns." Then, concluding his long homily as with an afterthought, he gave in one brief sentence his own philosophy and the secret of his power over Fate and men: "It must not be forgotten that he who suffers conquers, and that daily resisting and conquering is the school of triumph, and is the road to the heroism of tomorrow."

Could this inaugural address, delivered before nearly five hundred students at a Service academy just brought into being, by a Director completely new to his duties, have been bettered by any Commandant at England's Sandhurst or any Commanding Officer at America's West Point? Like 'Rosa Dartle' in Dickens' *Bleak House*, I am drawing no conclusions but merely asking for information. In accordance with his character, that of a 'Roman Spaniard' and a soldier devoted to his métier, Franco had thrown himself with his characteristic driving force heart and soul into his new job, and this flare continued, so much so that the fame of his Academy crossed frontiers, brought international visitors and notabilities, and evoked international tributes.

During the three years that he was permitted to direct the Academy, he was enabled to fulfil a long-cherished wish to visit military academies in other lands, spending two 'busman's' vacations in Berlin and Dresden respectively, and in November, 1930, attending the French staff course for generals and colonels at Versailles, where one of the lecturers was the then middle-aged Marshal Pétain, of whom Spain was to hear and see much a decade later, and Europe a lot more after that, and another was Marshal Foch.

It is perhaps fruitless at this late date to speculate to what higher degree of efficiency and fame Franco might have raised the General Military Academy at Saragossa had he been allowed to

---

* *hidalgo*—"son of something."

carry on his work there for a decade in the spirit in which it was begun. As Director he combined qualities uniquely joined in one man: a first-class strategical brain combined with an unparalleled (in Spain at any rate) knowledge of military strategy, an un-equalled record of valorous service on the field of battle re-inforced and supported by a deep love of tradition, and a trans-parent spirit of patriotism which evoked the willing devotion of the generous-hearted Spanish youths who passed through his hands.

Fate and destiny had other plans. Country-wide municipal elections, whose ultimate results were to show a substantial majority in favour of the Monarchy, through Republican bounce and agitation following the anti-Alfonso vote in the cities, brought about its fall overnight. The King, bowing to the storm, while abdicating none of his rights agreed to 'make himself scarce' (which Franco has resolutely refused to do, perhaps with the royal example and its aftermath ever in mind) and on the night of April 13th, 1931, within a few hours had left Madrid and Spain, on whose beloved soil he was never again to set foot, for his last years in exile. The Queen and the royal children followed next day, not from Cartagena by Spanish warship like the King, but in a special train bound for Hendaye which they discreetly joined at the station of El Escorial, within sight of that massive monastery-palace-mausoleum the plan for which Philip II drew up on his return to his native land sometime after a year's residence in London as King-Consort of barren and unhappy Mary Tudor.

Public men are judged by their actions and decisions in times of vital emergency. It may be unprofitable but it is only human to wonder to what extent modern Spanish history might have been saved its most tragic chapter had the King stood his ground and refused to budge at the dictate of the first returns in municipal elections: and had the Leader of the Opposition in the Republican Cortes, Calvo Sotelo, listened five years later to the desperate pleadings of his wife on the night of July 13th, 1936, and declined the invitation of the uniformed *Guardias de Asalto*, or Republican Shock Police, unprovided with any warrant, to 'go for a ride' with them in a police coach. Don Alfonso, by one of those bold gestures that Spaniards are quick to appreciate, might not have lost his throne, and Calvo Sotelo might not have lost his life in an official car, shot in the back of the neck. In either eventuality, civil war might have been avoided.

"Both men should have sat tight," said the former *Times* correspondent in Madrid for a quarter of a century, my good friend Ernest Grimaud de Caux, when I sought his opinion recently, "they acted as they did from motives of mistaken patriotism."

Had the Monarchy not fallen—and the speed and manner of its fall staggered the Republican elements in the country no less than the general public—the future of the subject of this study would without doubt have been materially different, for that there would have been no 'Franco Spain' goes without saying. When the Republic did come in, Franco lost no time in proclaiming his allegiance to the new régime, even though it had been ushered in so unceremoniously without general elections or plebiscite—as King Alfonso's cousin told me in 1932, the late Duke of Santa Elena, who had driven through howling and gesticulating crowds right up to the gates of the palace—by "mob vote".

On April 15th Franco promulgated a special order of the day drawing the cadets' attention to the fact that "a Republic having been proclaimed in Spain, and the highest powers of the State being assumed by the Provisional Government, it behoves us all at this moment to co-operate with discipline and the solid virtues so that peace may reign and the nation may adjust itself through the natural legal channels." He further declared that soldiers should stand aside from politics and think only of the nation.

These declarations of his own position and that of the Academy, namely, to be above all politics, made, however, no impression on the later Republican War Minister, Manuel Azaña, a former Civil Service clerk who had claimed public attention some months earlier by asking his supporters at a party gathering held in the Madrid bull-ring whether they were to be governed any longer "by monkeys"? The descriptive adjective most favoured by Madrileños for himself during his tenure later of the offices of War Minister, Prime Minister, and President, was *"pachyder-maous"*—although I once heard him described by a colleague with whom I attended the debates in the Republican Cortes as "a man of cold passion". Azaña, who, I learned from a Spanish source, was dismissed as a cadet from the Toledo Alcazar for unnatural practices and thereafter conceived a hatred for all things military, could see no useful purpose in the Academy, and little enough in its conscientious Director, whom the new Government regarded with the same suspicion as they regarded the entire army. He accordingly closed the General Military Academy at Saragossa by decree, and kept its ex-Director out of employment for a twelvemonth.

Franco's farewell speech to his cadets, given exactly three months after the establishment of the Second Republic, is well enough known in authoritarian Spain; no apologies are therefore offered for reproducing some extracts from it here, over twenty years after it was made, especially as it reveals some of his methods:

> The General Military Academy [said its pre-Civil War Director] has functioned for three years . . . years through which we lived by your side, educating and instructing you, and attempting to forge for Spain the most competent and honourable staff of officers that any nation can hope to possess. We had the real satisfaction on that road of thorns when the most capable foreign experts lavished warm eulogies upon our work, studying and praising our system and setting it up as a model among modern institutions of military training. . . .
>
> We studied our army, its faults and its virtues, and correcting the former, we have increased the latter, while noting a real evolution in procedures and systems. Thus we saw rigid and out-of-date textbooks succumb before the pressure of a modern Faculty, conscious of its mission. . . . The entrance examination, automatic and anonymous, previously open to intrigue and influence, were not debased by recommendation and favour. . . . The machine is in pieces, but the work lives on. You are our work, the seven hundred and twenty officers who tomorrow will be in company with the common soldier, whom you will guard and lead, who will be, without doubt, champions of loyalty, gentlemanliness, discipline, the fulfilment of duty and the spirit of sacrifice for country, all qualities inherent in the true soldier, among which stands out above all discipline, that sublime virtue indispensable to the life of any army, and which you are bound to keep as the most precious of your possessions. . . .

And at once the speaker, introducing a personal note into his eloquent homily, reveals the keenness of his pang at seeing his proud creation, the fruit of long experience, intellectual range

and sheer hard work, shut down in the full tide of its usefulness.—
"*Discipline! . . . which shows its true worth when the mind advises
otherwise, when the heart fights to rise up in spiritual rebellion, or when
the command is arbitrary or erroneous.* This is the discipline which we
inculcate in you. This is the example which we offer you."

The speech, breathing as it did the spirit of profound patriotism,
allied to something like an heroic self-mastery, did not please at all
Señor Azaña, who mentally—and it maybe, actually—put a
black mark against the name of him who had uttered it, later
placing it with others at the bottom of the promotion lists.

When I interviewed Azaña, on behalf of a British national
daily the year after these occurrences, in the Cabinet's room
of the Cortes, after walking unannounced into the War Office off
the Plaza de Cibeles and past the two armed sentries at the garden-
gate to secure an introduction from his surprised Military
Secretary which I made use of within the hour, the Republican
Prime Minister had only one phrase on his lips in reply to all my
questions: "*Es mentira*—it's a lie!"   I wish now that I had brought
into the conversation Borrow's *Bible in Spain*, of which Azaña
did the first Spanish translation.

Chapter Twelve

THE PATRIOT (*continued*)

I T WOULD BE BETTER, PERHAPS, for the professed, or intended objectivity of this study if there could now be revealed some nefarious or treasonable activities of "this man", this deposed, sacked, and frustrated Director of one of Europe's most successful Military Academies: some plotting against the legitimate Government, some underhand traffic with international Fascism, or indirect negotiations with the Axis dictators who must have been watching developments in Spain with particular interest at this time as these were following the same pattern as social unrest and Communist agitation and infiltration had done in Italy and Hungary and Bavaria after the first World War. Considerable research in archives and by personal enquiry have, however, so far yielded me no evidence of such activities: nothing, in fact, beyond a rumour that appeared in a London daily that Generals Goded and Franco were "believed to be involved in some plot". This rumour seems quickly to have petered out.

After a year kicking his heels at the will of the Minister for War, Franco was at last given the command of the infantry brigade garrisoned at Corunna. This was in 1932, in January of which year I first arrived in Spain to take up foreign correspondence work in Madrid. The liberal and enlightened character given to the Republican régime by its famous Constitution, which "outlawed war" yet brought a murderous internal strife and rancour into public life everywhere by the tacit or active encouragement given to subversive elements, had been wiped out by the introduction of the "Defence of the Realm Act", which was never repealed during the whole life of the Republic. At a stroke this measure swept away all the proudly boasted 'democratic liberties' of the Spanish people, and Spain became, in fact, a Police State in which fear, tyranny and injustice stalked the land. That under the present régime the *Fuero de los Españoles*, the "Charter of the Spaniards", is reputedly suspended, and that the country is still technically under Martial Law, is a clear indication that democracy, as the West understands it, does not flourish—is never allowed to flourish—organically on Spanish soil. There are many *Calles* and *Avenidas "de la Libertad"* in Spain, but the boast is mostly wishful thinking, for the Spaniard is always disposed to interpret *"libertad"* according to his own particular wishes and political affiliations, which does not make for effective government or well-ordered living.

> The same arts that did gain
> A power, must it maintain——

as the Puritan poet Andrew Marvell wrote after Cromwell's return from Ireland.

As a patriot, a 'green incorruptible', Franco was *persona non grata* to the quasi-Liberal and the Leftist leaders of the calibre of Azaña, Indalecio Prieto, with his non-committal expression and dangerous smouldering eyes, Albornoz, short of stature and of indifferent presence, the Republican Minister of Justice, the genial but unscrupulous Fernando de los Ríos, Minister of Education, with whom I had a pleasant chat once in his office in the Calle de Alcalá, the dark horse Casares Quiroga, the firebrand Margarita Nelken, and the 'pink revolutionary' Victoria Kent, with English ancestry. Even far Galicia was considered too near to the capital with Franco there for Government Ministers to feel over-safe in carrying through their drastic programme, and in 1933 the youngest general was transferred as military commander to the Balearics, where, despite growing anxiety for his country and a sudden access of despair at the pass to which it was being steadily brought, he profited by the occasion to work out a complete plan for the defence in time of war of those delectable islands. The instant effectiveness of the scheme was proved, in a manner not envisaged when it was drawn up, when the Balearics withstood, better perhaps than did any other part of the realm, the severest test when the national crisis did come, decisively defeating a determined invasion of Communist elements from Valencia.

There seems to be small doubt that at the time of his transfer to Palma, Franco was giving serious thought to the question of resigning from the army and entering politics in the hope of being of more use to Spain and in a more effective way. It was even reported that a delegate of the Popular Action Party from Madrid had approached him at his headquarters in the 14th-century Palacio de la Almudaina, with the offer of a sure seat in the next Cortes if he decided to stand. Whatever idea, however, he entertained at this time of changing his profession, was finally abandoned in the same place and he remained in Mallorca until he was urgently called back to the capital by a new War Minister, Don Diego Hidalgo, in the late autumn of 1934 to advise on military measures to subdue the most serious threat which had up to that time arisen to the Second Republic, indeed to the very life of the country. Simultaneously, as if concerted by prior plan, a Separatist rising in Catalonia and a Communist-inspired rising of the miners in Asturias, both of a dangerous magnitude, had broken out at the two opposite ends of Spain. "Ancestral voices", and something much more modern and ruthless, were "prophesying war".

Had the ears of the rest of western Europe been metaphorically attuned, as in actuality are those of Red Indians who we are told placed them to the ground in times of emergency or threatening war, to the ominous rumblings coming from 'emancipated and liberated' Spain, these coincident uprisings would have carried over land and sea a conviction of their true significance—that a revolution of the proletariat was impending. The ostensible reason advanced for the twin outbreak was the overthrow of a Socialist Government in a general election and the return of a Rightist majority led by the able head of C.E.D.A., Señor Gil Robles, who should in fact, had the President acted constitutionally, have been asked to form the government.

This unexpected check to the hopes and designs of the Extremists roused them to fury; indeed, the extreme Left-wing leaders like Indalecio Prieto and the 'Spanish Lenin', Largo Caballero, openly threatened an armed rising, for which secret stores of munitions had been assembled in different parts of the country for many months in anticipation of just such a check. For when the *vox populi* went against them and contrary to their revolutionary doctrines, the extremist leaders were not prepared to accept the popular verdict.

With Catalonia and Asturias in a state of rebellion and anarchy, the life of Madrid was now paralysed by 'snap' strikes in the essential services. While twenty thousand dissident miners marched on Oviedo and Gijón with arms reported to have been landed at night on the rocky Cantabrian coast by Soviet ships, the citizens of the capital were deprived of water and light and simple necessities such as coffee and milk. Lenin's prophecy, that Spain would be the next Soviet State, appeared on the point of being fulfilled. "There is no need to destroy Europe," Stalin had remarked ominously after Lenin's death; "it will destroy itself."

Into the heart of the alarming internal situation came at urgent Ministerial summons the 'exiled' commanding general of the Balearic Islands. And the contemporary records demonstrate that it was Franco's cool, collected and utterly effectual handling of this perilous crisis which more than ever marked him out as the predestined leader in the now inevitable struggle for national survival against the octopus-like embrace of the Leftist influence, although still two years away was the ultimate 'show-down'.

Condemnation, abuse and embittered attacks have been heaped on Franco's head in partisan literature for the sharp lesson he administered to the sinister forces engaged in the uprisings. In the north particularly, no quarter was given to the anarchic elements in the cities by the Government troops, which included now for the first time forces from Africa; concentrations of Communists and anarchists, and Asturian '*dinamiteros*', were shelled from the sea and on land driven from the key positions they had taken up. But such ruthlessness as was used needs to be viewed in the light of the emergency, which was now a nation-wide emergency with the soul and future destiny of Spain—and incidentally of western Europe—as the pawn.

Franco brought his strategical expertise and his unique experience in battle to the task of stemming internal anarchy ("Spain is rapidly moving towards a condition of complete chaos," wrote one foreign observer at this time). And the Republican War Minister himself, the quick-witted Diego Hidalgo, paid tribute to the qualities of the man he had called in as a last resort:

> Devoted entirely to his profession [he wrote] he possesses in a high degree all the military qualities, and his activities and capacity for work, his clear judgment, his understanding and his culture, are always ready for the call of arms. Of his qualities the greatest is his concentration on examining, analysing, enquiring and developing problems. A carefulness which impels him to be minute in details,

exact in service, correct in observation, strict and demanding in discipline, and at the same time understanding, calm and devoted. . . .

One has to pinch oneself to realise that it was a Republican, and a Minister of the Second Republic at that, who authorised this tribute to a general for whom Azaña had had no use.

Franco extinguished revolt at both ends of Spain when the fate of his country hung by a thread, and he learned a great deal in the course of the operations which do not appear in books about the Republican era. He discovered from where the northern rebels got their arms, and he discovered the true nature of the propaganda which had been inculcated into them since the coming in of the régime. He knew now, what José Antonio Primo de Rivera had been preaching in and out of the Cortes for two years, that the enemy Spanish patriots had to confront with unity and the utmost resolution, if the country was to be saved, was not only to be found in those Spaniards willingly or involuntarily led away by an alien ideology, but was hydra-headed and infiltrating into their midst day by day, week by week. He had seen militant Separatism and its aim face to face in Catalonia, favourite hunting ground of Bakhunin's particular brand of anarchism, and militant Communism in naked action in Asturias. His future thought was to be shaped and moulded by this experience and by this knowledge. "One could not be expected to be neutral *in thought*", many citizens of countries neutral in the 1939-45 war have said; similarly, a patriot's thoughts were his own.

His year as Commander-in-Chief in Morocco (1934), his appointment as Chief of the General Staff to Gil Robles during the latter's brief term as Minister of War, in which capacity he attended the funeral of King George V in London, were but episodes in a Preamble to the final tragedy, Civil War.

Early in the fateful year, 1936, he was exiled again, this time as Captain General to the Canaries. But before he sailed for Las Palmas from Cadiz to take up his duties, he met for the first and only time the leader of the Phalanx, who, all unknowingly, had before him but a few more months of life. The subject of their conversation at this dramatic meeting has never been revealed, but one may be reasonably certain that it did not concern Madrid's new *Frontón*, nor the art of *cante hondo*, the 'deep song' of the Deep South, whose foremost male exponent today is Juanito Valderrama.

BOOK TWO

"Bear what thou canst; pow'r cometh at man's need."
THE GOLDEN VERSES OF THE PYTHAGOREANS

Chapter Thirteen

WHAT IS THE 'FALANGE'?

AN EYE-WITNESS OF THE SCENE when Hitler left the railway coach at Hendaye after his ten hours' fruitless parleyings in 1940 with Franco in an attempt to bring Spain into the war on the Axis side and secure uninterrupted transit to Gibraltar for the Nazi tanks, describes how the *Führer* cast his familiar peaked cap on the ground and jumped and stamped on it in rage and exasperation. Hitler, in any case, as all the world knows, was quite lacking in self-control and when thwarted in his designs became as infuriated and ruthless as any Asiatic tyrant, so that it is credible enough that after being astutely played like a big fish by the Spanish leader for an entire day he should have emerged from the ordeal with frayed nerves and in a filthy temper.

Franco, on the other hand, is a man who has gained over himself an iron mastery, and it is this quite un-Spanish quality above all others, perhaps, which gives him his personal and spiritual ascendancy over his countrymen and countrywomen. The proverb which says that he who would dominate the many must first learn to dominate himself was perhaps never better exemplified than in this Galician Spaniard of insignificant stature who for nearly two decades has held the fate of his country in the hollow of his hands.

Only once, so far as my researches have carried me, did that full self-control desert him, when a leading Phalangist brought forward the recommendation during a meeting of the National Council at El Pardo that its *centurias* "should be armed, like the Army". The mere suggestion put Franco into a towering passion. Was it not enough, he shouted, that Spain should have undergone the horrors and sufferings of a ferocious Civil War through the indiscriminate and criminal arming of opposing groups, that the recommendation should be seriously proposed for the arming of the quasi-national *Falange*? Not content with telling the Phalangist leader in forthright terms what he thought of his idea, it is said that Franco then had him incontinently gaoled for two years—but I have been unsuccessful in finding any confirmation of this latter story. In 1937 Franco had Hedilla, a leading Phalangist, tried for inciting opposition.

"The Monarchists hate the *Falange*, and the *Falange* hate the Monarchists," a new Civil Governor remarked to me as I sipped a glass of his excellent *Tío Pepe* and nibbled a handful of *almendras* one Sunday morning in his pleasant home in one of the northern provinces. "And," he added, "among the younger Phalangists there is a trend back to Republicanism." On a previous Sunday I had been present in the Paseo de Coches in the Retiro park in Madrid—originally the rose-garlanded royal park of the Palace of Buen Retiro, where Velasquez painted his famous portraits of Philip IV and maybe his 'four-square' masterpiece *Las Meninas*— at a parade of seven thousand Phalangist youth in celebration of the Day of their patron, St. Ferdinand, 13th-century King of Castille and the liberator of Seville from the Moors. Some of his royal garments in perfect preservation are to be seen today in the royal convent of Las Huelgas, near Burgos—and also the 'camp' crucifix carried at the decisive battle of Las Navas de Tolosa (1212).

One group wore white ski-ing dress, but all the rest were clad in grey shorts and blue stockings, blue shirts and the scarlet Carlist red berets which looked like so many huge poppies as their wearers knelt down in the road for the *Misa de Campaña*, or Field Mass, celebrated by a Phalangist chaplain on a raised platform containing an altar. Later an eloquent address was delivered from this platform on the life and example of St. Ferdinand by the Head of the Phalangist *Frente de Juventudes*, Elola, who dragged in a withering reference to "Winss-tun Churr-cheel", who had recently denied in the House of Commons that he had given any promise during the war that Gibraltar would be returned to Spain in return for her neutrality.

For a detached observer like myself it was not particularly reassuring to see the old Fascist salute of the raised right hand being given by the recipients of good-conduct medals and new banners as they made their way to the tribune, where their salutes were returned and each youth clasped in the Spanish embrace. I was reminded of the swastika-beflagged parades of the pre-war Nazi *Jugend* at the Feldernhalle, in pre-war Munich, and down the broad handsome Ludwigstrasse, where, in the Press Tribune on the "Day of German Art", I had twice sat for two hours opposite Hitler, Goering and Goebbels installed in the official stand below the equestrian statue of Ludwig I in the Odeonsplatz, during all of which time the hypnotic strains of *Deutchsland Über Alles* flooded the circumambient air from the loudspeakers. The exuberant shouts and songs of the homegoing Spanish Phalanx boys, which percolated into the quiet, colour-filled rooms of the stimulating Modern Art Exhibition in the Retiro, to which I next turned my attention, were, too, an equally uncomfortable reminder of the Nazi chants and slogans I used to hear on pre-war summer days on the white, dusty roads of the Bavarian alps as Hitler's conscripts and potential killers and torturers carried out their training amid the paradisial setting of the Isar valley, between the Brauneck and the Geierstein.*

Yet I knew well enough, none better for I was living in Spain at the time, that the Spanish Phalanx had been founded on October 29th, 1933, and the first parade held in the great court-yard of the Escorial, expressly to counter increasing disorder under the Second Republic and the growing menace of Com-munist infiltration. During the first four months, for example, of the Popular Front Government, Spain endured 113 general strikes and 218 partial ones, and 170 churches, 69 clubs and the offices of ten newspapers were set on fire, and attempts made to burn 284 other buildings, 251 of them churches (to quote from the official statistics accepted by responsible British correspond-ents). Priceless treasures of art and architecture belonging to the

---

* Whilst I was working on later sections of this book in the shop of Josef Eibel, local printer at Lenggries, in the Bavarian Alps, he volun-teered three pieces of information: (i) that Hitler had planned World War II from the year he attained power, 1933, "and left no other alternative than national bankruptcy"; (ii) that American propaganda in Germany since war ended had been "overdone" and that the actions of the occupying forces were not always in line with the democratic precepts they professed, and (iii) that the de-Nazification Courts had terminated their functions prematurely. "It is now," he declared, "that the true Nazis are insolently proclaiming their allegiance. Those who made an honest mistake gave it up long ago." Eibel was in Hitler's attack on Poland and invasion of France, where he was seriously wounded.

10

national patrimony, besides such imponderable spiritual riches as the heart of St. Francis Xavier, the 'Apostle of the Indies', which perished in the burning by a Madrid mob of the historic Jesuit church in the Calle de la Flor, were destroyed or otherwise lost for ever. Writing in the *Journal de Genève* on January 17th, 1937, the former President of the Spanish Republic, D. Niceto Alcalá Zamora, who had been overthrown by a treacherous move of his Prime Minister, Manuel Azaña, whom I once interviewed for the London *Daily Telegraph* in the lobby of the Cortes, himself declared that this Left-wing Government had "obtained power by violent means." "With my illegal removal," he added,, 'the last obstacle was overthrown on the road to anarchy and all the violences of Civil War."

The founder of the Phalanx, the late José Antonio Primo de Rivera, eldest son of the former Dictator, General Primo de Rivera, Marqués de Estella, had certainly got the idea from Mussolini's Blackshirts, but then Italian Fascism, I also knew well enough, had itself come into being as a counter to post-war Communist influence in Italy and after the considerable port of Civita Vecchia had actually been declared a Soviet. Phalangism grew in Spain, where its guiding inspiration was honest patriotism and a desire for social justice, because it seemed the only remedy for what looked like becoming, and did in fact become, a dictatorship of the Left.*

If one of the slogans of the new patriotic formation was "*Por el Imperio hacia Dios*—By (or through) the Empire, towards God"— predicating an ambition in the direction of national resurgence and territorial expansion, the better known "*Arriba España*" was no more chauvinistic, and no less truly patriotic in concept, than the watchword, "Wake Up England!" which King George V made his own when he returned from his voyage round the world as Prince of Wales. Moreover, it dated back to the centuries of the Reconquest, as did also the symbol of the yoke and arrows, which was part of the insignia, signifying unity, of the Catholic Monarchs.

If the manner in which the whole Western world swallowed hook, line and sinker, the Republican (and International Com-

---

* "In the political ranks of the Phalangists were youth and vigour, and in the forefront of their programme reforms for which the country was waiting".—E. Allison Peers in *The Spanish Dilemma*.

munist) propaganda line regarding the origin and true significance of the Civil War must go down in history as one of the
most monstrous deceptions ever imposed on a credulous mankind,
the labelling as "Fascist" of all Spanish patriotic and traditional
movements represents an equally nefarious triumph for the
Soviets. For it was in obedience to a Cominform directive that
the parrot-cry of "Fascist" was directed by all agents and organs of
international Communist publicity against any and every
patriotic *national* activity in any European State which did not
favour, of intent or tacitly, the Soviet designs. This fact is abundantly confirmed in the "Secret Documents Detailing the Plan for
the Establishment of a Soviet in Spain", clause 2 of which
provided for the starting "on the same day as the said movement,
the world-wide agitation to be named 'anti-Fascist' " and clause 9
of which entrusted one of the Madrid "cells" (No. 25) composed
of active members of the Police Force, "with the task of elimina-
ting the prominent political and military men likely to play an
important role in the counter-revolution".

It is worth while to examine a few of the recorded sayings of
José Antonio Primo de Rivera, extracted from his published
speeches and articles in the *Obras Completas: Edición Cronológica*,
published by the Dirección General de Información in Madrid in
1952, as indicating the purpose motivating his action in forming
and developing the *Falange Española Tradicionalista*, afterwards
merged with the *Juntas Ofensivas Nacional Sindicalistas*, or J.O.N.S.,
founded in 1931 by Onésimo Redondo and Ramiro Ledesma
Ramos (both later assassinated by opponents), whose Twenty-Six
Points were adopted by General Franco in their entirety as the
basic policy for the present authoritarian régime in Spain.

Thus, in May, 1936, two months before the outbreak of the
Civil War and five months before his own 'liquidation' in the yard
of the modern prison at Alicante, this thirty-three-year-old
Madrid barrister wrote: "We stand before the imminent menace
of a barbarian invasion, one of those historical cataclysms that
regularly operate as the colophon to every age." (A few months
later General Queipo de Llano declared that every thirty years
Andalusia suffered "a political earthquake.")

Three years previously in the Cortes, where he represented the
drovince of Cadiz as independent member, José Antonio said:

". . . the members of this youth, of which I form part, consider it not merely a bad thing that there should be a dictatorship of the Right or a dictatorship of the Left, but even that there should be such a thing as a political Right or Left at all". And in another speech: " . . . when we, the men of our generation, look about us, we find a world in moral ruin; a world split by every kind of differences; and as regards what concerns us most nearly, we find a Spain in moral ruin, a Spain split by every kind of hatred and conflict".

"It seems abominable to us," he declared before the Popular Front elections in 1936, "that the fortunes of Spain should have to be staked every two years on the hazards of the poll; that every two years we should put on the tragic show in which by dint of shouting, bribery, inanities and insults everything permanent in Spain is jeopardised and the concord between Spaniards is rent asunder." Franco himself was to claim later that democratic elections in Spain were never honest. "A century and a half of Parliamentary democracy," he told the famous war correspondent, Christopher Buckley, who was afterwards tragically killed in Korea (Franco sent a message of condolence to the British Ambassador for conveyance to the dead man's family), "accompanied by the loss of immense territory, three civil wars, and the imminent danger of national disintegration, add up to a disastrous balance sheet, sufficient to discredit parliamentary system in the eyes of the Spanish people."

Speaking in the Cortes after the Catalonian Separatist rising of 1934 had been quashed and the Communist revolt in Asturias defeated, both, it cannot be denied, by the prompt measures taken by General Franco, urgently recalled from enforced retirement by the Republican War Minister, Don Diego Hidalgo, to cope with the dangerous situation, José Antonio, revealing what was at the back of his mind, declared: "Neither the Spanish State nor Spanish society would have defended themselves vigorously against the revolution, had there not entered into play the factor which always looks unforeseen to us, *but which never fails to make its appearance on historic occasions*, namely, the hidden genius of Spain, which, now as ever, housed within military uniforms . . . has once again, *now as ever*, given Spain back her unity and her peace. . . . This heroic military vein has saved us *the same as ever*, and must once more regain its paramount position" (my italics).

In the event of anarchy usurping the functions of responsible government in Britain or the United States, the intervention of the armed forces in support of the police would likewise be inevitable.

Finally, from the prison to which he had been sent on a false pretext by the Madrid Government, the prison he was never to leave alive, he addressed a "Letter to the Armed Forces" which was smuggled out by a sympathiser in which sentences flash and coruscate like instantaneous light in an all-encompassing darkness. "What is at stake," he wrote, "is the very existence of Spain as an entity and as a unity. The present peril is precisely equivalent to that of a foreign invasion . . . the foreignness of the movement that is laying siege to Spain is betrayed by its watchwords, by its slogans, by its aims and by its sentiments. . . . Weigh your awful responsibility. Whether Spain shall continue in being depends upon you."

The doomed patriot would echo that doggerel on the wall of the cottage at Rijnsburg where Spinoza, direct descendant of Spanish 'Marrano' Jews, once lodged with the surgeon, Hermann Homan, and wrote his *Short Treatise on God, Man and his Well-Being*:

> Alas! if all men were but wise,
> And would be good as well,
> The Earth would be a Paradise
> Where now 'tis mostly Hell,

and the *cri de cœur* of the Taoist mystic Chuang Tzu: "Alas! man's knowledge reaches to the hair on a hair, but not to the things of eternal peace."

Of such calibre was the founder of the Spanish Phalanx, as pure a patriot as Egmont or the Duc d'Enghien, whom Napoleon caused to be judicially murdered ("worse than a crime, it was a blunder") and such the man who, on November 19th, 1936, conducted his own defence before the Tribunal sitting on an upper floor of the Alicante prison, and by a "masterpiece of forensic oratory" (to quote from the long report next day in the Leftist *El Día* of Alicante) saved the life of his brother and fellow-prisoner, Miguel, today Spanish Ambassador in London, but not his own. His speech profoundly moved his hostile judges and the members of the public admitted to the Court-room, but the Madrid government had decreed his death ("acting on instructions from Moscow" announced my guide at the prison) and there was no escape. Of such a stamp was this noble Spaniard of thirty-three who was led out at dawn the next morning to face with serene and Christian fortitude a firing squad with "two Phalangists on one side and two Requetés on the other":

> Condemned yesterday to death, I pray God that if He does not still spare me from coming to that last trial, He may preserve in me up to the end the seemly submission with which I contemplate it and that in judging my soul He may apply to it not the measure of my merits but that of His infinite mercy [from the *Last Will and Testament*].

One morning in January, 1952, I traced on the high parapet wall of the prison courtyard at Alicante the track of the fusillade which had killed José Antonio on that November morning nearly twenty years before, and stood in the single cell where he had spent five months completely *incomunicado* and without reading matter of any kind, in the power of his implacable enemies. "I heard the shots which ended his life," remarked the driver of the car in which I travelled from El Ferrol del Caudillo over the mountains of León to Madrid two years after this Alicante visit: "I was imprisoned there too, and I saw him taking exercise with the guards in the prison yard the day before his death—he was never allowed out with the others."

"What was his bearing?" I enquired.

"Absolutely tranquil," the man replied, "he was the calmest and bravest of us all."

One sometimes hears the view expressed in Spain that if José Antonio was to return today to the scene of his former patriotic labours "he would disown his creation, the *Falange*", but, like most casual opinions, that is an oversimplification of the issue. Owing to the intensity with which Spaniards live and follow their interests and avocations, all political movements in Spain gravitate toward extremes. And the Phalanx he created is no exception; in fact it is propelled towards extremism by the fact, explained to me by Spaniards themselves, that many extremists, including former Anarchists and Communists, have found their way into its ranks. Doubtless it is this fact that gives rise to the anti-British tone of many articles in the Phalanx Press, for the view is widely held among the die-hard members of the organisation, and by a great many others for that matter, that the United Kingdom deliberately misinterpreted the true issues of the Civil War and retarded if not deliberately impeded the inevitable Nationalist victory at a heavy cost in Spanish lives and in widespread hunger and misery.

"It makes my blood boil to read some of the articles in *Arriba*," Sir John Balfour exploded before me in the Embassy one day; while one of His Excellency's subordinates, a commercial secretary in his office on the third floor, contented himself with exclaiming somewhat inelegantly, when I called for a chat later, that "they", *i.e.* the lads of the Phalanx, "hate our guts—they hate the reputation of our Ministers and civil servants for incorruptibility and integrity and the fact that Britain still has an Empire." He pooh-poohed the idea that the present régime had greatly improved the lot of the workers with welfare, health and pensions schemes with the view that it was "on paper, all paper". And again I was assailed by the conviction that the only way to understand Spain is to love Spain, and the only way to understand the Spanish is to become one of them in mind and spirit. Too many of the British in Madrid are content to enjoy all the delights that a well-paid job in Spain offers and to criticise at every turn the people and the régime. Ignorant and ill-natured attacks on Spain in the British Press, and insulting cartoons which are happily now far less frequent than they were, have been borne for years by Spaniards and their leader with exemplary patience and dignity.*

---

* ". . . as a whole, British families living in Spain gave one the impression of exiles, with one eye always on the postman bringing the English mail, much less interested in the fascinating people and places around them. . . . Not less noticeable was the indifference to Spanish affairs shown, in their private capacities, by the staffs of Embassies and Consulates. Their aloofness struck a chill. Here were the Spaniards . . . striving to work out for themselves a new way of life under conditions which should have aroused a fellow-feeling in any Englishman. Yet they seemed always to be regarded by the Britons in Spain as 'those curious foreigners' and the sort of comment one heard upon the most momentous political happenings could always be expressed in the formula: 'Dear me, what *will* they do next?' "—(E. Allison Peers, *The Spanish Dilemma*, pp. 105-6).

Personally, I do not care about seeing on the threshold of nearly every village in the Castiles an iron post bearing the huge Phalangist emblem of the yoke and arrows, but I know that the inspiration behind the choice of the emblem was at the outset entirely patriotic, for the yoke and arrows were part of the coat-of-arms of Isabella and can be seen today, just as they were painted in her own time, on the arbour-posts of the incomparable Generalife gardens above the Alhambra at Granada after its capture from the Moors, below the motto she adopted for herself and Ferdinand: "*TANTO MONTA, MONTA TANTO Isabel-como Fernando*"—("What belongs to you belongs to me".)

Franco met the founder of the Spanish Phalanx only once, in the house of a mutual Madrid friend, just before he left to take up his command in the Canary Islands. What passed between them at this meeting has never been revealed, and probably never will be now that one of the two men is dead. But that these *varones*, both a hundred per cent Spaniards and fearless traditionalists, must have made a powerful impression on each other goes without saying:

> For there is neither colour,
> Border, nor breed, nor birth,
> When two strong men stand face to face,
> Though they come from the ends of the earth.

The *Caudillo*'s references to José Antonio are always couched in affectionate and laudatory terms; but the real tribute, and enduring evidence of what the present régime owes to the founder, is the fact that Franco is himself Chief of the *Falange Española* and that the régime is organised and wholly based upon its "Twenty-six Points", "The Programme of the New Spain", evolved and propounded years before the Civil War, the "War of Liberation", was fought out. The Phalangist hymn, *Cara al Sol* ("Face to the Sun") is always played after the royalist National Anthem in radio programmes in the three Madrid transmissions and in the excellent provincial broadcasts.

Speaking as far back as May, 1939, Franco told a mass gathering of women Phalangists, whose very efficient *Sección Femenina* is responsible for reviving national interest in the captivating regional dances and folksongs throughout Spain, that the

country would embark "on no mad adventures". "I want Spain," he declared, "to become a fortress of peace." Some years later the United Nations, in full assembly, passed a resolution by a large majority branding Spain as "a danger to peace", and promptly advocated, at Poland's suggestion, the withdrawal of all Ambassadors from Madrid! (On October 29th, 1953, the Generalissimo told a mass gathering of 150,000 Phalangists that Spain had emerged triumphantly "from an international conspiracy to isolate her"). . . .

One day at Irún, the northern frontier station, my friend Señor Fernández, head of the Tourist Bureau there, said to me: "German officers from Hendaye used to come into my office on the station here in 1940 and sound me as to whether Spanish public sympathies were preponderantly with the Phalangists. I knew, of course, they were spies, sent to find out what our reaction would be to a sudden German drive through Spain to take Gibraltar. I used to tell them: 'Well, there may be a hundred thousand sympathisers, or there may be double that number. But then there may be twenty-eight million Spanish people who don't sympathise with the *Falange*. That would be awkward for you!'."

By a clever stroke of political strategy Franco calmed the fierce and turbulent spirits of the rival patriotic bodies, the Traditional Carlists, the Nationalist Phalangists, and the *J.O.N.S.* by fusing them all into one single organisation, a *Falange Española Tradicionalista y las Juntas — Ofensivas Nacional Sindicalistas* (what a mouthful!) which is today the single political body allowed inside the country. "There are terrific tensions operating under the surface ", a Secretary of Embassy in the Spanish Foreign Office confided, pulling his fingers until they cracked in vivid illustration, "but each cancels out the other—and Franco floats on the top". Franco, in fact, sits on a three-pronged stool, the three 'legs' being respectively the Army, the Church, and the *F.E.T. y de las J.O.N.S.*

During a six-day National Congress of Syndicates (the twenty-four official trade unions of Spain) in November, 1953, the *Caudillo* told the forty nominated delegates that they were the "base of the régime" and compared the "constructive work" of the Syndicates with what he called the "ineffectual activities of the international Trades Unions gatherings".

What *are* the 'twenty-six points' on which the structure of the modern authoritarian Spanish State has been raised? They deserve study for a right understanding and evaluation of the new dynamism which has taken hold of the nation and which bids fair, under the continued guidance of the "little Gallego", the "Roman Spaniard", the "Pro-Consul", Francisco Franco, to forge Spain once more into a First-Class Power and the strongest champion of Western Christendom against an Asiatic menace which has inherited the untameable ambitions of Attila, Genghis Khan, and Hitler combined.

Here they are, from the official Spanish translation:

PROGRAMME OF THE NEW SPAIN
THE 26 POINTS OF *FALANGE*

COUNTRY — UNITY — EMPIRE

1. We believe in the supreme reality of Spain. To strengthen it, elevate it, and improve it, is the urgent collective task of all Spaniards. In order to achieve this end, the interests of individuals, groups and classes will have to be remorselessly waived.

2. Spain is a destined unity in the universe. Any conspiracy against this unity is abhorrent. *Any form of separatism is an unpardonable crime.* The existing constitution in so far as it encourages any disunity, commits a crime against the destiny of Spain. For this reason, we demand its immediate abrogation.

3. We have a will to empire. We affirm that the full history of Spain implies an empire. We demand for Spain a pre-eminent place in Europe. *We will not put up with international isolation or with foreign interference.* With regard to the Hispano-American countries, we will aim at unification of culture, of economic interests and of power. Spain claims a pre-eminent place in all common tasks, because of her position as the spiritual cradle of the Spanish world.

4. Our armed forces, on land, on sea and in the air, must be as efficient and numerous as may be necessary to assure Spain's complete independence at all times and that world leadership which is her due. We shall restore to the armies on land and sea, and in the air, all the dignity which they deserve and, following their ideal, we shall see to it that a military view of life shall shape Spanish existence.

5. Spain will seek again her glory and her riches by means of the sea. Spain must aspire to become a great maritime power for her defence and for her commerce. We demand for our Motherland an equally high standing for our Navy and our Air Force.

6. *Our State will be a totalitarian instrument in the service of National integrity.* All Spaniards will take part in it through their family, municipal and syndical functions. *No one shall take part in it through any political party.* The system of political parties will be implacably abolished, with all that flows from them—inorganic suffrage, representation by conflicting parties, and parliament of the familiar type.

7. Human dignity, the integrity of man and his liberty, are eternal and untouchable values. *But only he is free who forms part of a strong and free nation.* No one will be allowed to use his liberty against the unity, strength and liberty of the country. A rigorous discipline will prevent any attempt to poison, disunite or influence Spaniards against the destiny of the Motherland.

8. The National-Syndicalist State will permit every private initiative which is compatible with the collective interest of all, and will even protect and encourage beneficial enterprises.

9. In the economic sphere we imagine Spain as *one gigantic syndicate of producers.* We shall organise Spanish society in a corporative manner by means of a system of vertical syndicates with branches of production in the service of national economic integrity.

10. We repudiate any capitalist system which ignores popular necessities, dehumanizes private property and huddles workers into shapeless masses ripe for misery and despair. *Our spiritual and national sense also repudiates Marxism.* We shall organize the impulses of the working-classes, led astray today by Marxism, by exacting their direct participation in the great task of the national State.

11. The National-Syndicalist State will not cruelly ignore economic conflicts, and therefore will not stand unmoved in face of a domination of the weakest class by the stronger. *Our régime will make class-war radically impossible,* inasmuch as all those who co-operate in production will be part of an organic whole. We abhor, and will prevent at all costs, the abuse of one partial interest by another and anarchy in the field of work.

12. *The first object of wealth*—and our State will affirm this—*is to better the people's conditions of life.* It is intolerable that great masses of people should live miserably whilst the few enjoy every luxury.

13. The State will recognise private property as a lawful means of fulfilling individual, family and social ends, and will protect it against the abuses of the great financiers, speculators and money-lenders.

14. We uphold the tendency towards nationalization of the Banking services and also, through the medium of Corporations, that of the big public services.

15. *Every Spaniard has the right to work.* Public bodies will, as a matter of course, assist those who are unable to find work. Until we have built up the new structure, we will maintain and intensify all the advantages which have been afforded to the worker by the existing social laws.

16. Every Spaniard who is physically fit has the duty of working. The National-Syndicalist State will not extend the slightest consideration to those who do not engage in any definite employment and aspire to live like invited guests at the cost of the effort of others.

17. *At all costs the standard of life in the country must be raised.* It is the permanent spring of the life of Spain. To this end, we bind ourselves to carry out without hesitation the economic and social reform of Agriculture.

18. We shall enrich agricultural production (economic reform) by the following means:

(*a*) By assuring for all products of the soil a remunerative price.

(*b*) We shall insist that a great part of what today is absorbed by the towns in payment for their intellectual and commercial services shall be returned to the land so that it may be sufficiently endowed.

(*c*) By organizing a real National Agricultural credit scheme which, by advancing money at low interest to the labourer on the security of his goods and harvests, will save him from usury and the domination of political bosses.

(*d*) By spreading the teaching of agriculture and cattle-breeding.

(*e*) By arranging the allotment of land according to its conditions and with regard to the possible disposal of its products.

(*f*) By arranging tariffs so that they shall protect agriculture and the cattle industry.

(*g*) By the acceleration of irrigation works.

(*h*) By rationalizing the units of agriculture in order to suppress both the large neglected estates as well as small properties which are non-economic because of their poor return.

19. We shall organize Agriculture socially by the following means:

(*a*) By redistributing cultivable land in order to set up family properties and energetically stimulate the syndication of labourers.

(*b*) By ending the misery of the human masses who today wear themselves out in ploughing sterile land, and who will be transferred to new cultivable land.

20. We shall embark on an untiring campaign to increase the importance of raising cattle and reafforestation, taking severe

measures against any persons who may place obstacles in the way, going so far as *the temporary compulsory mobilization of the whole of Spanish youth for this historic task of reconstruction of the National wealth.*

21. The State will be empowered to expropriate without compensation any property which has been illegitimately acquired or enjoyed.

22. The reconstruction of the communal land of the villages will be one of the first objects of the National-Syndicalist State.

23. *It is the essential task of the State, by means of a rigorous discipline in education, to build up a strong and united National spirit and to instil into the souls of the future generations happiness and pride of country.* Every man will receive a pre-military education in order to prepare him for the honour of being incorporated in the National and Popular Army of Spain.

24. Culture will be organized in such a form that no talent shall run to seed for want of economic means. *All those who deserve it will have easy access to the University.*

25. Our movement will incorporate the Catholic spirit—of glorious tradition and predominant in Spain—in the national reconstruction. The Church and the State will arrange a Concordat defining their respective spheres. But the State will not permit any interference or activity which might lower its dignity or the National integrity.

26. The Spanish Traditional Phalanx and the J.O.N.S. desires a new order of things, which has already been set out in the principles announced above. Its methods are preferably *direct, ardent and combative.* Life is a battle, and must be lived with a spirit alight with service and sacrifice.

The key passages of this remarkable document, on which the whole structure of 'Franco Spain' has been built, I have emphasised in italics. On the face of them, they would not appear to furnish any justification for the disgraceful U.N.O. resolution that Spain was "a danger to peace". To an unprejudiced mind the programme might even recommend itself as the outward manifestation of a deep patriotism similar, shall we say, to that which inspired the framing of the American Declaration of Independence.*

---

* In the Madrid Municipal elections held in November, 1954, 55 per cent. of the voters supported Phalangist candidates, the highest individual total being 232,980 for the chief of the Phalangist Youth Front, Elola, whose speech I had heard in the Retiro park.

Chapter Fourteen

CHURCH AFFAIRS

ONE OF THE MORE FAMOUS AND FATUOUS of Azaña's public statements when he held the high office of Prime Minister under the Republic was that "Spain had ceased to be Catholic". I was living in Madrid at the time and in a position, therefore, to note the stupor—or was it a silent contempt?—with which the asseveration was received by the devout citizens, who crowded the churches in even greater numbers than before. If, instead of such a patently unreal attitude, he had said that Spain had ceased to be clerical there might have been some foundation for the announcement, for while the average Spaniard cannot escape his Catholicism, which is part and parcel of himself, and is Catholic to the bone, he is at the same time, by his very individualism, strongly inclined to anti-clericalism.

It is impossible to visit present-day Spain for any time at all without discovering that this Catholicism, a thoroughly sincere and devout piety, is an integral part of the daily life of the people. I have heard from the Duchess of Nájera, who was caught with her children in San Sebastian at the outbreak of the Civil War and only succeeded in escaping with them to France by boldly confronting the militia tribunals at Irún, that most of the seriously wounded Government troops who had boasted of having thrown overboard all religious beliefs asked for a confessor and the last rites, "just in case" as they naively put it.

The eldest of the three grandchildren of the Generalissimo and Doña Carmen Polo de Franco was named "María del Carmen Esperanza Alejandra *de la Santísima Trinidad y Todos los Santos*" at the El Pardo christening.

The hold of the priesthood and the Church over the minds and imagination of the people—that is, the power of the image of Christ crucified and the hunger for eternal salvation—has led to a great deal of nefarious propaganda and misunderstanding in other countries, where ill-informed critics never tire of talking of the

158

'wealth' of the church in Spain and the 'illiberal' character of ecclesiastical education. If there is some restlessness among more intellectually advanced Spaniards at the somewhat rigid forms of the latter—and the newest catechism makes it a mortal sin "to read Liberal newspapers"*—the overriding tenets of the religious establishments in hospitals, in education, care of the poor, and in the missions have, since the Inquisition ceased functioning, always been in Blake's words: "Mercy, pity, peace and love". The Jesuits, the "army of the Church" as they have been called, are not as black as they are garbed. "Unswerving in their work for God," remarked a Spanish lady I accompanied to Mass one Sunday to the Jesuit church in Corunna, "they live lives of heroic self-sacrifice and their influence is all good." But the fact that the Jesuit Universities are allowed to confer their own degrees undoubtedly leads to some abuse and confusion.

A compelling illustration of the innate Catholicism of the Spanish race was provided by Señor Azaña himself, an *Enciclopedista* and professed atheist, under whose Presidency hundreds of churches and religious houses were burned and thousands of priests and religious murdered. When he lay dying at Bayonne in 1940 he sent for the Archbishop (which, as an ex-President of a friendly State, he had a right to do), made a full confession, received Extreme Unction, and died in the bosom of the traditional Faith.

An even more remarkable illustration was given by the extremist leader Largo Caballero, who was so far to the left as to be practically indistinguishable from an out and out Communist (documents discovered in Spain prove, in fact, that he was in close touch with the Kremlin), and under whose aegis every Madrid church was closed to worship, with the exception of the French chapel in Claudio Coello Street, and the majority despoiled of their sacred vessels and pictures. He likewise died fully reconciled to the faith he had rejected, in the German concentration

---

* "The back page of the Madrid daily *El Liberal* in the days of the Republic," said to me in Madrid an Englishman who has spent half a lifetime in Spain, "used to be exclusively devoted to dubious advertisements." And as early as the first year of Republican administration I myself witnessed an epidemic of frankly pornographic literature sold freely on the streets of the capital.

camp to which he had been transferred from his French hide-out by the Nazi occupation forces.

Under the rule of these nominal Republicans, and 'Liberals' like Alejandro Lerroux and Fernando de los Ríos, the Jesuits were first expelled from the country, and then the Law against Congregations passed and many Catholic schools closed. No priests or religious orders were permitted to teach unless authorised by the State, with the immediate result that in 1933 thirty-six thousand children were on the streets in Madrid alone.

On the outbreak of the Civil War the priests were all imprisoned and no less than six thousand of them, with thirteen bishops and thousands of monks and nuns, were barbarously assassinated. Their full names, classified under the towns and dioceses where they met their violent deaths, may all be found in the *Guía de la Iglesia* for 1954, which I examined in no less a place than the British Embassy in Madrid.

What was the object of this repressive Law of Congregations?— what was the purpose of the wholesale murders? The object and purposes were identical with those pursued in all other lands which international Communism designed to bring under its yoke, namely, to put an end to organised religion.

"If the Nationalists had not won the Civil War religion in this country would have been uprooted and destroyed." This opinion was expressed to me, not by a Spaniard or by one ignorant of the background of the Civil War, but by the Embassy's First Counsellor, Mr. Bernard Malley, C.B.E., great Hispanophile and *Hispanista*, who has spent more than half a lifetime in Spain where he is the confidant of high and low and known far and wide as 'Don Bernardo'. He himself suffered imprisonment by 'the Reds', and only regained his freedom with difficulty because of his nationality.

"The Church here knows that its debt to Franco is immense," he said, "for not only did he save it alive, but he has restored all church property confiscated under the Republic and re-established prerogatives of the ecclesiastical authorities, and made the teaching of religion compulsory in all the schools and universities, with the single exception of those students for whom 'non-Catholic' parents request exemption." Yet, despite or because of this realisation the Church in Spain today is chary of showing itself too closely allied with the régime. It is a fact that its most outspoken critics are found among the ecclesiastical authorities, and it was from the bishops that the suggestion came that some relaxation of the press censorship might be introduced.

Franco's insistence that he should enjoy the royal prerogative of having a canopy borne above him on Church ceremonial occasions when he is present—a prerogative which Alfonso XIII rarely exercised—carried the day, but not with too enthusiastic support from the clergy. The other privilege on which he insisted, of submitting to the Pope his own 'short list' of candidates for vacant bishoprics, was backed with more cordiality, although the Holy Father has the last word in the appointments.

The rigidity of outlook and narrow-mindedness which have characterised the sway of Cardinal Segura has been tempered recently by the Papal appointment of a 'Coadjutor-Archbishop', which considerably curtails his power, if not his forthright criticism.

But all interior and most lay criticism of Franco in his relations with the Church was silenced in 1953 by two events of outstanding importance in the history of contemporary Spain. The first of these was the signing on August 27th of that year of the Concordat between the Holy See and the Spanish Government; the second was the announcement of the award by the Pope to the Head of the Spanish State of the Supreme Order of Christ, the highest honour in his power to bestow and at present only held by two others, of royal blood. The Concordat, which was virtually the ratification of a series of previous agreements resulting from the Nationalist victory, by which the fallen were designated as having died "for God and for Spain"—those of June 7th, 1941, July 16th, 1946, December 8th of the same year, and August 5th, 1950—set out in thirty-six Articles and a Protocol the circumstances in which the full and unfettered exercise and practice of the Roman Catholic Faith and religion should be permitted in the most Catholic land of Spain.

If the Head of the State is, however, immune from all but verbal criticism by Spaniards in Spain, such immunity is not always extended to the régime. Something like a sensation was caused in the country some months ago by the clandestine spreading of copies of an article which had appeared in a leading French monthly review calling in question various academic and other recent State appointments, notably to the rectorships of

11

Madrid and Salamanca Universities, and indicating that the time was ripe for a 'liberalisation' of the régime. A Spanish priest, a fellow-passenger on the *Highland Brigade* from Tilbury to Vigo last September (1954), told me that the belief was sometimes expressed that the movement *"Opus Dei"* was behind the article, but no such activity has been acknowledged. The author of the article, Calvo Serer, a staunch Catholic and Professor of the Philosophy of History at Madrid, held a high position under the *Consejo Superior de Investigaciones Científicas* and the editorship of its extremely high-brow monthly review *Arbor*. Once, at the Spanish Institute in Eaton Square, London, I had been present at a lecture by Calvo Serer whose audience on that occasion had consisted of only one other individual besides myself.

"This is bad," he had said, with disappointment, and I had commiserated with him on the paucity of the attendance and had later invited him to lunch. It was then that he had confided his hopes of being instrumental in bringing Spain and Britain closer together "for the good of Europe", and with this end in view had asked for a list of the names of some notable writers and thinkers whom he could invite to lecture in Madrid. I never heard if the invitations actually went out, and now it is too late for as the outcome of his indiscretion he has been deprived of his editorship and his connection with the Council and his activities are confined to his professorial duties at the University.

If there was no criticism of Franco in the article which got him into trouble, there was nevertheless a good deal behind it of personal feeling and hostility about some appointments within the personal choice of the *Caudillo* . . . Spain's critics maintain that the people remain under the thumb of the priesthood, and are kept in bondage by their Faith. But on more than one occasion, at some ordinary service in a church serving the poor and the struggling, observing the singleness of devotion, a spontaneous surge of emotion has been followed by the thought, "If any people is saved, this people will be." For religion is the hygiene of the soul; the solvent for what is immortal, or immortality-desiring, in the human spirit.

Chapter Fifteen

BACKGROUND TO FEAR

IN THESE DAYS OF INCREASING FRATERNISATION between East and West, of cultural exchange visits between the Comédie Française and the Bolshoi Ballet and semi-official trips to Moscow and Peking by the Leader of Her Majesty's Opposition in company with Dr. Edith Summerskill, M.P., and other Labour luminaries, any national newspaper or periodical would be amply justified in offering a substantial prize for the discovery of the real authorship of the following analysis of the meaning and methods of Communism. Is it a translation from a Spanish Nationalist publication on the origins of the Civil War?— an outpouring from the Phalangist Press in Madrid?—extract from a speech by Senator MacCarthy or one of his henchmen of the Committee Enquiring into Un-American Activities?—or a leading article from a London Right-Wing organ?

Communism is exceedingly astute and its tactics are manifold: it avails itself of every means to win followers. Communists even present themselves as good Catholics in order to succeed in winning the confidence of simple people. They who by nature are sowers of discord and war, dare to organise "pro-peace" campaigns, claiming to take the lead among nations, while from day to day they secretly search for arms and day and night operate factories for armaments and military equipment. They take advantage of dissensions between employers and workers, make use of family divisions, and, with the sole purpose of attaining power, create anarchy within nations by false promises to workers and peasants, promises which they never keep, for when the Communist régime is introduced workers and peasants are in worse conditions than before because the Master State is the most cruel of all Masters . . . the worst tyrant of all who have attained tyranny.

Communists in their eagerness to deceive carry magazines with fascinating pictures pretending to reveal the happiness of the "Soviet paradise", but never publish those of their concentration camps, where millions of human beings work as if they were, not slaves, but worse than beasts of burden; human beings who are systematically assassinated as soon as they are unable to produce, whether because of old age or because their strength has weakened, weighed down by suffering and disease.

There is not a single Code of Justice which makes it obligatory to seek peace with a power which has converted millions of human beings into slaves, and which is systematically trying to banish the name of God and human dignity from the earth. . . .

Communism takes advantage of prevailing economic inequality to seduce those who have nothing. But it also foments scarcity of food and of the most necessary means of livelihood, in order to exasperate the poor and make them believe that, in such a miserable situation, the Communist régime would be able to improve their condition. But the truth has always been otherwise: when Communism reached power in Russia in 1918, far from remedying the misery of the peasant, there followed such hunger and want that all nations sent subsidies and food to that poor people who were dying by thousands, and the sending of food-stuffs had to cease because Russia's new rulers seized for themselves what Christian fraternity and sentiment sent for those poor people who were starving to death and millions of whom perished. A similar picture of desolation scourged Hungary at her first Communist fall, and an even more frightful one scourged Communist China.

"Millions of whom perished—" . . . Yes, and not all by calculated starvation by any means. It was the talented pianist daughter of the great Russian composer, Glazounov, who suddenly exclaimed to me in anguish in Paris one day last Spring, in the flat she shares with her mother and writer-husband in the narrow rue Boissy-le-Vent off the Bois de Boulogne: "This régime has murdered twenty million Russians," and she repeated the astronomical figure incredulously—"*twenty million!*" Well, she should know for she lived many years under it, until her late father, taking advantage of a Continental conducting engagement of his own works, sought refuge for himself and his family in France.

That, according to Lord Russell of Liverpool, until recently Assistant Judge-Advocate in Germany, twelve million men, women and children were likewise murdered by the Nazis in the occupied countries during the war (vide *The Scourge of the Swastika*: 1954) only serves to indicate that life in our own times has retrogressed to the age of the roving saurians and the sabre-toothed tigers. . . .

The passage quoted at the beginning of this chapter is not from any Spanish Nationalist or Phalangist publication, nor literary emanation of 'MacCarthyism' in the United States, nor from any British Conservative newspaper. It is extracted from the Pastoral Letter addressed at the time of national crisis last year by Mariano Rossell Arellano, Archbishop of Guatemala, "To our Venerable Brethren, the Most Illustrious Members of our Metropolitan Chapter, to the Priests of the Secular and Regular Clergy and to all the faithful of our Archdiocese".*

At about the same time as this ecclesiastical homily appeared "among the faithful" in strife-torn Guatemala, right on America's doorstep, the former United States Ambassador to Republican Spain from 1933 to the end of the Civil War in 1939, Mr. Claude G. Bowers, published his impressions of that time: that is, from fifteen to eighteen years after the events which the book sets out to describe in fact happened.†

Every man of honest intentions is entitled not only to hold but of course to express his point of view, and, above all, his impressions of any given time or experience. Indeed, it is almost a duty to do so for an Envoy of a Great Power serving in a foreign land during a time of tragic civil conflict. But it is surely indicative of the manner in which the whole Spanish issue in modern times has been bedevilled by obdurate reasoning and passionately-held convictions that the former Plenipotentiary of the United States in Spain from 1933 to 1939 can still solemnly maintain that it was no Civil War in the usual meaning of the term but a war of oppression waged by Hitler and Mussolini," and declare, with complete inconsistency, that "Non-Intervention was the plan through which the European democracies aligned themselves . . . on the side of the Fascists against the Spanish Democracy." That is, the European democracies aligned themselves with the Axis dictators whom they were to fight to the death a few months later!

What is equally thought-provoking in the light it casts on the

* "Only the other day a Swedish freighter, *having taken Polish arms to Guatemala* (my italics) was ushered into KeyWest for enquiry."—*The Times*, August 20th, 1954 (from 'turn-over' article, "From our Special Correspondent").

† *My Mission to Spain: Watching the Rehearsal for World War II*, by Claude G. Bowers (New York: 1954, Simon & Schuster).

'blind spot' which characterises so much of British and American thinking about the Spain of that time is that an outstanding journalist of Herbert L. Matthews' international reputation should confirm in a review of Mr. Bowers' book which appeared in the New York Times Literary Weekly that "in all this Mr. Bowers is absolutely right." Certainly, this forthright approval is qualified by an admission that the book is "passionate, biassed, provocative" and contains "an appalling number of mistakes"; but the confirmation stands.

Once, when I was lunching with him in Fleet Street, I asked Douglas Hyde, the former News Editor of the Communist *Daily Worker* and now the celebrated author of the book *I Believed*, whether he could say from personal inside knowledge that international Communism brought about the Spanish Civil War: he replied, "Undoubtedly."

But one of Mr. Bowers' own countrymen, of an even longer acquaintance with Spain than himself, has expressed a totally dissimilar viewpoint to his own of the Civil War's true origins, and the real significance of the "crusade" led by Franco to make Spain safe, not, it is true, for democracy, but for ordinary living. Thus, Mr. D. Kirkwood, a former Associate-Editor of the *International Review*, who was in Spain at the same time as Mr. Bowers, gives a different picture in his essay: *Spain: Genius, Faith, Glory*:

> The Second Spanish Republic [he writes] was the prelude to civil war.Why? Because, while giving expression to and encouraging the development of nearly every divisive force within the Spanish nation, it failed to provide the necessary counterbalance of great leadership, and the unifying force of a great ideal. The Left, which dictated the new Constitution and dominated government under it in the first and last of its five-year life, was itself united only in what it wanted to destroy; there was no agreement in what it wanted to build. How could there be, when it included a Republican Left and a Republican Union, Socialists both moderate and extremist, Marxists loyal to Trotsky and to Stalin, as well as Syndicalists and Anarchists? There were leaders among these men *who frankly proclaimed their intention of using the Republic to bring about Revolution.** But the revolution they sought was never for Spain as a whole. Probably that is why the Left encouraged regional autonomy for

---

* My italics.

Catalonia, the Basque provinces, and Galicia: a fragmented Spain would be easier to conquer.

Certainly the plague of riots, strikes and assassinations that accompanied the Republic was in accord with accepted principles of revolutionary procedure. In the first four months after the victory of the Popular Front in the elections of February 1936, there were 113 general and 218 partial strikes; successful firings of 170 churches, 69 clubs and 10 newspaper offices; and attempts to fire 284 other buildings, 251 of which were churches. . . . Spanish generals began to consider whether the Spain they had sworn to defend was not dissolving before their eyes.

This passage has warranted quotation at length mainly because of its conclusion: ". . . the Spain they had sworn to defend". For that pointer means, if it means anything, that the concerted military rising which marked the opening of the civil war was in lealty to an oath—an oath solemnly if automatically taken by officers of the Spanish Armed Forces to defend with their lives Traditional Spain, the Spain of history, the *united* Spain won by their forefathers in seven centuries of struggle; but not, be it noted, a Sovietised Spain nor an anarchist Spain.

How often has this basic and wholly valid explanation of the action of the Spanish generals, led by Sanjurjo, Franco and Mola in July, 1936, been given to their readers by any British or American newspaper or periodical? It is my belief that it has never been given to this day. "In Spain," says José C. González-Campo Dal Ré in the Madrid quarterly *Política Internacional* for December, 1951 (my translation)—"In Spain, the army, loyal to the purest traditional essence, took up arms against the advance of Communism and Anarchy. At its head, seconded by all the sane elements of the Spanish people, General Franco was placed . . . (whose) ideology was not influenced by Fascist theories, but by traditional and patriotic concepts."

In the autumn of 1946 I made a journey of more than two thousand miles in Spain. I visited Soria, Burgos, Valladolid, Avila, Mérida, Seville, Cadiz, Malaga, Granada, and Jaén, where the entire Cathedral chapter were murdered in the Civil War from Bishop to altar-boy, and crossed the highest mountain ranges, the Cordillera Central and the Cordillera Penibética, still evoking the old Roman provincial identification, with the Sierra

Nevada. From Santa Fé, last camp of the Catholic Monarchs before the fall of Granada, and the scene of Isabella's melting to the seven-year-long pleas of Columbus for royal sanction of his foolhardy dream to sail westwards to 'Cipango', I drove up to the eternal snows of La Veleta and Mulhacén over 10,000 feet above the sea along the highest motoring road in Europe. When passing from the Don Quixote country of La Mancha I negotiated the majestic Pass of Despeñaperros, the site of important finds from the prehistoric and Iberian-Roman eras, and the natural boundary between north and south; and crossed the rivers Duero Arlanzón, Alberche, Tagus, Guadiana, Guadalquivir and Genil.

In the winter of 1952 I made a journey of equal length to the west and by coastal road round to Alicante, returning to Madrid from Valencia in eight hours by the magnificent road over the Cuesta de Contreras.

During these long tours it was impossible not to compare the conditions prevailing everywhere of alert official protectiveness, general civic orderliness, and the individual's complete freedom from sudden armed attack, to those which had been the customary experience in these same regions when I had travelled that way in the time of the Republic. Murder was then of almost daily occurrence in broad daylight in the streets and squares of the big cities by young 'pistoleros', who were as often as not allowed to get away scot free by the Guardias de Asalto to 'beat up' and burn churches and convents and wantonly fire the rich southern orchards, olive groves and wheatfields. "There is order . . ." In 1946, and for years before that, order had returned to Spain, the maintenance of which is the first duty of any government.

"Communism," the much-reviled Head of the Spanish State said in a sentence which has stuck in my mind from some speech he delivered in Madrid last year, "is not one evil, but a compendium of all the evils." The Leader of Her Majesty's Opposition, and some other Labour Members of the British Parliament, do not apparently share this view; they are much more impressed (from the reports of their visits to Moscow and Peking in August, 1954) by Malenkov and Mao-Tse-Tung than by the Christian leader of Spain, the true 'Defender of the Faith' in the West, who, deny it who can, stemmed the Communist drive at Europe's heart as the Islamic drive was stemmed at Poitiers and Soisson.

Let me conclude this chapter with some pertinent extracts from a recent publication by a former Scottish member of the International Brigades who fought for two years against the Nationalist Forces. In *Spain and the West* the author, Mr. Hamish Fraser, writes:

Today none but the slaves of the Kremlin cherishes any illusions about these new (*i.e.* 'People's) 'democracies'. But when the first such régime was in process of being established, all Europe was deceived. . . . Such was the enthusiasm of the working class movements of Britain and France that even now the effects of the deception remain.

Spain was the country chosen by the Kremlin as a sociological laboratory wherein the formula of a 'people's democracy' was first put to the test. Spain was not slow to react. The heroism of traditional Spain, combined with the apathy and indifference of those Spaniards whom the Kremlin endeavoured to enslave, made it impossible for the new Soviet technique to succeed within the Iberian Peninsula. As one who served for nearly two years in the army of the Republic I know such to be the truth—as does every ex-International Brigader. . . .

The truth is that the only reliable units in the service of the Republic, apart from the Communist International Brigades, were such divisions as were composed of and led by Spanish Communists, and for that reason a victory for the Republic could not but have been a victory for International Communism. But for the Nationalist resurgence, Spain today would be but another 'People's Democracy', and the peaks of the Pyrenees but the spikes of yet another Soviet Iron Curtain.

One final quotation, which would seem to provide further conclusive answer, from a former Communist combatant in the Civil War, to ex-Ambassador Bowers' thesis and to Mr. Herbert L. Matthews' unreserved approbation of it:

The Spanish 'Civil War' was in fact the bloodiest of all Soviet internal aggressions, Spain's losses in both blood and treasure being proportionately very much greater than our own losses in World War II.

What was the "Fascist cut-throat" and "despicable tyrant" up to on the eve of this "bloodiest of all Soviet agressions"?
Vamos a ver—Let us (go to) see.

Chapter Sixteen

'LIKE TENERIFE OR ATLAS, UNREMOVED'

I T IS NOT THE PURPOSE OF THIS BOOK to investigate at any
length the story of the Spanish Civil War, its true origins and
its tortured course to a conclusion which has never been fully
accepted by the Europe which it undoubtedly saved. Detailed
and documented studies by incontestable authorities have long
been available in such books as *The Spanish Tragedy* by the late
Professor Allison Peers, *Spain's Ordeal* by Robert Sencourt, and
in *World War in Spain* and *Spain: 1923-1948* by Arthur F. Loveday, and in other works by writers of opposing sympathies. The
latter author, particularly, who traces direct Communist activity in
the Peninsula as far back as 1930 (Russian anarchist activities began
with the century, Gerald Brenan demonstrates in his *Spanish
Labyrinth*), as Chairman of the British Chamber of Commerce in
Spain for many years, wrote from full and first-hand knowledge,
of the country and the people.

Of much more recent date, Sir Robert Hodgson, K.C.M.G.,
Britain's first accredited Agent to General Franco in 1938, has
published his own memories and impressions with authoritative
sections on Gibraltar and Tangier, in his *Spain Resurgent*. In Spain
there are Tomás Borrás' books *Chekas de Madrid* (Editorial
Nacional, 1944) and the massive testimony of the *Causa General:
La Dominación Roja en España*, issued by the Ministry of Justice,
with, as I have already pointed out, copious illustrations from
photographs found in Republican archives of the Soviet *chekas*
implanted in Madrid and Barcelona, and elsewhere of some of the
tens of thousands of victims of the Terror, and of secret Communist documents planning a proletarian revolution on the
Bolshevik model for July, 1936. These testimonies ought to
prove convincing enough even for the ex-United States Ambassador, Mr. Claude Bowers, that the Civil War was in fact a death-
grapple between Spanish patriotic and traditionalist elements and
infected Socialism and conspiratorial Communism, as truly as the

American Civil War was a struggle *à outrance* of the harder-headed materialistic North against the traditional, more easy-going and more cultured South, whose negroes were by all accounts happier and more contented under the feudal order obtaining there before Abraham Lincoln than they have ever been since in their qualified freedom. Which is not to say that human bondage in any part of the earth is anything but iniquitous.

The Left-wing deputies in the Cortes, growing increasingly menacing under a Right-wing majority, raised a clamour early in 1936 for a dissolution of parliament, and finally the Republican President, Niceto Alcalá Zamora, yielded to the extremist pressure for new elections, which incidentally brought about his own downfall, for he was shortly afterwards removed from power by an extremist vote. He gave afterwards in Paris, when the 'pachydermatous' Azaña had stepped, or been pushed, into the presidential shoes, his own version of the true character of the elections, and afterwards published them in the *Journal de Genéve*. "In spite of the syndicalist reinforcements, the Popular Front obtained only a few, a very few, more than two hundred seats out of a total of 473," he declared. "Thus it became the biggest minority group, but did not secure a majority in parliament. It managed, however, to obtain this majority by hurrying through two stages of procedure, in defiance of all legality and with utter disregard to scruple." So much for "the Legitimate Government of Spain"....

Before leaving Madrid at this time to take up his new post in exile General Franco saw both the President and Manuel Azaña, the Prime Minister. To all his warnings of the reality of the dangers immediately confronting Spain, Alcalá Zamora could only repeat, parrot-like, in his musical falsetto that "the revolution was crushed in Asturias", which blindness to actuality in the responsible Head of State is on a par with the attitude to Hitler and Nazi Germany of Britain's pre-war Ambassador in Berlin, Sir Neville Henderson, who wrote in despatches to the Foreign Office in the spring of 1939 that Germany "wanted peace very badly" and that "of all Germans, believe it or not, Hitler is the most moderate so far as Danzig and the Corridor are concerned"*. Azaña contented himself with remarking that "he himself was the revolution", and that he cared little for the advice of generals.

---

* *Documents on British Foreign Policy, 1919-39.*

Franco was later invited by conservative groups to stand for Cuenca, where elections had to be held again, but he declined with a statement which revealed clearly enough his complete disbelief in the honesty of the plebiscite: "When the funds of the workers' organisations are devoted to political bribery, the purchase of arms and munitions, and the hiring of gunmen and assassins, democracy as represented by universal suffrage has ceased to exist." When the Civil War was in full spate he declared that "the teachings of the false prophets have accomplished the moral assassination of a people".

As the exiled *Commandante-General*, Franco (looking, in the press photographs of the time, preternaturally serious, as well he might) sailed in February, 1936, accompanied by his wife and their daughter, María del Carmen, then aged nine, for the Canary Islands, where his official residence lay between the vast banana plantations of the Orotava Valley, backed by the soaring volcanic peak of the Teide (over which view Alexander Humboldt had waxed lyrical more than a century earlier) and the gleaming sapphire sea beyond Santa Cruz de Tenerife. Spain had been brought to the edge of the abyss, but all the lawlessness and all the plottings were camouflaged under the designation of 'democracy', the familiar 'Popular Front' cry whenever any felonious blow was contemplated against human liberty, national or individual.

. . . it was part of the technique of Communism (writes Loveday in *Spain: 1923-1948*, p. 99) to work behind the scenes, to support socialist and more moderate left-wing candidates to parliament with their votes, instead of presenting candidates of their own, until the time comes when, as the 'Popular Front', they can seize power. Then there was to come the next and last step in communist action, the dictatorship of the proletariat.

And Loveday goes on to make the significant revelation that the British Foreign Office, which was for years, and still is, far more allergic to Spanish traditionalism than to Communist internationalism* (witness its surprise and consternation when the

---

* It negatived all requests from Madrid to the British Council for me to be sent to Spain to lecture because—as I was informed by the lectures-manager himself, an old friend and fellow Philhellene, in his Mayfair flat—I was considered "pro-Franco", although the Spanish Head of State is not once mentioned or referred to in my book *Spain Everlasting*.

French Chamber of Deputies, after four years of dithering, rejected the European Defence Community by the *bloc* voting of the hundred Communist members, which could have been predicted a year before), "rejected" an exact translation of secret documents discovered in Spain detailing the plan "for the Establishment of a Soviet in Spain". (Document No. 1 ends thus: "The orders are for all anti-revolutionaries to be immediately executed". Document No. 2 gave fixed dates "for starting the subversive movement" and named the ministers of the first Spanish "National Soviet". Document No. 3 recorded the decisions taken at Valencia on May 16th, 1936, by "the Revolutionary Committee for Spain" and "Delegate of the Third International, Ventura" . . . "to start, on the same day as the said movement, the world-wide agitation to be named 'anti-Fascist' so as clearly to express that the whole proletarian class is behind the movement". There was also a reference to a meeting to be held "at the premises of the International Library" at Chamartín de la Rosa, outside Madrid, attended by, among others, "Thorez", "Auriol" and "Dimitrov", the originator of the 'Popular Front' façade idea). . . .

All first-hand accounts of Franco at this time of mortal crisis for his country agree that, outwardly at any rate, his serenity and imperturbability were unaffected in the Canaries by the threatening situation, by the fact that he was surrounded by spies and walked in daily danger of assassination. "As I have always regarded my life as a gift," he had told me at El Pardo, "I have never worried overmuch about my personal safety."

> During his visit to England to attend the funeral of King George V (wrote Mrs. Dora Leonard de Alonso on July 20th, 1937, in the old *Morning Post*) he realised that he missed a great deal through not knowing the language, and determined on his return to the Canaries to set about studying it. He looked around in Tenerife for an English teacher . . . Franco earned my whole-hearted admiration and affection. He used to take his lessons three times a week, 9.30—10.30. He wrote two exercises for 'homework' three times a week and five out of six of the exercises were about golf, which he had taken up after his arrival. He got to read and translate amazingly quickly, but he found English hard to follow. . . .

It was at this time that he wrote his famous letter of warning to the War Minister in Madrid, Casares Quiroga—a sinister figure whom I once met at a reception in 1933—about the true state of feeling in the army both as regards the injustices being done by the government to serving officers with fine fighting records, and on the growing uneasiness in face of widespread acts of extremism.

As a preponderance of people everywhere still, eighteen years after the event, cling to the belief that Franco and his fellow-generals rose in irresponsible and selfish rebellion against "the legitimate Government" (despite Churchill's published acknowledgement that "Franco was a Republican general who gave full warning to the Spanish Government of the political anarchy into which they were drifting"), it will do no harm, and might conceivably do some good in the international sense, if an extract from the letter is reproduced here: "Those," wrote the *Commandante-General* of the Canary Islands to the 'Excelentísimo Señor' War Minister—"who paint the army as hostile to the Republic are not telling the truth; those who are accusing the army of conspiracies, in their turbid passions are deceiving you; those who are misrepresenting the uneasiness, the dignity and the patriotism of the army, making it appear as the symbol of conspiracy and dissatisfaction, are rendering a miserable service to their country. . . ."

In Tenerife Franco was watched day and night, his mail censored, his telephone messages intercepted, and surrounded by spies organised by hostile local authorities. Near the *Capitanía*, strange silent figures would be observed to glide from behind palm trees or bushes, volunteers who had offered their services to kill the general, his wife and daughter, who, however, had been warned of the projected attempt by the Civil Guard and faithful friends. Unknown to himself officers of the garrison, on the initiative of Colonel González Peral, of the general staff, formed themselves into a permanent personal guard, and even the times of his public appointments were changed, without Franco's knowledge. Three definite attempts to assassinate him were made, at La Laguna, at the flower festival in Valle de la Orotava, and by three men on July 13th, who were frustrated in their efforts to scale the garden walls and reach the residence by sentinels who put them to flight.

In the event, it was not Franco who was killed, but the military commander of Las Palmas, General Amando Balmes, who accidentally shot himself with a revolver when at target practice outside the town. It was July 16th, 1936. The War Minister had agreed to Franco's telephoned request for permission to go to Las Palmas to attend the funeral, and at half an hour after midnight he embarked on the small inter-island ship at Tenerife with his wife and daughter, carrying merely a small valise containing a black suit.

The brave and brilliant Calvo Sotelo, ex-Minister and Leader of the Opposition in the Cortes, was dead, murdered by State police reputed to be acting on government orders. The tocsin had sounded for traditional Spain—rise or perish!

Less than twenty-four hours after General Balmes' funeral Franco was airborne en route to his old fighting ground, Spanish Morocco, wearing his black civilian suit and carrying his general's uniform on his knee in a brown paper parcel, while in all the islands his first Manifesto to the Nation was being read in the streets and cafés. As this historic document has never been published, in translation, to this day, so far as I am aware, I venture to give it to the English-speaking world as providing the final and conclusive answer before God and history to the long familiar charge, still enjoying world-wide currency, that Franco and his fellow-generals "murdered Spanish democracy". The translation is my own.—

Spaniards! To whoever feels a holy love to Spain, to those who in the ranks of the Army and Navy have made profession of faith in the service of the country, to those who have sworn to defend her from her enemies with their lives ("hasta perder la vida"), the Nation calls you to her defence. The situation of Spain is each day that passes more critical; anarchy reigns in the majority of her fields and villages; authorities nominated by the Government preside over, where they do not foment, the revolts. The pistol and machine-gun annul the differences between groups of citizens, who are maliciously and treacherously assassinated without the public authorities imposing peace and justice. Revolutionary strikes of every nature paralyse the life of the Nation, destroying and ruining her founts of wealth and creating a situation of hunger which drives the workers to despair. The monuments and artistic treasures are the object of the most rancorous attacks of the revolutionary hordes, obedient to the orders they receive from foreign sources ("directivas extranjeras") who count on the complicity or negligence of governors or officials. The gravest offences are committed in the cities and the countryside, while the forces of public order remain permanently billeted, corroded by the despair which provokes a blind obedience to leaders who intend to dishonour them.

The Army, the Navy, and other Service institutions are blackened by the vilest and most calumnious attacks, precisely on the part of those whose duty it is to guard their prestige. The states of exception and alarm only serve to muzzle the people and to keep Spain ignorant of what goes on outside the gates of her towns and cities, thus equalling the imprisonment of pretended political adversaries. The Constitution, suspended and weakened for all, suffers a total eclipse; neither equality before the law, nor liberty oppressed by tyranny, nor fraternity when hate and crime have substituted mutual respect, nor unity of the country menaced by territorial rendings more than by regionalism, which their own authorities foment, nor the integrity and defence of your frontiers, when in the heart of Spain one hears foreign broadcasts predicting the destruction and partition of our land.

The Magistracy, whose independence is guaranteed by the Constitution, suffers equally persecutions which enervate and interfere with it, receiving the hardest blows to its impartiality. Electoral pacts made at the cost of the integrity of the country itself unite to overcome the Civil Governors and civic strongholds in order to falsify the records and shape the mask of legality which dominates us. Nothing halts the appetite for power, neither illegal destitution of moderating elements, glorification of the revolutions of Asturias and Catalonia, both shattering blows at the Constitution which, in the name of the people, is the fundamental Code of our institutions. To the revolutionary spirit and blindness of the masses deceived and exploited by Soviet agents, who conceal the bloody reality of that régime which sacrificed to its existence twenty-five million persons, are united the malice and negligence of the authorities of every order, who, protected by a negligent power, lack the authority and prestige to impose order and the sway of liberty and justice.

Spaniards! Is it possible to consent one day more to the shameful spectacle we are giving to the world? Are we to abandon Spain to her enemies by cowardly and treacherous behaviour, handing her over without a struggle and without resistance? This? No! Let the traitors do it, but we, who have sworn an oath to defend her, will not do it. Justice and equality before the Law we offer you; peace and love between Spaniards. Liberty and fraternity in place of libertinage and tyranny. Work for all. Social justice, raised to the head without resentments or violence, and an equitable and progressive distribution of riches without destroying or endangering Spanish economy. But, before all of this—war without quarter to political exploiters, to the deceivers of the honest labourer, to the foreigners and would-be foreigners ("extranjerizantes") who direct and influence them with intent to the destruction of Spain.

In these moments Spain entire is avid for peace, fraternity and justice; in

Aged 33. 'The Victory smile'. A rare African war photograph of the occupation on October 2, 1925, of Axdir and the house of Abd-el-Krim, showing Colonel Franco wearing wide sun-hat, inspecting hill positions just captured from the enemy troops

(Photo: Diaz Casariego)

'. . . the over life-size representations of Lenin and Stalin were removed from the Alcalá and the Gran

every region the Army, the Navy, and the forces of public order rise up to defend the country. The energy in the maintenance of order will be in proportion to the magnitude of the resistance offered. Our impulse is not determined by the defence of some bastard interests, nor by the desire to retreat on the road of History, because the Institutions, be they what they may, must guarantee a minimum of common life among citizens who, despite the cherished illusions of so many Spaniards, we have seen defrauded . . . with an anarchical reply whose reality is imponderable. . . . The spirit of hate and vengeance holds no lodging in our breasts; from the unavoidable disaster which some legislative experiments must suffer, we shall know how to save whatever is compatible with the interior peace of Spain and her desired grandeur. . . . Spaniards: Long live Spain! Long live the honourable Spanish People! — El Comandante General de Canarias. *Santa Cruz de Tenerife, at 5.15 a.m. on July 18th, 1936.*

Six months later, on December 5th, *The Times* published a letter pleading against any recognition of Franco—who two months previously had been elected Head of the Nationalist Government and Chief of all the Armed Forces—jointly signed by "Sir Richard Acland, M.P., the Duchess of Atholl, Gerald Bullett, G. D. H. Cole, R. H. S. Crossman, M.P., A. D. Hall, M.P., Professor Lancelot Hogben, Aldous Huxley, John Ireland, Geoffrey Le Mander, M.P., J. B. Priestley and V. S. Pritchett."

Which of these distinguished persons had any knowledge whatsoever of the real causes of the Spanish Civil War, such as are given in Franco's first Manifesto above?

Chapter Seventeen

STRANGER THAN FICTION

THE RECORD OF HOW FRANCISCO FRANCO OF SPAIN was enabled in July, 1936, to leave the Canary Islands for Spanish Morocco in a privately-chartered British plane piloted by a British pilot, Captain C. E.W. Bebb, makes one of the most fantastic adventure stories of modern times. Ever since his arrival there in February, he had been a marked man to all Spanish Marxist, Anarchist and the Left Republican elements.

Four principals were involved in the preliminary negotiations, which culminated, as the world knows, in shortly placing the exiled Commander-in-Chief of the islands at the head of all the Traditionalist and Nationalist forces in Spain, thus saving the Peninsula from the imminent sovietisation that threatened it. These were: the British historian, editor and publisher, Douglas Jerrold (whom I encountered by strange chance in Whitehall Court only two hours before this chapter was written); Luis Antonio Bolín, for eight years before the Civil War London correspondent of the Madrid newspaper *A.B.C.*, for a decade and more after it the hospitable and very able Director-General of the Spanish State Tourist Department to whom I am beholden for much kindness, and now Information Counsellor at the Spanish Embassy in Washington; Señor de la Cierva, the Spanish aeronaut and inventor who lost his life in an air crash in 1936, and Major Hugh B. C. Pollard, a Sporting Editor of *Country Life*, a world adventurer with experience of Moroccan, Mexican and Irish revolutions, and, according to *Who's Who,* "an authority on modern and ancient firearms".

Jerrold, a staunch Roman Catholic who had made a special study since the time of the Monarchy of the situation in Spain, and who for years was a voice crying in the wilderness in regard to the devil's brew being steadily brought to boiling point there, was frequently visited in his London office or club by notable Spaniards like the late Don Antonio Goicoechea, the Marqués del

Moral, and Señor de la Cierva. Believing that Spaniards would never be fascists because "they are God's last protest against the Machine Age", he declared his conviction, in *Georgian Adventure*,* that "Spain during the fateful months which followed the 1936 elections was saved by José Antonio Primo de Rivera's Phalanx. There were, it is said, only twenty thousand. But it was enough".

Of Franco himself, Jerrold later wrote: "Having talked with him, I realised, as everyone does, that that in itself is a privilege. He may or may not be a great man as the world judges, but he is certainly something a thousand times more important—a supremely good man . . . a man of great charity."

Jerrold has given his own historic account of the meeting which settled the Nationalists' predicament of how they were to get Franco to Spanish Morocco to take up the leadership of the African army in the nation-wide revolt headed by the "Lion of the Riff", General Sanjurjo, soon afterwards to be killed through the crashing of the plane taking him from Portugal to Madrid to assume its overall direction. With Luis Bolín and de la Cierva, Jerrold was inveigled out to lunch at Simpson's, in the Strand, where, with some difficulty a table was secured out of earshot of neighbours. . . . "And then it happened," he writes.

"I want," Bolín suddenly announced, "a man and three platinum blondes to fly to Africa tomorrow."

"Must there really be three?" Jerrold asked.

"Well, perhaps two would be enough," Bolín replied.

Jerrold telephones, "Can you fly to Africa tomorrow with two girls?" to Pollard, who answers, characteristically

"Depends on the girls."

"You can choose," says Jerrold; "I'll bring two Spanish friends down to see you this afternoon," adding a rider to the effect that there was only one point to mention: "The aeroplane may be stolen when you get there. In that case you come back by boat".

When I saw Pollard (the narrative continues) I took him on one side and explained to him, with an assurance that I could not possibly have justified, that his aeroplane, containing the self-styled English tourists, would be stolen, if the anticipated crisis arose, at the

---

* *Collins*, 1937.

Canaries, to take General Franco to Morocco. . . . Round the table
we got down to business. Passports, money, the route to Casablanca.

Then began the most arduous search of all. Pollard's daughter was
to be one of the party, but the other girl was out—no telephone
enquiries could locate her. All that was known was that she was
delivering chickens somewhere and that she hadn't got a passport.
And so the Last Crusade began on a hot July afternoon with four
men searching frantically up and down Sussex lanes for a girl
delivering chickens and who had not got a passport.

On July 9th Captain Bebb, of the Olley Airways at Croydon,
who later published his own account of the adventure, was
commissioned to fly to Las Palmas on secret mission *via* Casablanca,
where Bolín himself would await Franco's arrival. Major Pollard,
(whom the late Rudolph Timmermans identifies in his book on
Franco, published in Zurich in 1937, as "*ein Englischen Lord*"),
his daughter Diana, and her friend, Dorothy Watson, who had
reached the islands on the 15th, remained in their hotel at Las
Palmas, when Franco, walking to the plane at dawn on July 18th,
carrying his uniform in a brown paper parcel, went to his destiny
accompanied by two aides, the aviator Señor Villalobos and a
relative, Lieut.-Colonel Franco Salgado.*

There was one brief halt at Agadir, where the travellers
remained undiscovered by some Spanish service airmen who,
recalled by the Government, were on their way from Spanish
Guinea to the mainland, and another at Casablanca where he
found Bolín whom he sent off on a special task to Lisbon: and, at
seven o'clock on the morning of the 19th the new leader was
changing into uniform as the British plane circled the Alcazaba at

---

*By an extraordinary chance, not uncommon in Spain where each day is
an adventure, I found myself seated one Sunday morning last October
in a café in the Calle de Serrano, Madrid, beside a British Consul
on leave from South America who, as a youth, had been one of a party,
which included his father, then Consul at Las Palmas, seated with
General Franco in a local hotel nine hours before the flight to Tetuan.
The previous day he heard islanders discussing at a bar the arrival of
the plane. "It's just like the English to land here without papers," one
of them remarked, "they think they own the earth; I shall remove the
propeller after dark." Said my informant: "Spain's fate in those hours
hung by a hair's breadth." He added that only a few days before, when

Tetuan, to land a few minutes later among a group of waiting officers, whom Franco greeted with the one slogan: "Blind faith in victory" which he kept right through the "war of Liberation".

At that time, and for some considerable time afterwards, his followers on the mainland had little else to pit against the mobilised might of the proletariat.

The fact has long been proved beyond peradventure by the discovery in Spain of secret documents detailing "The Plan for the Establishment of a Soviet in Spain"—extracts of which have already been given and a full translation of which lies before me at the present moment—that a Red revolution was planned to follow the election in May of Azaña as President in place of Alcalá Zamora in the Crystal Palace of the Madrid Retiro park. The Socialists and Communists then present, according to contemporary press reports, "gave the clenched fist sign and sang the *Internationale*." This mass revolution the generals decided to forestall by a narrow margin, but it was the assassination of Calvo Sotelo on the night of July 13th which actually sparked it off. The Republic then had three separate Ministries in twenty-four hours, whereupon the Anarchist, Andrés Nin, declared: "The Government does not exist; it can do no more than sanction what is done by the masses", the masses, including the most hardened criminals from the prisons, having been indiscriminately armed by their leaders. . . .

What was the precedent for this rising of the military party in defence of the very life of the country? It was the Napoleonic invasion and the subsequent struggle for independence, which began in 1808. In this struggle—a landmark in Spanish history— the forces of the nation rallied round the army, which was the spearhead of resistance, and the population fought to the last gasp against the most powerful army in the world, a heroic stand tragically immortalised by Goya in his grimly realistic cartoons, *Desastres de la Guerra*.

Another manifestation, characteristic of the political life of

---

clearing up family papers in Las Palmas, he destroyed the detailed diary record kept by his father of the events preceding the flight ("you could have had it otherwise," he said), and confided that his Spanish mother was born in the same house in El Ferrol as Francisco and Nicolás Franco.

Spain, recurred throughout the 19th century—the military *pronunciamientos*. Between the uprising in Valencia in 1814 and the period of autocratic rule, there occurred the Riego rebellion of 1820, the mob riot of July 7th, 1822, the insurrections at La Granja in 1836, the part played by the army in the Carlist wars, the *pronunciamientos* of Narváez in 1843, of O'Donnell in 1854, and General Prim in 1866, Pavía's *coup d'état* in 1874 and that at Sagunto in the same year.

These were the most outstanding of the events that show the role constantly played in Spanish politics by the army, despite the fact that it was also engaged during most of that time in wars in Africa, Cuba and the Philippines. It is true that this interference in the internal political affairs of the country, together with the series of military reverses, made the army somewhat unpopular with the people; but the reason for the army's action was not as might be charged, ambition on the part of certain generals so much as the necessity *to break up frequent situations of political deadlock which the political parties, lacking both popular support and constructive policies, were incapable of resolving.*

The matter may perhaps be best summed up by stating that during the 19th century the army was closely involved in the political affairs of the nation, in which it was one of the most powerful influences, and that it continues right up to the present day, and certainly did so during the steady deterioration of living conditions under the Second Republic, to reflect and interpret the fundamental feelings of the people, and to respond to the political exigencies of the nation. As was seen even during Franco's time in Africa, the Spanish army had been modernized since the loss of Cuba and brought to a state of unusual efficiency. This was demonstrated when the use of the ancillary services, the landings at Alhucemas, and the low-flying operations of the Air Force, all represented important advances even from the point of view of world military technique.

At the present time it is true to say that the Spanish army has almost completely abandoned its traditional political role, devoting its undivided energies to the task of national security and to seeing that the nation is fully prepared against the eventuality of war. Nevertheless, its broad foundation on all strata of the community establish it as one of the vital elements, if not the most vital, in the life of the nation.

The rising of the military in July, 1936, against active and long-standing foreign interference in Spain's internal life, reflected overwhelmingly the *will* of all the better elements of the nation who not only saw, but had actually experienced, no alternative to increasing chaos, anarchy and general disorder.

It was high time to impose *"orden en el país"*.

Chapter Eighteen

THE LEADER

TOWARDS THE END OF AND IMMEDIATLY AFTER the last World War a literary friend holding a senior post in the Research Department of the British Foreign Office, in reply to suggestions of mine that Spanish patriots had no option but to revolt in July, 1936, or see their country become a Communist state, would wag his head wisely and throw out dark hints of references in secret archives to pre-Civil War Franco plots and later post-Civil War pro-Axis moves. Today no excuse exists either for mystery or mystification, for the entire records so far as Germany and Italy are concerned of Franco's moves and actions, both throughout the Civil War and during the course of World War II, have been laid bare and made available for general reading in the Ciano papers and in the far more important evidence published in 1951* in *Documents on German Foreign Policy 1918-1945, from the Archives of the German Foreign Ministry.*

Of this monumental publication, Volume III, Series D, bearing the title, "The Spanish Civil War", lies before me at the present moment, and from a careful reading of the first analytical list of documents, and of the documents themselves, certain definite facts emerge, the most significant of which are these.—The secret German Foreign Office records afford no evidence whatever of any association between Germany and Franco, or indeed any of the Spanish generals or opposition leaders, prior to the outbreak of the Civil War, or of any approach by them, direct or indirect, to Hitler. On July 24th, 1936, that is one week after the African garrisons had revolted, the German Consul at Tetuan advised the Foreign Ministry in Berlin that General Franco had told him during a conversation that day that "the Nationalist uprising was necessary in order to anticipate (*sic*) a Soviet dictatorship which

---

* By His Majesty's Stationery Office, London.

was already prepared".* The Consul reported to Berlin next day that "the military revolt had been planned for some time, but action was only begun *when Russian ships carrying arms for the Communist insurrection arrived in Spanish ports*" (my italics). "I shall save Spain at whatever cost from Marxism," Franco told a special correspondent of the London *News Chronicle*—could it have been Arthur Koestler?—only five days afterwards.

Other captured German documents provide evidence that a flow of arms and aircraft into 'Red' Spain had already started, not only from Soviet Russia but also from France under the Popular Front Government of Léon Blum, and that Franco's own first attempts to obtain a few troop-transport planes from Germany were decisively turned down by the German Foreign Ministry, and the Director of the Political Department later urged "that no arms shipments to the rebels be considered". It was only after the personal delivery sometime later to Hitler (at Bayreuth, after a performance of *Tannhäuser*) by Bernhardt and Langenheim, German citizens and business men resident in Spanish Morocco, of a letter from Franco that any German help was given to the Nationalist cause in Spain.

From where else could the Nationalist patriots have obtained help or sympathy in their desperate eleventh-hour enterprise to defeat the Communist conspiracy for the subversion of the peninsula if not from Germany and Italy, both of which countries had had first-hand experience of Communist-imposed régimes after World War I? Certainly not from Great Britain or the United States, who were at that time—as well as the bulk of their peoples—completely hoodwinked regarding the 'democratic' foundations of the Popular Front Governments; indeed, the British Foreign Office and the Trades Union Council, the whole of Labour and a good deal of Conservative opinion have remained blind ever since to the true nature and significance of the Spanish conflict.

In this last part of July, 1936, almost the entire corps of Spanish

---

* The following September Franco was telling the representative in Spain of a German Export organisation that "as a soldier he had felt it his duty to prevent the Bolshevisation of Spain", and that "the Red Government had systematically destroyed the Army in order to give Bolshevism a free hand". (p. 84).

naval officers, some four hundred odd, had been killed by their lower decks, allegedly on orders from the Ministry of Marine, and warships from Cartagena and Cadiz under the command of Sovietised crews were careering about off Ceuta and Tangier in an attempt to blockade Morocco. In the meantime a few Italian planes arrived at Tetuan, and with these the transfer of the Spanish African army to the mainland began. Months later Ciano complained to Hitler that "Franco had declared that if he received twelve transport or bombing planes he would win the war in a few days" but that the supply "had grown into more than a thousand planes, six thousand dead and fourteen billion lire".

In the democratic countries the question continues to be posed —it is a question which, although dead, obstinately refuses to "lie down"—as to whether it would not have been better for the opponents of the Spanish Government to express their opposition through constitutional channels. To this, my friend Don Aurelio Valls—and as a Spaniard of that generation, born in Brighton and educated in England, he should know—replies in his valuable little publication issued by the Office of Diplomatic Information in Madrid, *The Spanish Controversy: Sixty-four Questions on Spain:*

> Many Spaniards had tried in good faith, through several general elections held during the Republic, to uphold the new régime until they had to resort to violence against violence. Even the moderate party called *Acción Popular*, which had tried to influence the Republic through democratic channels, was completely overwhelmed by violence. The Republic, on the other hand, never knew democratic freedoms, and the law *"de Defensa de la República"* abolished the civic liberties. When the police leave the field to the gangster, and even line up with him, there is no other course of action for the victim than to resort to violence himself.

Concerning the leadership of the Traditionalist forces, with the elimination by police assassination in Madrid of the potential 'civilian *Caudillo*', the brave and brilliant Calvo Sotelo, and the death shortly afterwards in a plane crash of the next in line, Sanjurjo, the choice fell between the next senior generals, Mola and Franco. Mola, who was in command of the Northern Army, had not the political sagacity, the prestige nor the popular following of Franco, although he did covet the leadership and sometimes had a crack at Franco for not following his advice; it was therefore to "Paco", "Franquito", "el Comandantín", "Al Mansur", or "the little Gallego" that all eyes turned for resolute guidance and steadfastness in the hour of supreme crisis. That he did not fail them, but from the first moment of the inevitable struggle displayed the qualities that have marked out the born leader of men from the beginning of history is a tribute alike to the leader himself and to those who turned instinctively to him in their and Spain's moment of peril.

When, in the grand old city of Burgos in October 1936, at the age of 43, in the throne room of the grey-walled Captain-General's palace, near the 14th-century church of San Gil, Franco was invested with the title of Generalissimo of all the Armed Forces and "Head of the Government of the Spanish State" by the President of the Junta of National Defence, the white-haired and snowy-bearded General Cabanellas, he accepted the solemn charge with the historic words: "You have placed Spain in my hands, and I assure you that my hand will not tremble. With your help I will raise Spain to a lofty height, or die in the attempt."

The historic *Salas Capitulares* of the 12th-century royal convent of Las Huelgas, fabulous keystone of Old Castile, a mile and a bit southwest of Burgos, where many Castillian kings and queens and their offspring are buried, was the colourful scene of his later election in 1938, when, fresh from the victory at Teruel in the biggest battle of the Civil War, where 280,000 men were engaged, 70,000 on each side with an equal number in reserve, with the war already won but with fighting still continuing and all Catalonia still awaiting liberation, Franco took the oath as "Head of the Spanish State and Prime Minister". The then Primate of all Spain, the late Cardinal Gomá, officiated, in the lofty and barely furnished stone hall still hung to this day with the beautifully preserved green wall tapestries given by the convent founders, Alfonso VIII and his English Queen Eleonora, daughter of Henry II. . . .

The American journalist, Abbe, whom I have mentioned before, gave a vivid pen picture of Franco at this time, "running a war, conducting affairs of State and a Civil Government, dealing with foreign nations, and occasionally snatching a little sleep—living between his desk and nearest camp, with meagre meals thrown in", which is valid also as a description of him after he had moved his headquarters to the Episcopal palace in Salamanca's magnificent central *plaza*, and indeed for the duration of the internal convulsion which many Spaniards at first thought would last no more than three weeks. The famous British war correspondent, the late Sir Percival Phillips, reported somewhat confusedly that Franco "was at his desk for sixteen hours daily", and Mr. Randolph Churchill, in an interview published in the London *Daily Mail* on March 1st, 1937, wrote: "You don't have to be in Spain for more than a few days to realise the power behind him is a straightforward Nationalist and patriotic movement. The issues at stake transcend party lines." In this interview Franco reminded his interlocutor that "we Spaniards are a proud and ancient race". "The Spain which played so glorious a part," he added, "in carrying the treble torch of discovery, conquest and civilisation into the New World is not going to be the first to see it extinguished in Europe." He was proud and grateful, he told Randolph Churchill, that it should be his lot in saving her "from the worst form of barbarism that has ever menaced her".

To look at, he is of medium height,* handsome, dark-eyed and haired (wrote Arthur Loveday, who was in turn granted an interview in Salamanca in May, 1937), with a small military moustache, and somewhat bald on the forehead. His eye is bright, clear and smiling, and he has those outward signs of greatness—tranquillity, imperturbability, with plenty of time at his disposal to discuss matters at leisure with the foreign visitor, even during the time when he had on his shoulders a thousand miles of battle front, and the rebuilding of the Spanish State.

But this tranquil and imperturbable mien that he presented to the innumerable newspaper correspondents and international visitors who were always seeking interviews with him during these critical years, was not always conspicuous when he was wrestling alone, or with his battle-front commanders, far into the night on strategical or ordnance or commissariat problems. From more than one source I have heard that he was in the habit when planning an attack or a whole campaign of biting up his pencils, and that his aides would carry off clandestinely as souvenirs the chewed remains when the Generalissimo at last retired to rest.

---

* The exact stature of the Spanish Leader is 5 ft. 3½ ins.

The documents from which quotations have already been given reveal that both Malaga and Almería were the scenes when they fell of Nationalist excesses, but that Franco learned from these experiences and made very sure when Bilbao fell after a siege of eleven weeks that only picked troops, and those in small numbers, were allowed to enter the great Basque city and port, when the opposing forces had been driven across the Nervión. In considering the executions carried out by the Nationalists at Badajoz, Malaga, Almería (which the German cruiser *Deutschland* had ruthlessly shelled in retaliation for a 'Red' plane's attack on the *Leipzig* in Iviza harbour) and Algeciras, however, it must be remembered that by this time all Spain, both 'red' and 'white', was ringing with stories of the horrible crimes being committed by undisciplined hordes in the regions nominally under the control of Government forces against men, women and children, priests, monks and nuns, who perished in their thousands upon thousands under circumstances of nameless horror and cruelty.

What does as impartial and firm a friend of Spain as the late Professor Allison Peers say regarding the Popular Front and the overthrow of "the legitimate Government"?

> . . . it would have been a disaster for Spain had the cause of the Popular Front triumphed. In the first place, though its apologists did everything possible to represent it as standing for 'pure Republicanism', the democratic Republic died twenty-four hours after the outbreak of the mainland risings, when, in defiance of the 1931 Constitution, the extremist groups prevented President Azaña from appointing the Prime Minister of his choice. . . . A Republican victory, then, would have meant a new upheaval in Spain, in which the Republican minority would inevitably have been crushed and the Proletarian Revolution would have reigned supreme.—*The Spanish Dilemma* (pp. 14-15).

No halt to the torturings, murders and massacres was ever called, or even advised by the Soviet Ambassador to Republican Spain, Marcel Rosenberg, to whom an emissary of the Republican Government of the moment attended daily for guidance and instructions in his quarters, almost opposite the world-famous Prado Museum, in the Savoy Hotel (now demolished) where, incidentally, I was present in 1932 at a luncheon given to H. G. Wells. At the time of the propaganda outcry over Guernica, which, when the Nationalists had gained control in 34 out of the 50 Spanish provinces and were soon masters of 36 capitals, Franco declared on July 14th, 1937, was "not bombed by Nationalists but fired by the Reds", the Generalissimo waxed righteously indignant that "newspapers now crying aloud, remained silent when in Madrid, under the presidency of the Red Government, over 60,000 innocent beings were murdered without any motive other than the whims of a militiaman or a servant's dislike".

In Barcelona, said Franco on this occasion, the anarchists had committed the same number of "horrible murders"; in Valencia the figure was twenty-thousand. This, he pointed out to the unheeding world, "was not war, but crime". Towards the end of the same year he informed a representative of the British United Press that more than two million persons in Government-held territory were card-indexed "with proof of their crimes, and with names and witnesses".

Well might George Edinger declare with commendable impartiality in the *Daily Herald* that . . . "Spaniards do not sink their differences, not even in the face of the enemy".

L'idée de l'Espagne, the French Academician, Jean Cassou, had pointed out years and years before the Civil War, *est dense comme les métaux les plus denses, compacte, résistante et profonde . . . nous devons être reconnaissants à l'Espagne d'avoir assumé, par les déséquilibres qui la composent et la déchirent, le visage tragique de l'humanité.*

Chapter Nineteen

THE LEADER (*continued*)

A CIVIL WAR MYSTERY still awaiting clarification is why the Ambassadors of the Great Powers, including the British Envoy, the late Sir Henry Chilton, remained outside Spanish territory, at St. Jean-de-Luz and Biarritz, when the Republican 'façade' President, Azaña, and the Spanish Government, or rather 'Governments', stayed on in Madrid right through the summer heat. It was surely their duty, or the duty of the Foreign Ministers of their respective countries to order them, to be near the Administration to which they were accredited. Being so far removed from the centre of things, how could they know, or report at first-hand to their respective chiefs that, in actual fact, responsible rule in Spain had broken down and that in its place reigned chaos, red terror and ruin?—that, in accordance with this situation, recognition should be suspended of the Spanish Government until the outcome of the struggle to restore order was placed beyond doubt. Such a course might have brought hostilities to an end in a week; it would certainly have put an end to the daily and nightly mass murders by irresponsible militia and the armed rabble and released criminals in the cities and the *campo* where the pseudo-Republican fiat ruled.

At the British Embassy in Madrid, there was only a subordinate official, the Passport Officer and pro-Consul Milanés, a conscientious and ingratiating Maltese whom I knew well during my first spell in Spain and a musician of no mean order (he was entertaining in his flat in Calle de Hortaleza on the last occasion I saw him, in 1949, Sir Malcolm Sargent). He only was left to deal with the chaotic situation and the hundreds of British refugees who swarmed for protection into the Embassy grounds and buildings, until the arrival of a Chargé d'Affaires, the late Sir George Ogilvie Forbes, gave him a respite from his onerous responsibilities which he carried out with exemplary efficiency and *sang froid*, but which, I personally believe, shortened his life.

Similar mental and administrative confusion on the part of the Powers was manifest from the start in the hypocritical policy of Non-Intervention, which, after the pouring into Spain first of Communist agents, then of Communist volunteers, and then of munitions from Soviet Russia, followed by German and Italian aid to the Nationalists, could not be imposed or honestly carried out; while the obstinate denial of belligerent rights undoubtedly prolonged the war at the cost of countless lives.

Although the elected Leader had hoped at the beginning for a speedy victory over the forces of disruption and anarchy, he had clearly envisaged the likelihood of a protracted struggle, even before he took the British plane piloted by Captain Bebb from Las Palmas to Tetuan. "If the coup fails," he told his companions on the flight, "there will be a long and bloody civil war; the enemies of Spain are many and they are powerful." The factors which destroyed the chances of a quick decision and the possible voluntary abdication of power by the Left-wing leaders, factors which decisively changed the whole course of the *alzamiento*, or rising, were the cardinal mistakes made by certain of the generals, by Fanjul, Batet and Goded, who disobeyed orders, were defeated and summarily shot.

From Tenerife, after the murder of Calvo Sotelo, Franco had written to Fanjul, who was commanding the Madrid garrison, urging upon him the vital importance for the maintenance of order of sallying out with his troops into the streets and squares of the capital, but the letter miscarried and Fanjul remained in the Montaña barracks, on the Paseo de Rosales, not far from University City, like one hypnotised until the investing mob brought from somewhere an old field gun, mounted it on a handy lorry and stormed the barracks through the subsequent breaches made in the wall, massacring the majority of the garrison where they stood. He paid the penalty for his indecision later before a militia firing squad, after the death sentence had been passed by the Supreme Court judge who presided, actually a Nationalist sympathiser brought reluctantly to Madrid to conduct the trial, who was reported to have declared later, when dealing with the purely juridical aspect of the circumstances, "I have never signed a warrant with a calmer conscience."

Goded and Batet, who flew in to Barcelona and Valencia, committed errors of timing and strategy for which they too paid

Aged 43. Generalissimo of the Armed Forces. A photograph taken immediately after the relief of the Toledo Alcazar with Colonel (later General) Moscardó, in the bullet-scarred *despacho* where the stronghold's heroic defender had refused its surrender in exchange for the life of his 16-year-old prisoner son

(Courtesy of Instituto de Cultura Hispánica)

Aged 60. 'Paterfamilias'. The Head of the Spanish State and Prime Minister photographed in the grounds of El Pardo palace, the grace and favour residence he inhabits with Señora Doña Carmen Polo de Franco, with the two elder children of their only daughter, the Marquesa de Villaverde

(*Photo: José Campúa, Madrid*)

with their lives. Thus, within a few days of the opening of the nation-wide conflict the entire Mediterranean coast was lost to the Nationalist leader, from the French border as far as Gibraltar, with Barcelona, Tarragona, Valencia, Alicante, Murcia, Cartagena, Almería and Malaga, and on the Atlantic coast Huelva, with, in the interior, the cities of Lérida, Cuenca, Guadalajara, Alcalá de Henares, Toledo (in part), Cáceres and Badajoz, and in the north Gijón, Santander, Bilbao and San Sebastian as well as the passes over the Cantabrian chain of mountains.

This situation did not indicate a well-laid plot on the part of Right-wing patriots; rather did it look like hasty planning and premature action, with inadequate and faulty means of communication.

During these critical first weeks the writ of the *Movimiento Nacional* ran only in Spanish Morocco, a strip of Andalusia with the important cities of Cadiz, Granada, Cordoba and Seville, which city the commanding general, Queipo de Llano, had held by a supreme stroke of bluff with a few hastily assembled soldiers, Corunna, Pontevedra and Vigo in the north, with Salamanca, León, Palencia, Valladolid, Burgos, Pamplona, and Saragossa, Vitoria, Logroño, Huesca, and Jaca.

It was the link-up at Badajoz of General Mola's northern columns with the southern army, composed mostly of legionaries from Africa which had struck north under General Yagüe in a sweeping advance from Seville northwards, which gave Franco the consolidation of his left flank, thus freeing the whole frontier with Portugal on whose benevolent neutrality he knew he could reply. "If Spain goes Communist," Dr. Salazar, the Portuguese Prime Minister is said to have declared when the Spanish Civil War broke out, "Portugal may follow within two months." Yet, despite this threat endangering Portugal's vitals, the records reveal that Whitehall put considerable pressure upon the Lisbon Government to dissuade it from affording any active help to the Nationalist cause, even going so far as to warn Salazar that the provisions for mutual assistance in the ancient Treaty of Friendship between England and Portugal were by no means necessarily operative in this case.

Although, on all the evidence, the relief by Franco, or rather by General Varela's column, of Colonel (now Lieut.-General)

13

Moscardó,* Colonel in Command of the Infantry Academy, and his "thousand men and boys" and many women and children, besieged for seventy days and on each of them 'stormed at with shot and shell' in the Toledo Alcazar, postponed the expected fall of Madrid, thus prolonging the war by three years, it was undoubtedly this dramatic and most characteristic Spanish feat, resounding throughout the free world, which gave the Nationalist cause the moral initiative which it never lost and electrified the generous and patriotic youth of the country with crusading fervour. This feat, and the undying story—for heroism is the patrimony of all mankind—of Moscardó's last telephone conversation from the Alcazar with his doomed son of sixteen, who had fallen into the hands of the investing militia and was shot by them on his father's refusal to surrender the fortress in return for his son's life. . . .

". . . *Then give a* Viva España *and die like a man, my son, for I will never surrender the Alcazar.*"
"*That is easy, papa. A long embrace, papa.*"
"*A long embrace, my son. . . .*"

"What you have done," said Franco in the half-ruined courtyard of the Alcazar, standing before Pompeo Leom's toppled bronze statue of Charles V, to the skeleton-like defenders assembled to hear him, "will not be forgotten by Spain. You have a place among our ancient heroes. You have given a glorious example to the new Spain which will arise from these ashes and ruins." He embraced the garrison's commander and pinned upon his breast the Laureate medal of San Fernando, which was collectively awarded to the entire garrison. Today, every guide at the Alcazar is a veteran of that epic defence.

It is simple enough now, when following with maps the war situation as it existed in Spain at the end of July, 1936, to see that it was then a matter of touch and go for the scattered Nationalist adherents, with nought but a small strip of Andalusia, the Balearic Islands, and a larger strip in the north so far in their hands. "Blind faith in victory", was Franco's admonition, and the

---

* He lies gravely ill as I write (September 30th, 1954) at Laredo on the Bay of Biscay . . . . after receiving the Last Rites, he made a complete recovery.

situation needed just that to keep faith in ultimate victory, despite the appointment by Great Britain in July, 1937, of Sir Robert Hodgson as British Agent "to the Government of Nationalist Spain", and of Monsieur Bérard as French Agent, and later of the aged Marshal Pétain, Franco's old mentor at the War College at Versailles, as French Ambassador.

Before the great Aragon offensive less than half the country was liberated, with all Asturias still to be won; but after that offensive the picture was different. With the successful outcome of the fiercely fought war in the north and of the battle of Teruel in the bitter winter of 1937, where prodigies of valour were performed on both sides, and where the defenders continued their embittered fight even from beneath the ruins of the city, the final issue of this appalling civil war was no longer in dispute, although more fierce battles were to follow in 1938.

There remained the liberation of Catalonia, and the long-deferred fall of Madrid. "It would be a crime against the historical unity of our nation," Franco told a representative of the *New York World Telegram* on February 3rd, 1937, "if we left Catalonia to the fate which has overtaken it, for Catalonia is as much a part of Spain as Lancashire is of England." To all true Spaniards he could speak in the spirit of Shakespeare's

> Nought shall make us rue
> If we to our own selves do rest but true.

As the legendary Castillian conquistador, the Cid Campeador, had done nine hundred years earlier when warring against the mud-tide of Moorish occupation, Franco too would drive right through to the Mediterranean coast, thus cutting in half his opposing forces.

In that brave and brilliant, but at the same time disgusting, depressing and distressing book *Homage to Catalonia*, the late George Orwell, writing as a volunteer fighter in Spain in the ranks of the Trotskyist P.O.U.M. anarchist organisation, speaks of the sinister tensions existing in Barcelona at this time, providing all unconsciously one of the severest indictments against the Left-wing elements in all Civil War literature. The following passages are taken at random from the book of a man who sympathised wholeheartedly with the 'revolution of the proletariat' and was himself gravely wounded in the throat while fighting against "the Fascists" on the Aragon front.

No one who was in Barcelona then, or for months later, will forget the horrible atmosphere produced by fear, suspicion, hatred, censored newspapers, crammed jails, enormous food queues, and prowling gangs of armed men. (p. 157).

It was the first time that I had been in a town where the working class was in the saddle. Practically every building of any size had been seized by the workers and was draped with red flags or with the red and black flag of the anarchists. Every wall was scrawled with the hammer and sickle and with the initials of the revolutionary parties; almost every church had been gutted and its images burnt (p. 2).

Since the beginning of the war the Spanish Communist Party had grown enormously in numbers and captured most of the political power, and there had come into Spain thousands of foreign Communists, many of whom were openly expressing their intention of 'liquidating' anarchism as soon as the war against Franco was won (p. 167).

Here, then, were the naked forces of violence and anarchy against which the generals had risen in revolt 'at five minutes after twelve'; this was the dragon which Francisco Franco of El Ferrol, in far Galicia, had sworn to kill or die in the attempt; and before Madrid fell a million Spaniards were fighting for the same ideals.

To Spaniards (wrote a correspondent in the London *Daily Telegraph*, as recently as August 12th, 1953) the Civil War was not an attempt by force of arms to decide an authoritarian rather than a democratic form of government, but a defence of Christianity against anti-Christ and decency against bestiality. . . . In 1936 it was difficult for us to realise that the capture of the Iberian Peninsula was the first step in the Communist plan to occupy Europe by force. . . .

A catastrophic period in Spanish history, involving the death in battle, by violence and assassination of a million Spanish men and women and the temporary ruin of a key European country, is adumbrated in the opening words of poor Orwell's much-vaunted *Homage to Catalonia*:

In the Lenin barracks in Barcelona, the day before I joined the militia . . .

Madrid capitulated at last, after a heroic defence which also won its meed of world admiration. The over-life size portraits of Stalin and Lenin were removed from Calle de Alcalá and Gran Vía, and other Communist emblems quietly taken down before Franco's last laconic official war bulletin was broadcast: "The War is over". When the liberating army, quickly followed by *Auxilio Social* with its soup kitchens and Red Cross services, entered the Spanish capital they found only eight of Madrid's forty large churches intact "and all the precious ornaments and vessels dispersed and melted".

In historic Granada a fortnight later the victor remarked that the Spanish Empire had been born with the final defeat of the Moors, and that that day the unity of Spain was reaffirmed "with the defeat of the Marxist hordes".

Spain had once again saved herself from the advance of alien ideals, and Europe by her example, even though that example was unacknowledged and, in many quarters which should have known better, was utterly condemned.

Chapter Twenty

'HÁBIL PRUDENCIA'

"**P**REJUDICE OF ONE GROUP of people against another group," I read one day last spring in a dry analytical pamphlet* which came my way while attending a Unesco Congress in Paris "has existed in most parts of the world and at all periods of history":

> It has not been universal, in the sense that all cultures or all peoples have displayed it; but it has been prevalent enough to serve as a basis for conflict between nations and between groups within a nation. It practically always involves discrimination, which means mistreatment of people without their having done anything to merit such mistreatment. It has thus been a source of human unhappiness and misunderstanding wherever and whenever it has arisen. Although certain individuals have exploited prejudice to gain political power or economic advantage for themselves, there is no example of a whole people advancing themselves or their civilisation for a long period of time on the basis of it. It has been, rather, a blight from almost every standpoint.

It would not, I suppose, be an exaggeration to say that in this present tragic century we absorb prejudice with every reading of a daily newspaper, with almost every news broadcast or political commentary—of race against race, of nation against nation, of one religion at the expense of another religion, of one system of government compared to another system, of 'democrats' against 'authoritarians'. But of all kinds and characters of prejudice which have existed since the Night of St. Bartholomew, when "more people perished in a few hours than during the entire Spanish Inquisition",† it would be hard to discover a more obstinate and deliberately blind attitude than the world-wide prejudice which

---

* *The Roots of Prejudice*, by Arnold M. Rose, Professor of Sociology at the University of Minnesota. Unesco publication.
† 64 Questions on Spain; O.I.D. Madrid, 1953 (p. 10).

has existed against Spain and Franco ever since the national *Alzamiento*, or rising, of July, 1936.

"When Spain is mentioned," I said the other day to a Madrid friend of many years, "most of my compatriots think of the Inquisition, the 'Invincible' Armada, Franco's rebellion against the 'legitimate Government', and bullfights".

"And when England is mentioned," he retorted with a grin, "Spaniards think of Elizabeth I, *fútbol*, Mister Attlee, and *Drak-ee* (Drake) who was nothing but *un bandido, un pirata*," (adding as an afterthought that Philip II was a fool to give the command of the Armada to the ageing and timid Duke of Medina Sidonia, that Don Juan of Austria, victor of Lepanto, should have had it "but Philip was jealous of his popularity").*

Perhaps no ruler in European history has been called upon to support and to survive a greater, more sustained and more widespread campaign of prejudice than has "this man" Francisco Franco Bahamonde who is only now, after eighteen years as leader of the Spanish nation, beginning to be recognised outside Spain as something more than a vulgar usurper and military mountebank avid of power for its own sake, but as a true patriot and a statesman of historic stature.

This statesmanship and this patriotism he has demonstrated since his election by his peers as Head of the State on October 1st, 1936, by the policy he and his Governments have carried through with resolution and efficacy despite all obstacles and hardship. The policy of Franco covered two phases: firstly, consolidation of peaceful rule at home with steady reconstruction of the devastated areas and gradual improvement of the workers' lot under conditions of law, order and security which the country had not known for quarter of a century; and secondly, a proud and stoical resistance, in which he carried all the people with him, to outside interference in Spain's internal affairs and to world pressure inspired by the intrigues of the defeated leaders and international Communism to get rid of him and overthrow his régime. This was followed by steady consolidation of Spain's

---

* "What foolish nationalism educates us to think of the Spaniards of the sixteenth century as if they were evil-doers, and our seamen engaged in a mission to put things right."—Michael Swann, *Temples of the Sun and Moon* (p. 20).

position abroad and cautious expansion of her influence in international affairs, with an implacable stand against the world-wide Communist conspiracy as the governing inspiration.

Michel Clerc, a special correspondent of *Paris-Match*, to whom reference was made in the prologue to this book, has described the Spanish *Caudillo* as 'a Roman Spaniard', and in his attitude to his immense responsibilities and his general direction of State affairs, Franco would certainly seem to have taken as models the great Roman Pro-Consuls of *Hispania Tarraconensis* in the time of Augustus. This has been evident particularly in the individual political system he has consistently forged since the end of the Civil War and to which he gave the name *"Hábil Prudencia"*, a way of intelligent prudence and enlightened caution which has in the long run yielded immense dividends.

With the disastrous legacy on his hands of two unsuccessful Republics and three civil wars in the course of a hundred years, and with exact knowledge of Soviet backing of the 1934 revolts in Asturias and Catalonia and in the ensuing preparation of Spain to be the first Communist State in occidental Europe, Franco reached the decision to cry quits with the nineteenth century and to re-orientate his internal policy to the authoritarian system under which the country rose to greatness and international weight before the effete Bourbon Charles IV and his decadent Queen, María Luisa of Parma. . . .

Spain's economy in 1939 was in ruins like a great part of the country, agricultural production had reached its nadir, and the vaults of the Bank of Spain were void of gold, for fifty-million pounds worth of bullion had been sent out, mostly to Moscow by the Left-Wing leaders. Hunger, poverty and starvation, stalked a greater part of that sun-drenched land which King Alfonso 'el Sabio' described in the 13th century as a terrestrial paradise. And a second World War was soon to bring to Spain's very frontiers the armoured and avaricious might of Nazi Germany.

Heroism, stoicism and frugality had been innate Iberian qualities from time immemorial; they were those that most impressed the Roman legionaries and soldier settlers in Mérida, Itálica and other Roman towns in Spain. And these qualities were still conspicuously in evidence when Casanova travelled leisurely through the country at the end of the eighteenth century:

> The landlord smoked his paper cigarettes nonchalantly enough, blowing clouds of smoke into the air with immense dignity. To him poverty was as good as riches; his wants were small, and his means sufficed for them. In no country in Europe do the lower orders live so contentedly as in Spain. Two ounces of white bread, a handful of roast chestnuts or acorns, suffice to keep a Spaniard for a day. (Vol. VII. *On the Road to Madrid*).

All Spain's internal and external crises and difficulties Franco confronted with his seemingly ineradicable serenity and imperturbability, on his chosen ground of 'Hábil Prudencia'. On this level he met and defeated Hitler at Hendaye and Mussolini later at the San Remo meeting, while giving lip service—effective lip service at the time it must be admitted—to the Axis with enthusiastic pro-German speeches and some sort of veiled promise to become a belligerent 'sometime'. On the same plane he summoned the whole nation to withstand the Kremlin-inspired international campaigns of venom and calumny, world boycott, and the self-damaging United Nations' decision of December, 1946, to call for the withdrawal of Ambassadors, and the later cruel denial of all Marshall aid at the insistence of France and Britain.* It was on this political 'rock' that he raised his three-tiered foreign policy of the Iberian *bloc*, an unbreakable brotherhood with Portugal, *Hispanidad*, or the close fraternal understanding with the sister-nations of Latin America, and the series of pacts of friendship and commerce with the Arab states in the Middle East.

"At the last hour," said Spengler, "it has always been a platoon of soldiers that has saved civilisation." That 'platoon of soldiers' had saved modern Spain in her hour of supreme crisis, and very possibly France and continental Europe into the bargain, and all

---

* "To eliminate Spain from this Act (*i.e.*, the Marshall Plan) is nothing but a shameful and stupid appeasement of the Reds in Moscow and the Reds in our own department of State and Trade. Moscow will take Spain's exclusion as a moral victory for herself."—Statement by Senator Okonski in the American Congress, March, 1948, as quoted by George Bilainkin in the London *Contemporary Review*, November, 1953.

the poisoned wells of international prejudice, hatred, misunderstanding and rancour would not and could not alter that historic
fact.

> *Soy el amo de la burra,*
> *Yen la burra mando yo;*
> *Cuando quiero digo arre,*
> *Cuando quiero digo só.*

> (I am the master of the donkey,
> And I command the donkey;
> When I want I say 'go',
> When I want I say 'stop'.)

One day Britain and the United States would understand and
truly evaluate Spain's and Franco's achievement. Until then
Spaniards would tighten their belts, as they had done before in
their long history; time counted less in a land in daily and
intimate relations with eternity. "This man" could give to his
countrymen in their own thought-forms and musical language
Shakespeare's

> Come the whole round world in arms,
> Nought shall make us rue
> If we to our own selves do rest but true.

A Spanish writer, Mariano Daranas, writing on "The Franco
Mystery" ("*El Misterio Franco*") on the eighteenth anniversary
last October of Franco's assumption of power, expressed the view
that the modern age does not record a career analagous to his, "so
fruitful in gaining objectives so varied, a capacity so extraordinary
in the direction of public affairs, after the collective ruin of a
country and compromised by the veto of the most powerful
international coalition that the centuries have seen," who,
"without change of convictions or of tactics, has passed from
an imposed solitude ("*la soledad incomunicada*") to the international
summit."

M. François Piétri, French war-time Ambassador in Spain and
a resident for several years afterwards, claims in *Mes Années
d'Espagne*, 1940-1948,* that Spain's war-time record was, if

---

* Paris, 1954; Librairie Plon.

anything, more satisfactory than the behaviour of the other neutrals, Switzerland, Turkey and Sweden. "He discounts Franco's hostile speeches," to quote from a *Times Literary Supplement* review, "as being a necessary cover; and he recalls that after Italy went over to the allies the Spanish Government steadfastly refused to recognise the Government set up by Mussolini in northern Italy."

The reviewer tempers his impartial presentation of the book's substance with the opinion that "the facts recorded in official documents of the period before the Battle of Britain tell a different story than Piétri's statement 'as an established fact' that at no moment during 1939-45 did General Franco intend launching Spain into the war". But Franco has himself categorically declared that "at no time had I the slightest intention of taking Spain into the war on the side of the Axis". Are we to believe, then, that this is a lie, whatever pro-Axis lip-taxes he may have paid to keep Hitler at bay? We can, if we like, add that reservation he made to Hitler which is found in the captured German documents of World War II—"because I fear my own annihilation in the event of an Allied victory."

As early as March 19th, 1938, he said in an interview with a representative of the Havas international news agency that "not an inch of territory will be detached from Spain for the benefit of foreign powers after our complete victory", and the 'united kingdom' of the Spains today fulfils to the letter that undertaking given at a time when the European Press was 'revealing' secret promises of the eventual cession of the Balearics to Italy and of the Canaries to Germany!

In point of fact Spain did not enter the war, despite the sop of 'non-belligerency', and at the Nuremberg trials Jodl cited as one of the three chief causes of Germany's defeat "General Franco's repeated refusal to allow German armed forces to pass through Spain to take Gibraltar". In short, 'Hábil Prudencia', which simply meant the best interests of Spain before everything else, outwitted both the Axis and the Allies, and its greatly under-estimated author not only escaped annihilation but today bids fair to become one of Europe's and the world's key arbiters in the unending struggle with Asiatic and atheistic Russia for the soul of mankind.

Since 1951, (to return to Bilainkin), United States officials on the top rung have thrown overboard all the weary war-time phrases used for years about Spain and Franco. Reflections about Franco's Government constituting a danger to world peace are treated by them like yesterday's chewing gum—to be unceremoniously spat out. . . . Mr. MacVeagh (*i.e.*, the former U.S. Ambassador) until his fabulously foolish withdrawal last March by the new Republican Government, was having talks and more talks with Franco and with the elusive Foreign Minister, Don Alberto Martín Artajo, former journalist. Mr. MacVeagh came to and left Madrid with a deservedly prodigious reputation as one of the major stars in international diplomacy. Great Britain has, on the surface, continued to treat Spain as she did in 1944, as a dreadful apparition on the European horizon. . . .

Chapter Twenty-one

GIBRALTAR—'THEIRS OR OURS'?

WHEN I WORKED IN INDIA as Assistant Editor of an English daily newspaper in Delhi, in 1929-30, one of the expressions most frequently used by Mahatma Gandhi in his public and wayside discourses, and particularly during his almost biblical Salt March to the Sea, which I followed day by day in accounts in the *Hindu Times*, was that what he looked for above all else in Britain's dealing with India was "a change of heart". That change came with the years, but only after a second World War, and the voluntary and valiant co-operation on Britain's side of two million Indian soldiers, had enforced on the British Labour Government led by Mr. Attlee profound heart-searchings and a new attitude towards Indian Nationalist aspirations.

It is a similar "change of heart" that Franco seeks in Britain's attitude to Spanish sentiments regarding Gibraltar, whose original capture by the then allied British and Dutch forces after a three-days' siege on July 24th, 1704, was made in any case in the interests of the Archduke Charles of Austria, but "Sir George Rooke, the British Admiral, *on his own responsibility* (my italics) caused the British flag to be hoisted and took possession in the name of Queen Anne."*

"Gibraltar," the Head of the Spanish State told the late Christopher Buckley, correspondent of the London *Daily Telegraph*, in an interview given at the El Pardo palace on January 31st, 1949, "will always constitute a shadow between our two countries. It is a part of Spanish territory, and British occupation has been described by many Spanish writers as a permanent thorn embedded in the heart of Spain."

Two years later, on May 28th, 1951, in reply to a question from Ward Price, who was interviewing him on behalf of the London

---

* *Encyclopedia Britannica.*

Daily Mail, as to "what Spain was prepared to exchange for Gibraltar" Franco remarked with audacious frankness: "When you have lost your pocket-book you do not expect to have to give something up for its return." By dealing justly with the question of Gibraltar, he added, Britain would win the sincere friendship of Spain, as "the main problem before us is to defend Europe and maintain unity". Always that emphasis on "unity".

Certainly, Spanish friendship is worth the winning, although some distinguished Britons do not seem to think so, judging from a number of incredible pronouncements published in England on Gibraltar in justification of Britain's position there. Thus, Sir David Kelly, a former British Ambassador to Soviet Russia, writing in the London *Sunday Times* on May 1st, 1954, while agreeing with an earlier opinion of Sir Winston Churchill that the "fundamental interests of Britain and Spain are identical", declared that Spain had no "ethical or historical claims" to Gibraltar. "Historically," Kelly affirmed, perhaps with tongue in cheek, "Gibraltar is not a part of ancient Spain. Until A.D. 711 (*i.e.* the year the Moorish warrior El Tariq invaded Andalusia at the head of seven thousand Berbers and Arabs) there is no evidence of permanent human habitation; the oldest inhabitants are the famous monkeys whose presence suggests a primitive connection with Africa."

But Kelly completely, maybe deliberately, ignored Spain's *geographical* claims, for Gibraltar is neither an island nor attached by any tongue of land to Africa. He seems to have taken the lead for his equivocal attitude from an equally incredible Letter to the Editor to which the same paper had given first prominence some months earlier from no less a person than a former Governor of Gibraltar, Sir Alexander Godley. In this letter Godley pleaded that "the geology and flora are more African then European. The partridges (the letter went on) are chestnut as in Morocco, while at some kilometres distance they have red feet. The well-known monkeys are Berber, and there are other characteristics more African than European." So there are, for that matter, in Malta, which was in occupation by the Carthaginians among many other races for no inconsiderable time.

But what nonsense it is for such reputable and well-known Britons, whose knowledge and intellectual endowment should save them from teleological snares, to attempt to bolster up

Britain's claims to permanent occupation of the Rock, which is only fifteen minutes' walking distance away from Spain, by such specious arguments, which were inevitably torn to shreds with native irony and devastating humour by Spanish writers. They might have saved themselves from ridicule by taking the road from La Línea de la Concepción right into Casemates, in the heart of Gibraltar town, or by referring to M. Déperet's testimony before the Academy of Sciences in Paris in 1918:

> It was formerly supposed that Gibraltar was connected with the African shore during or after the Pleistocene Ice Age, but the trend of opinion is now towards the view that the connection must be Pliocene at the latest. Reference used to be made to the occurrence of Barbary apes on the Rock, but it is now thought that these were introduced by Romans or Moors; no fossil remains of them have been found in any caves or breccias. Neither the surviving nor the fossil Pleistocene fauna suggest an African connection . . . mammalian remains are essential European.

Better still, a visit might have been paid to the Peñón de Ifach, some hundreds of miles along the coast from San Roque, the town to which the entire Spanish population of Gibraltar emigrated after its capture by forty-four English and Dutch men-of-war, which preserves to this day the original flag bearing the coat-of-arms granted to Gibraltar by Queen Isabella I in the 15th century. For at Ifach, opposite the ancient Iberian town of Calpe, there rises a "little Gibraltar" exactly reproducing the lineaments and massiveness of the Rock, and joined like Gibraltar to the Spanish mainland by a narrow isthmus. It might be argued that this *peñón* is also "more African than European" and that therefore Spain has no just title to it!

When such weak, untenable arguments are propounded by leaders of British thought, one of them a former Governor who must often have passed from Gibraltar into Spain, although perhaps never by land, it is scarcely to be wondered at that what Franco looks for from Britain is a "change of heart" where immodifiable British occupation of the Rock is concerned.

As I faced the Spanish Leader one morning in the early summer of 1954 in his spacious study-cum-reception-room in the quiet El Pardo palace, I admitted to him that there was both ignorance and real incomprehension among my countrymen on this difficult question. "But," I added, "there is also real incomprehension among the Spanish, Your Excellency, regarding the depth of British sentiments and convictions in the matter. The English are not ordinarily emotional or demonstrative, but they *are* emotional over Gibraltar and almost everyone possesses strong sentimental feelings about continued British representation there." As the Generalissimo listened with friendly expression to my imperfect Castillian I told him that I had been surprised when explaining the Spanish patriotic attitude to friends at home to discover how demonstrative they could become, and how agitated. "The feeling is deep-seated, I assure you," I concluded, "and perhaps psychological, since we would have a sense of insecurity if Gibraltar were returned to Spanish sovereignty— like losing the trusted protector of the family interests."

Franco replied to this that he had always appreciated Britain's overseas responsibilities and the need to maintain sea communications with her far-flung Empire, but that the world of the twentieth century was radically different from that of the nineteenth century. "In the past," he said, "England kept the peace of the world with her fleet—her navy patrolled the seven seas. Now she must share that responsibility with the United States and other Powers, even with Russia. The seas are open to all peoples, peace-loving or otherwise.* Therefore indefinite British occupation of Gibraltar is today an anachronism, her attitude is unrealistic, and she should understand the justice of Spain's claims and our sensitivity in the matter in the interests of good international relations and of European defence."

I was reminded of a conversation I had had in the autumn of 1946, outside his office on the quayside at Algeciras, with Don Raimundo, a Spaniard who told me that he had seen the preparations in the Bay for the Allied invasion of North Africa, Quite possibly, although he did not say so, he had also witnessed the departure from that very quayside of the Nazi general, Lange, who visited Gibraltar disguised as a civilian worker in 1941 (I have read a Spanish translation of his own account of the visit as

---

* "Britannia does not rule the waves alone. . . . It is as good partners with our friends that we shall maintain the freedom and independence of a great Power." Sir Oliver Franks, in the first Reith Memorial Broadcast for 1954 (November 7th, 1954).

published in a German newspaper) and took photographs of the fortifications and defences from a small Leica hidden in the lining of an old jacket. As I stood with Don Raimundo on the quay gazing across a sheet of oily, sunsplashed water at the great leonine outlines of the Rock, he countered my question as to whether Spanish forces ever seriously considered having a crack at it during the war with the dry remark: "Franco knew very well that the moment either the Germans or his own troops attacked Gibraltar the Canary Islands would be occupied by the Allies within twenty-four hours." As though in reply to a question of his own, he added that Spain could never have survived her long drawn-out Civil War but for the fact that she was "fundamentally an agricultural country". "Had we been predominantly an industrial country," he added, "we should have been done for."

At the time when the subject was filling columns of the uncensored Press of Britain and of the censored Press of Spain, all hingeing on the approaching visit to her loyal subjects in Gibraltar of Queen Elizabeth II, Britons in various stations of life sent letters to London editors asserting that it was only a small and vociferous portion of the Spanish people which really wanted its return, and that the large majority of the Spanish nation were quite indifferent. Here, again, was evident self-delusion and wishful thinking, for, as I have had the opportunity of testing in conversations up and down the Peninsula with representatives of all classes and categories, Spaniards of all political views and opinions are at least united in the one argument that Gibraltar is a part of Spain. Even that outstanding Spanish Liberal and confirmed Anglophile, Don Salvador de Madariaga, who maintains an uncompromising stand against the present Head of the Spanish State, is at one with his fellow-countrymen in this respect at least, for he points out in his standard work, *Spain*, that "it is impossible for any Spaniard not to want Gibraltar returned to Spain".

For honest-minded Britons the deep Spanish sentiment regarding our hold on Gibraltar should meet with a more logical and sympathetic understanding than the claims of Greek Cypriots to *Enosis*, for union with all the other Hellenes, despite the downright assertion of one of their most determined supporters, Thomas Anthem, in his recent "factual exposition of the . . . crisis which

14

threatens to rupture the relations of Britain and Greece"—"I know enough of the situation to be convinced that sooner or later Britain will be obliged to get out. If anybody doubts this, let him think of India, Persia, Egypt, Ireland and the rest. We should get out now with grace, and in doing so retain the good-will and friendship of the friendliest of all peoples, the Greeks."

Shortly after I had read this 'exposition' on Cyprus by Mr. Anthem I saw a news film in which a hundred and thirty thousand Greeks were shown demonstrating in—unconscious irony!—Constitution Square, Athens, while the Greek Archimandrite harangued them on the injustice of the British demand for "perpetual sovereignty over Cyprus", (where a Greek lady from Alexandria once told me that she had felt the ancient Hellenic spell of the island so profoundly in the Bay of Paphos that she had there and then divested herself of all her clothes and stepped into that classic foam which had given to mankind the legend of Aphrodite, the legend of beauty.) A hundred and thirty thousand demonstrators in Athens for *Enosis*, against ten thousand in Madrid on "this bloody question of Gibraltar", as the then British Ambassador to Spain had forthrightly remarked!

"We must all regret," wrote the Hispanophile Military Correspondent of the London *Daily Telegraph*, General H. G. Martin, in a leader-page article, "General Franco Puts the Screw on Gibraltar" on August 26th, 1954, "that Spain, with whom we have so many bonds of friendship and no real conflict of interest, should be our latest opponent in the cold war. In the battle for survival against Communism we stand together on the same side of the barricades."

As we sped [writes Anthem in his *Enosis* booklet] in our magnificent Viscount airliner, at 300 m.p.h. over the bay of Taranto and across the Ionian Sea into Greece, I could not help musing how fantastic it was that we British, occupying a group of islands in the north, which most foreigners imagine to be eternally surrounded by fog and mist, should have come to secure for ourselves such dominance and position in the Mediterranean Sea, and the ancient, historic lands whose shores it washes.

In the 19th century it was our policy to keep Russia out of the Mediterranean; earlier, in 1798, and subsequently, we kept the French out of Egypt so that they could not reach India by the back door. When, by the opening of the Suez Canal, the Mediterranean became the front door to the East, it became British policy to establish the Mediterranean as a highway for England to India and the Far East. We had grabbed Gibraltar, the Pillar of Hercules. In 1878 Cyprus came into our clutches as a result of what Disraeli described as "a thief's bargain" with the Sultan, and British forces landed at Larnaca . . . and hoisted the Union Jack in the place of the Turkish Crescent.

The Greek Note, signed by the Greek Premier, Field Marshal Alexander Papagos, submitted with the Government's appeal to the United Nations, stated, *inter alia*: "In 1915 the British Government . . . offered Cyprus to Greece on condition that the latter entered the war by the side of the Allies. Greece fulfilled this condition two years later, but the offer was not carried out." Franco and the Duke of Alba, then Spanish Ambassador in London, have declared that Gibraltar was offered to Spain in 1940 on condition that she remained neutral! "Perfidious Albion" say both Mediterranean peoples.

No small indication of the abyss of misunderstanding which today separates Britons and Spaniards was forthcoming in letters from other British correspondents who, remarking on the courteous silence maintained without any exception throughout Spain during the Queen's visit to the Rock, expressed the view that here was unmistakeable proof that Spain as a whole did not really want the return of Gibraltar. Of all the statements and opinions published in the British Press on the Gibraltar controversy at that time it was this particular declaration that nettled the Spaniards most as demonstrating a profound ignorance of the essential ingredients of the Spanish character—instinctive chivalry and courtesy to a woman, and a young woman at that, and a Queen for whom personally nothing but a charming respect and an almost affectionate admiration had been expressed by any Spanish writer in any Spanish journal, and a natural dignity in face of what they conscientiously regarded as an affront to the national pride. . . . The Spanish Vice-Consul at Gibraltar, while refraining from taking part in the official festivities, sent a personal bouquet to the Queen on his own account.

George Borrow, walking up Main Street at the end of his five years' adventurings all over Spain as agent of the British and Foreign Bible Society, was conscious of a fierce patriotic pride at the sight from his hostelry window of a military band beating the retreat in "a kind of square, in which stands the little exchange of Gibraltar," and the provincial accent of "the jolly ostler Griffiths",

"Dub-a-dub, dub-a-dub"—thus go the drums,
Tantara, tantara, the Englishman comes.

"O England!" apostrophised 'Don' George, "long, long may it be ere the sun of thy glory sink beneath the wave of darkness!" Yet even in Borrow's time, as he clearly indicates in Chapter 51 of *The Bible in Spain*, most of the inhabitants of the Rock were of Italian or Greek descent, with a number of Maltese, a few North Africans, and "between two and three thousand Jews".

The agitation in the Spanish Press over Gibraltar did not originate, as was claimed, with the celebrated approach by the Duke of Primo de Rivera, the Spanish Ambassador, to the Foreign Office, over the projected visit of Queen Elizabeth. It had been going on for at least three years, as I discovered for myself on working through some of the back numbers of the Madrid newspapers and the *Cuadernos de Documentos* No. 129 dated May 15th, 1952, and No. 639 of March 25th, 1954, issued by the Director General de Prensa on "The Illegality of the British Conquest of Gibraltar".

All this national ferment was, however, crystallised and brought to full and articulate expression in the forthright articles which appeared in the Phalanx daily *Arriba* above the pseudonym, "Macaulay", which everyone in Madrid knows is Franco himself. (When a new Ambassador from the Irish Free State was accredited to Spain whose name *was* Macauley, it was thought that Franco would adopt a different pen-name, or keep to his alternative pseudonym, "Hispanicus", but this did not happen.) The gist of Franco's argument fell under three heads: that the English conquest of Gibraltar was itself illegal, that Spain was not invited to take any part in the negotiations for its transference but merely asked to send envoys to sign the instrument of surrender in the Treaty of Utrecht, *viz.*: "The Catholic King does hereby for himself and his heirs and successors yield to the Crown of Great Britain the full and entire property of the town and castle of Gibraltar, together with the port, fortifications and fort belonging to them", and did so because they were "bad Spaniards"; and that the return of the Rock to Spain had been categorically promised, first by King George I to Philip V of Spain in a holograph letter dated June 1st, 1721 (a facsimile copy of which I have seen), and in more recent times by Sir Winston Churchill, then Prime Minister, at a luncheon at the Spanish Embassy in 1940 in return for Spain's refusal of facilities to Hitler's panzer divisions to storm it.

Some time before his death the Duke of Alba was asked the leading question by a Spanish journalist whether he stood by the accuracy of the telegram he had sent to the Foreign Office in Madrid immediately after the luncheon, at which Sir Anthony (then Mr.) Eden and Sir Samuel Hoare (as he was then), British Ambassador in Madrid, were also present. He replied that since his retirement he had ceased to take active part or interest in politics, but that he certainly stood by every word of the message he had sent.

"Of course, there was nothing in writing," a colleague remarked to me in Madrid when controversy was at its highest, "but obviously something must have been said; after all, it was only natural when Britain stood alone and Franco held the key to Gibraltar on the land side. Any Prime Minister at that time would have used every inducement to keep Spain friendly and neutral."

That Franco's repeated refusals of passage through Spain for the German forces, despite every menace and plea by Hitler and a special secret visit by Rudolph Hess six months before his abortive flight to meet the Duke of Hamilton in Scotland (Hess pressed for right of passage to Gibraltar for six German divisions "in exchange for food and territorial guarantees", a demand which like the others, was peremptorily refused despite the serious food situation) lost Hitler the war is now a matter of history, for it was clearly stated by Jodl, Chief of the German General Staff in evidence at the Nuremberg trials. It is scarcely surprising, therefore, if Franco feels that Spain has received treatment less than just from Britain, after 'promises' whose authenticity is attested by telegrams and documents available for inspection by accredited journalists in the archives of the Spanish Foreign Office. Among the callers was the well-known writer on diplomatic affairs, Mr. George Bilainkin, who gave a most enlightening account of his discoveries in the London *Contemporary Review* for November, 1953, in which he quoted the Spanish Foreign Minister's moving if breathless reference to the welcoming back into the European fold by the Allies of their late enemies and the continued cold-shouldering of neutral Spain:

> That is why this Spain, which was so badly wronged, which has been made to pay—what an irony!—much more dearly for its neutrality than the vanquished for their defeat; which as a reward for its heroic action against Communist barbarism has been cut off from the world; which has suffered hunger and want in its people's flesh owing to a blockade it did not deserve, and which has endured all those onslaughts precisely at the hands of the Western World whose cause it served, and at the instigation of that Soviet power which is the only real and terrible threat to peace—this Spain which loves Christian peace and serves the civilisation of the West at this solemn, historical moment, grants its amnesty to all the nations which offer it concord and is willing to forget its wrongs for the sake of, and to further, the common cause which is so seriously jeopardised.

"Lucharemos por lo que es nuestro—Gibraltar". I used to read the proud inscription, "we struggle for what is ours", each morning, painted in deep black letters on the wall of an educational institute as I made my way across the Plaza de España into the Avenida de José Antonio in Madrid. There are few, or perhaps none of the many frequenters of the British Club at number six of that glamorous thoroughfare who would, were they asked, agree to the return to Spain of Gibraltar, and it is certainly a very hard thing for any inhabitant of the British Isles to look at Franco's statements with an objective and supra-national eye. But the question needs to be faced squarely, without sentiment or prejudice, if Anglo-Spanish relations are ever to attain to that degree of confidence and cordiality which is absolutely essential for the effective working of Western defence from the North Cape to Tangier. And, irrespective of everything else, Spaniards claim that the treaty gave us no licence to use the land-strip between the boundary and the Rock.

"How would you like it if Spain owned Dover, or the Americans if we occupied Cape Cod?" a Spaniard asked a British newspaper correspondent.

"But whose seapower kept you safe from Axis-dominated Europe", was the retort, "and will protect you against Russia?" To which the Spaniard replied: "We are only too willing to let you use Gibraltar, and *all* Spanish bases, as an ally if you give Gibraltar back."

"But how can we be sure that you will be on our side?"

"*Hombre!*" exclaimed the Spaniard, "there is only one possible enemy in sight for a long time to come, and we are with you all the way on that."*

In an article from Gibraltar in the *Sunday Express* on November 21st, 1954, the Managing Editor, Mr. John Gordon wrote:

> The Queen should invite Franco's daughter to tea at Buckingham Palace. Those who know Spain say such an invitation would delight the whole nation, and do more to bring Spain and Britain into neighbourly amity than a year of political wire-dancing.

Some two years previously Franco's daughter had accompanied her husband, the Marqués de Villaverde, on a *private* visit to the United States; but President Eisenhower made them State guests for the entire period of their stay.

---

* As Sir John Balfour indicated to me at the British Embassy in Madrid (see *Prologue*), there is a kind of Portuguese Gibraltar in Spain—the small town of Olivenza, close to the Portuguese frontier, held by Spain since the time of the Napoleonic Wars and which she failed to return to Portugal even after the settlement reached at the Congress of Vienna. This was due to the duplicity of Godoy, the Spanish First Minister, who was a puppet of Napoleon. "Portugal has never seriously raised the matter," the Portuguese Ambassador to the Court of St. James himself told me, "in order not to disturb relations with Spain which, as is generally known, could hardly be improved."

Chapter Twenty-two

PORTUGAL AND SPAIN

I F THERE IS ONE CONCLUSION which the political and international convulsions of the present century have brought home
to every sane and thinking being on this afflicted planet, which
science would have us believe is 'a gigantic puff of gas in a vast
void' and which we know now is in any case one of billions of
stars whirling in inconceivable space, it is surely the utter fallibility
and casual opportunism of our politicians and statesmen. Were a
sentient being from another planet actually to land here from a
space ship (as has been legally attested before notaries in California
by four sworn witnesses)* and, after examination and analysis of
the story of two World Wars with forty million casualities and the
conferences at the end of the last one at Yalta, Teheran and Potsdam, by which the victorious Western Powers, on the late
President Roosevelt's recommendation, handed their temporary
ally but implacable enemy in space and time, Soviet Russia, two-
thirds of Europe as a springboard for the conquest of the rest, he
or she (if such a being were sexed at all) would certainly think
mankind on this planet mad. (And if there are a hundred and
seventeen words in that sentence the subject matter is worth it;
in a recent historical work Professor Arnold Toynbee has one
one hundred and forty words long.)

Outside the Communist States lack of prescience in a statesman
is not a capital offence, and all the world knows today that
Franklin Delano Roosevelt had a much greater predilection for
seeing Russia powerful on the European continent than Britain,
which the great American war-time leader, for all his professions
of blood ties and 'blazing' friendship, regarded with profound
suspicion.

But if such lack of prescience in statesmen is a human quality to

---

* *Flying Saucers Have Landed*, by Desmond Leslie and George Adamski
(Werner Laurie)—p. 192.

which they are, although they ought not to be, prone, an un-
blushing ignorance and a failure to study the published aims and
intentions of a potential mortal enemy are in quite a different
category of culpability. It was from the lips of a well-known
Conservative Member of the House of Commons, one day over
lunch in Whitehall Court, that I learned that a Foreign Secretary
had once confessed to a small gathering of Tory Members that he
had "never read the writings of Stalin, nor the works of Lenin or
Marx" previous to his first visit to Moscow, and therefore was not
really aware of the true meaning of Communism or of the
global aggressive strategy of the Kremlin. And it was from the
lips of the former Officer in Charge of Russian Intelligence at the
War Office, who later carried on investigations for the Foreign
Office, that I heard at first-hand of the reactions of the Premier
and Mr. Attlee to a talk he gave them at 10, Downing Street on
the true nature of Communism.

"For one hour," he told me in London, "I sat alone with the
Prime Minister and the Leader of the Opposition and explained to
them exactly what Communism meant, as I judged it from research and personal investigation over the past thirty years." My
informant produced for my inspection an identity card, printed
in Russian and bearing his passport photograph, which he
had extracted unperceived from the secret police files in the
Kremlin. "I explained the case of a landowner, one Mirsky, from
the Caucasus, whom I had met at an Allied international conference and who invited me to visit him on his estates." ....

" 'But I used to know your brother, I think', I said to him,
'Prince Mirsky. What has become of him?' My would-be-host
looked at me a bit sheepishly, and then replied: 'Well, you see, I
joined the local Communist branch and the leader said to me:
'We are very glad to welcome you here, Comrade Mirsky, but
before you can be regarded as a reliable Communist you must
betray to us two people who are near and dear to you'. So (said
Mirsky) one day I engaged my brother, who was not a member
of the Communist party, in conversation in a room of our old
manor-house where two N.K.V.D. men were concealed, until
he said something incriminating, and then he was arrested and
shot next day on the evidence of the two officials, and I took over
the estate.

" 'Very neat; but what about the second victim?' I enquired.

Mirsky smiled and opened his hands. 'After my brother's death
the branch leader said: "Now, personally I am satisfied of your
loyalty to the Party. But to convince Moscow you must betray
a second relative or close friend". Well, I had been engaged to be
married to a nice girl, Natasha, who broke it off when I joined the
Communists. So I invited her round to the manor to see me, and
unbelievably she came. I got her to talk, and again the N.K.V.D.
officials were there behind the heavy curtains. Eventually, she said
something critical of the Soviet rulers and was liquidated next
morning. After that the Party accepted me without further
demur' ".

"This," my informant said, "and other accounts, I gave to the
Prime Minister and the Leader of the Opposition. When I had
finished my explanation of the true nature of Communism, Mr.
Attlee remarked that such things could not happen in Britain,
and Mr. Churchill said: 'From what you say it seems to me that a
man could attain great power under such a system'," and the
speaker imitated the Churchillian lisp in an undeniably authentic
way! . . .

This lacuna in realistic understanding was certainly in evidence
in the apparent failure of the British War Cabinet to note the
real significance of the ten years' Treaty of Non-Aggression and
Friendship, known as 'Operation Bloc', which Spain made with
her sister-nation and neighbouring authoritarian State, Portugal,
ten days before she adhered to the anti-Comintern pact in July,
1939. The Treaty was one of the first fruits of the diplomatic
mission to Lisbon of Franco's elder brother (Rear-Admiral) Don
Nicolás Franco, who must almost possess the world record for
Ambassadors *en poste*, for he has been Spanish Envoy to Portugal
since 1937.*

---

* Franco is sometimes criticised in Spain for keeping his brother so long
at the Embassy in Lisbon, and a story says that an ill-wisher of Nicolás,
seeking to 'cash in' on this half-articulate public opinion, produced
before the Head of the State a copy of an illustrated Italian weekly
containing a page-photograph of the Ambassador in swimming trunks
seated on the Lido at Venice by the side of a comely signorina who was
wearing an abbreviated 'bikini'. As both the male and female of the
species are required to wear full-length bathing costumes on Spanish
beaches he thought that Franco would consider the picture of his

In the months of July, 1939, when presages in Europe all pointed to the imminent danger of a second World War, the Head of the Spanish State (by then recognised of their own free-will by all the Powers), had declared to representatives of the Portuguese Press that "Spain will never fight except for her honour or vital interest", and *after* the Allied Victory he stated that he "never had the slightest intention of entering the war on Germany's side". We have had an opportunity of examining the honesty of this confession, in the light of captured German documents and the published evidence of the Ciano Diaries and the book by Hitler's translator, Dr. Paul Schmidt. It is only necessary to refer here to the provisions of the Hispano-Portuguese Pact, by which the two High Parties undertook to commit no act of aggression or invasion against each other, with or without a declaration of war, and to respect each other's frontiers and territories.

Of far greater import to Britain, France and America, and of far greater significance to the ultimate outcome of the war: each Signatory solemnly undertook "to give no assistance to any aggressor against the other, and not to allow any attack, whether by land, sea or air, to be directed against the other from its own territory". Finally, each Power undertook "to enter into no pacts or alliances directed against the other, or aiming at aggression against the other", and to *"safeguard the principles of the Treaty in future treaties with Third Powers"* (my italics).

This Pact, viewed logically and with an inside knowledge of its sacred obligations as understood by the sister Iberian nations both ruled on similar authoritarian principles and one of whom had a binding alliance with Great Britain no less than seven centuries old, the oldest treaty of friendship and alliance in the Foreign Office archives, clearly demonstrated that Spain, even had she wished to, could not enter the war on the side of the Axis Powers without Portugal's assent, which of course, in view of the ancient Treaty, could never have been secured. Thus, the Iberian Peninsula, by the acumen and quiet statesmanship of the two respective Heads of State, had been forged into one strategic unity. This *bloc*,

---

brother at least undignified. But the *Caudillo*, after gazing at the illustration closely for some moments, merely remarked with a smile: "You know the trouble with Nicolás is, he's getting so fat!"

of the implications of which Hitler must have been at least aware
but not convinced, was further strengthened and reinforced by
the Protocol of 1940. But neither the Pact nor the Protocol
mentioned the Azores, where a hundred and fifty thousand fully-
armed men were kept always in battle readiness.

Accordingly, neither Mr. Churchill when he despatched
post-haste to Madrid Sir Samuel Hoare (later Lord Templewood),
who was essentially a politician and not a diplomat, nor the
German *Führer* when he sped through occupied France in his
bullet-proof coach to the Hendaye meeting, had on the face of
things deduced from the Pact (and from the Protocol) their
obvious and inescapable meaning, namely that Spain *could not*
voluntarily enter the war on the side of the Axis, for these Agreements expressly and of purpose aforethought obviated any such
possibility. ("The secret of good diplomacy is to know what is
at the back of the other fellow's mind," said Sir Harold Nicolson,
the author and ex-diplomat and biographer of King George V, in
a war-time address at the Royal Empire Society to which I
listened and a copy of which I had the greatest difficulty in
extracting from the Society for the then Spanish Ambassador in
London, His Excellency Don Domingo de las Bárcenas, who had
read the Press reports and enlisted my good offices. Only after
the then President, the Earl of Clarendon, K.G., had interested
himself in the matter was a copy forthcoming.) Even so anti-
Franco an authority as Lord Templewood admitted that the
agreement "was a definite sign that Spain wished to maintain her
independence and to keep the Iberian system out of Hitler's
continental system". (*Ambassador on Special Mission*, p. 58.)

Perhaps no aspect of Franco's foreign policy is so revealing of
his calculating Galician nature, or of the depth of his diplomatic
cunning, as these early war-time agreements with Portugal, for
while he haggled with Hitler and his brow-beating envoys month
after month, dangling like a carrot before a ravenous and
murderous mule a hypothetical undertaking that Spain would
'sometime' join Italy and Germany, his eastern flank was safely
covered and he himself knew beyond a peradventure of doubt
that Spain would remain neutral unless she were attacked or
invaded. "Only Franco's closest confidants knew right from the
start that he fully intended to keep Spain—bled white by the
disastrous Civil War—out of the World War," wrote Kees van

Hoek in an article which appeared in 1953 in the British illustrated weekly *Everybody's*, under the title, "Franco Rules Without Fear", the reading of which is rewarding.

Well might Hitler unconsciously reflect in his post-Hendaye seizures the biting proverb: *"Del agua mansa me guarde Dios, que de la brava me guardaré yo"*—("May God defend me from the still water, I will protect myself from the rough").

Franco has a temperamental kinship with Portugal, and the Gallego dialect, which he speaks more than passing well, is very similar to Portuguese. There is a distinct affinity between the inhabitants of Galicia and the neighbouring Portuguese, who are likewise addicted to canniness, the intelligent ones at any rate. When a Galician goes to see a lawyer, it is said, he always states his opponent's case first, and then, depending on the lawyer's opinions, he states his own.

In the summer of 1932 I was on holiday near the great Galician port of Vigo, at the historic and then unspoiled resort of Bayona, where the caravel *Niña* put in for repairs to a mast on the return of Columbus (who sailed on to Lisbon with the *María* and the *Pinta*) from the discovery of America—a bronze plaque on the *paseo* at Bayona records the fact—and where the Conde de Gondomar, the great Ambassador of Philip III to the England of James I, set sail for Greenwich, for the ancestral castle is only a few kilometres away in the village of Gondomar (his son fought Drake during one of his burning and slaying forays into Galicia.).

In Bayona at this time, where I used sometimes to exchange greetings on the beach with Bárbara Gondomar, the sister of the present Count and a direct descendant of the 17th-century Ambassador, an ex-Press chief of a Madeira revolution which preceded the advent of Dr. Salazar had found it expedient to take refuge. I had several talks with him and was struck by the fact that he seemed so completely at home in his new environment. It later transpired that he had fled from Funchal taking with him considerable financial assets to which apparently he had no prescriptible right.

As we know from the archæologists, the Iberian Peninsula was once inhabited by a single race, the "Ibo-orians", the short-statured, wiry, thick-skulled folk whose ancestors inhabited the "land

of the Ebro". (The country was given the generic name of
Sapan or *Span* by the early Phoenician traders, from the skin
of the marten which they procured from the peninsula in great
numbers). Accordingly, the blood and cultural ties linking the
Portuguese with the Spanish are closer than those between the
Welsh or Scots and certainly between the Irish and the English.

For sixty years, from 1580 to 1640, Portugal was actually under
the Spanish Crown, when, following the death of the Portuguese
King on the field of battle at Alcázarquivir, Philip II, whose
mother had been a Portuguese princess, was proclaimed heir to
the throne. Some historians aver, indeed, that if Philip had made
Lisbon the chief city of his Hispano-Portuguese kingdom,
instead of raising a brand new capital, Madrid, on the site of a
cluster of Mozarab dwellings with a Moorish Alcazar situated on
the high Castilian tableland, Portugal might still be a part of the
Spanish realm. But Philip had no wish to treat Portugal, an
autonomous State, as conquered territory, although even in the
time of the Catholic Monarchs, who fused all the disparate, proud
and jealous Spanish provinces and peoples into one nation by the
exercise of heroic will joined to a natural astuteness and a sense
of mission, it was one of Isabella's dearest wishes that the river
Tagus, which curves like a scimitar round walled Toledo, should
be made navigable all the way from Aranjuez to Portuguese
Belem, on the Atlantic.

> Spain has a community of ideals with Portugal at least as close as
> with Italy, and far closer than with Germany, while she is bound to
> Portugal as to no other nation by the combined ties of geographical
> propinquity, racial origin and linguistic, social and political history.
> In the Middle Ages Spain and Portugal had the same enemy, who
> had invaded them from the south, who threatened their Christian
> civilisation and whom they fought determinedly and successfully
> when not fighting each other. Today they have once again a common
> enemy with whom (though they are not at war with him) they
> maintain no diplomatic or commercial relations, who menaces them
> from the east, who offers no less of a threat to their Christian
> civilisation, and against whom they would no doubt be prepared
> at any time to take up arms together. . . . Between General Franco's
> National-Syndicalist State and the Corporative State of Dr. Salazar
> there is a great deal in common, and Portugal's sympathy with the
> Nationalist cause during the Civil War has frequently been acknow-
> ledged.—(E. Allison Peers).

Thus wrote one of the most eminent Hispanophiles and Hispanic scholars of our time during the 1939-45 war, and he added this pregnant observation indicating that his searching and essentially honest intelligence had probed to their inmost significance the Pact and the Protocol: "Is it conceivable that Spain will draw closer to Italy and Germany when this must mean moving farther away from Portugal?"

The Pact and the Protocol, which were renewed for a further ten years in 1948, and *Hispanidad*, 'the essence of things Spanish', involving the closer political and cultural association between Spain and all the daughter Latin-American States which had derived from the Motherland their culture, their laws, and their language (with the single exception of Brazil), represented the two chief pillars of Spain's foreign policy during the Great War. To all appearance and from all the evidence, their true significance was completely lost on the chief belligerents, each waiting with almost bated breath to see "which way the cat would jump" when the Pact and Protocol announced to whomever it might concern that the cat would not jump at all. . . .

The Treaty of Friendship and Non-Aggression between Portugal and Spain was signed at Lisbon on the 17th March, 1939. At that time, although the victory of the National forces of Spain was very near, the Civil War was still being fought. Furthermore, Hitler, strengthened and encouraged by the success of his daring methods, was preparing to impose his will on a weakened, disarmed, and irresolute Europe. Franco's decision to link Spain to Portugal by that Treaty was a fact of transcendent importance which revealed, to all who were capable of seeing clearly, what was to be the attitude of Spain. In fact, Franco showed that Spain would emerge from the Civil War free of any commitments other than those entered into with the Sister Nation in the Peninsula which, in the tragic hour of the clash between such radically opposed forces, had understood the true significance of the conflict.

But much more important than the Treaty of 1939 was the Protocol to that Treaty, signed in Lisbon on July 29th, 1940. Considering what was the situation in Europe at that time, with France and the rest of the European Continent crushed by the German forces, Hitler on the Pyrenees and preparing to attack Britain in her island, the fact cannot but be acknowledged that a new and firm step was taken by Franco to keep the Peninsula out of the War and free from Hitler. Under the terms of the Protocol, which began by confirming the provisions of the Treaty and by laying it down that the future action of the two peoples would be governed by it, Portugal and Spain undertook to "concert among themselves as to the best means of safeguarding their common interests to the greatest possible extent whenever events occurred or were to be feared capable of imperilling the integrity of their respective territories in the Peninsular, or endangering the security or independence of either party".

By this Protocol, Portugal and Spain asserted their firm intention to stop Hitler at the Pyrenees and if necessary to fight side by side against invasion of the Peninsula. There would be no repetition of the disastrous division which opened the way into the Peninsula for Napoleon, and which, only too late, was to be followed by the uniting of Portuguese and Spaniards under Wellington in the Homeric campaigns for the destruction and expulsion of what had been the invincible French Armies.

Hitler was under no illusion as to the significance of the Protocol of July 1940 between Spain and Portugal. His Ambassador at Madrid realised that Franco had taken up a clear position which he would be able to maintain thanks to his friendship with the other country in the Peninsula and the powerful and real military force which, on Spain's difficult terrain, was provided by an Army of young and well-trained men whose morale could hardly have been bettered. On the other hand, the role of Portugal in all this needs no explanation. Her line of conduct and the thought by which it was steadfastly governed proved to be invaluable.

During the darkest days of the World War, Britain had in Portugal the same friend she had always been able to count on. On the other hand, Portugal provided constant support for a firm stand on the part of Spain.

Portugal and Spain saw how a sound policy of good understanding, particularly in so desperately grave an emergency as that of 1940 and subsequent years, was to be crowned with complete success. Their joint efforts amounted to much more than the sum of their respective possibilities.

I have emphasised these paragraphs by placing them in italics because they record, word for word, a statement made to me, when this book was nearing completion, in the Chancery of the Portuguese Embassy in London by the Portuguese Ambassador,

Dr. Pedro Theotonio Pereira, who was for nine years (during the Civil War and World War) Envoy of his country in Spain. To him Sir Samuel Hoare (now Viscount Templewood), in his book *Ambassador on Special Mission*, pays tribute as "a colleague of outstanding ability and distinction" (p. 45). His Excellency, who may be said to have 'made history' by his negotiation of the Pact and Protocol, was good enough to remark of my earlier estimate of their true significance that it was "a hundred per cent right".

In the third week of October, 1948, the Head of the Spanish State paid an official visit to Portugal on board the battleship *Miguel de Cervantes*, which I used to see anchored off Santander, or disembarking leave-men on the mole at Cadiz, in the pre-Civil War days. The visit was ostensibly in return for the State visit paid to Spain by the Portuguese President, General Carmona, in 1929, when King Alfonso was on his throne. On arrival in the great central square of the Portuguese capital, "the finest arena for spectacle in Europe" as it has been called, although I should have thought that St. Mark's Square in Venice was a formidable rival, Franco was received with a 20-gun salute and the unconcealed enthusiasm of the entire population of Lisbon, clearly manifesting a solidarity of sentiment with Spaniards which was a pointer to the feeling of both peoples that blood was thicker than water, and that the type of régime which had saved Portugal from the abyss of anarchy and political chaos and given her economic and administrative stability should at least find understanding among the democracies when a similar régime was doing the same service for Spain. The opinion was also nationally articulate during the visit that Spain should be invited to join the Atlantic Pact, as Portugal was in it.

"While Europe heals its wounds," announced the venerable Portuguese President at the State banquet, "Portugal and Spain must be regarded as the preservers of the ideals of civilisation and the upholders of social discipline." The special correspondent of the London *Daily Express* described Franco at the time of this Lisbon visit as "a man who dreams up his politics and makes them true, a brown, laughing, vigorous man with a foundation of charm who takes a hack State meeting and transforms it into a great occasion".

When he returned to Madrid Franco was welcomed back by an

immense concourse of three hundred thousand citizens crowded
in the same vast square, the Plaza de Oriente, where, at the time
of the diplomatic boycott by the United Nations, a similar
gathering comprising representatives of all classes had greeted
him with the spontaneous slogan: "*Franco, Sí!—Comunismo,
No!*" "Spain," wrote a correspondent in the London *Daily Telegraph* at this time, "is the most politically and nationally united
country in Europe", while my friend of twenty years, William
Studdart, stated in a contemporary that the best service Britain
could give Spain was to leave her alone to work out her own
salvation. "Spaniards," he added, "must first solve the problem
which has perplexed them for a long time—how to reconcile
freedom with a respect for law and order."

Franco himself put his own position in a nutshell in his New
Year message for 1950: "Whether one likes it or not," he proclaimed, "Spain is destined by nature to be the key and life of the
West. Our political system is not transitory; every enterprise
needs a captain, and, as such, I am thoroughly conversant with
your needs." What remained of his life, he said, was dedicated to
their service. . . .

Chapter Twenty-three

'HOMBRE DE ESTADO'*

IN APRIL, 1939, THE LATE Field-Marshal Sir Philip Chetwode heard from Franco's own lips that he had "never executed a man for fighting against him, nor because of his political opinions." All those sentenced for civil crimes had been tried by legal courts, which led to "interminable arguments", for, in the typical Spanish manner, "neither side would give way a point to the other". Through the intervention of the British Commission for the Exchange of Spanish War Prisoners over which Chetwode had presided (to whom I had once lent the saddle-blanket of my horse when he was carried off the field after being heavily thrown at a jump during a meet of the New Delhi Hunt, under the mastership of the then Viceroy, Lord Irwin—today Viscount Halifax, K.G.) four hundred of the large number of prisoners who had been sentenced to death for proved crimes had had their sentences remitted.

For well over a decade now much capital has been made of the pro-German statements in Franco's wartime speeches—statements for which one may look in vain in the published collections of his addresses. And without doubt such propaganda twists as those given to the cession in 1941 of fifty United States' destroyers in return for a 99-years' lease of certain British Colonial bases, which Franco described as "the exchange of fifty old destroyers for a few bits of the crumbling British Empire", and the repeated declaration at one stage of hostilities that Germany "had already won the war" have continued to rankle in the minds of the British and American peoples.

A good deal of nonsense was published during and after the War about the token force Spain sent to fight on the Eastern front, the famed 'Blue Division'. The true meaning of that gesture was summed up for me in a remark made by a former

---

* Statesman.

member of it, brother of one of my earliest Madrid friends, and a
volunteer at 18. As we crossed the sands of one of the broad
Atlantic beaches near Bilbao for a swim on a June morning of
1949, he said: "We were not against England; we went to avenge
mothers and fathers, brothers and sisters, who had suffered torture
or death, or both, through the Soviet intervention in our Civil
War".

Yet hard words break no bones; and, as the American and
British Foreign Secretaries have consistently been telling Soviet
Russia ever since the war ended, "it is deeds that count". "The
unconditional surrender of France," said *A B C* in a revealing
editorial on the fifteenth anniversary of the Nationalist victory,
"placed us (*i.e.*, Spain) in one of the most difficult situations of the
century, incomparably more grave than in 1914." To the
Wehrmacht at Hendaye poised to drive straight through to the
Mediterranean, and the more and more imperative and high-
handed accents of Hitler's Ambassador in Madrid, Franco used
words as weapons and with them and nothing else held for three
years all Hitler's embattled might on Spain's defenceless frontiers.

As early as May 30th, 1939, he had declared at a mass demon-
stration of women Phalangists assembled in the gaunt but magnificent castle of Medina del Campo, in Old Castile, where Isabella
the Catholic died, that there would be "no mad adventures" and
that he "wanted Spain to become a fortress of peace". This
decision was reiterated two months later when, in an interview
with a correspondent of the Lisbon newspaper *Diario de Noticias*,
he said that Spain would remain neutral in the event of war "if her
territory, honour and vital interests are not affected".

The steady if subtle tenacity of Franco's foreign policy during
the Second World War was revealed by his choice of successive
foreign ministers—of the somewhat colourless Colonel Beig-
bedier, with his affable "wait and see" attitude, who, however,
went out of his way to be friendly to the British Ambassador, Sir
Samuel Hoare; Ramón Serrano Suñer, placed at the head of the
Foreign Ministry at a time when his pro-Axis bias was worth a
dozen divisions to Spain but who was held well in rein by his
Caudillo brother-in-law; the mild and slightly pro-Allied Count
Jordana who showed such distress when the American wartime
Ambassador, Professor Carlton Hayes, woke him up in the
middle of the night on the occasion of the Allied landings in

North Africa to hand over President Roosevelt's letter for the Head of the Spanish State; and, since Jordana's death in 1944, Don José Felix de Lequerica for a few months, and the *"buena persona"* and transparently honest Catholic gentleman, Don Alberto Martín Artajo, President of *Acción Católica*, who has been a tower of strength both to his Leader and to the régime.

Franco has never made any bones about the fact that he feels himself under no obligations of gratitude to the United Kingdom. In a talk soon after the war with the ardent Hispanophile Dr. Walter Starkie, whose work as British Council representative in Spain from 1940 to 1954 earned him the reputation in Madrid of 'Britain's unofficial Ambassador', the Spanish *Caudillo* courteously pointed out that the Nationalist victory owed nothing to British comprehension, and that only Portugal, Germany and Mussolini had demonstrated from the first days of the Civil War their understanding of the immense issues at stake.

Spain of the 18th July (*i.e.*, 1936) met international hostility. For the foreign chancelleries Madrid was the legitimate Government and the Burgos Government the rebels. In a few months the achievement of Franco and his representatives succeeded in changing the direction of affairs. The Republics of Guatemala and Salvador were the first two countries to recognise Franco on November 8th, 1936. Shortly afterwards Germany, Italy, Nicaragua and Albania followed with diplomatic representatives. In 1937 Argentina, the Holy See and Japan; in 1938 Honduras, Portugal, and in the first months of 1939 Ireland, Switzerland and forty other nations. The 'Black Legend', however, remained.—(From an *A B C* editorial of April 1st, 1954— my translation).

The late Marqués de Merry del Val, for so many years Spain's Ambassador to the court of St. James and a staunch and tried friend of this country, used these forthright words in an article entitled, "Neutral War Aims" which he contributed to the pre-War publication *Spain*:

At the supreme crisis of his national life he (*i.e.*, the Spanish Nationalist) found only misunderstanding and lack of feeling and support where least expected. . . . His surprise was great and bitter as he saw England, the just, the non-sectarian, the self-righteous, refuse even to examine the rights and wrongs of the case, or to give at least as much credit to the Cause fighting for the rescue in Spain of all that is dear to the Englishman's heart as to those who publicly professed their will to destroy the same ancient Christian civilisation which he jealousy preserves in his own land.

In March, 1946, a *Times* news report from Washington said an American White Paper had revealed that "in June, 1940, Franco promised both Hitler and Mussolini to enter the war on the side of the Axis on two conditions: that Gibraltar, French Morocco, a part of Algeria colonised and previously inhabited by Spaniards, be handed over to Spain, and that military and general economic and material assistance required for carrying on war will be made available to Spain". But, despite his appeasement of Hitler at the opening of the Hendaye meeting, when he said that "Spain would gladly fight at Germany's side" (what other sop could he have thrown to the tiger?), Franco always evaded coming to any agreement on a suggested date with the excuse of "the continued menace of the British Fleet, the incompleteness of Spain's military preparations, and the absolute inadequacy of Spain's resources".

According to Ciano's memoirs, Hitler complained bitterly and angrily of Franco's "unhelpful attitude" which he bluntly described as "hesitant and faithless", and later "heaped imprecations on Franco's head more virulent than those he employed even of Roosevelt and Churchill".

So much, then, for Franco's pro-German wartime statements and his "offers to enter the war on Germany's side". . . .

On March 15th, 1940, Franco, who had been living in the castle of Viñuelas, belonging to the Duke of Infantado, moved with his family to the El Pardo palace where he has remained ever since. In face of the immense tragedy of the Second World War, following so closely upon Spain's own mortal struggle, great works of reconstruction were planned and comprehensive measures of social welfare were put in hand. These works and these measures took over a decade to reach fruition; but no one can live or travel in Spain today without meeting on every side evidence of a powerful controlling creative impulse in the reconstructed towns and villages destroyed in the Civil War, in great new blocks of flats for fishermen and workers with communal canteens and recreation rooms, in fine new hospitals such as those outside Valencia and Corunna,* in new civic buildings

---

* I attended Mass only last Sunday (11-10-54) in the chapel of the latter, which contains four wings and six floors with the most up-to-date X-ray and therapeutical equipment, and accommodation for the

and town halls such as the imposing new *Ayuntamiento* at El Ferrol, in new modern barracks like the big stone and brick block which, however, appeared to be quite empty when I passed it a few months ago, opposite the ochre-coloured castle at Medina del Campo; in such a superb structural and artistic achievement as the recently transformed "plateresque" *Hostal de los Reyes Católicos* at Santiago de Compostela and undoubtedly today one of the world's finest hostelries. I was shown all over it in October with my friends the García-Duráns by kindness of the Director, Don Mario Sauvalle González, when we learned that six thousand workmen had completed the reconstruction in time for the Santiago Holy Year in 1954 by working day and night for six months. The result is certainly a revelation of taste and beauty, and of what modern Spain is capable.

Through years of unparalleled difficulty and crisis, of constant danger of invasion either by Germany or the Allies, of almost complete isolation from 1945 to 1950 (in 1946, Spain, then in the throes of a disastrous five-years' drought, was on the brink of bankruptcy I have heard from the lips of the Director-General of Commerce at that time), of world boycott, international persecution, denial of all economic aid, and deliberate misrepresentation of his achievements and of his aims, Franco maintained his firm leadership of the nation, holding it together through thick and thin. So much was this the case that in September of the year the war ended a British Liberal journal could say that "Spain today is in many ways better off than almost any country in Europe", while Franco himself pointed out that his country was "moving towards complete normal internal liberty".

Posterity may take a hard view of the outright rejection by the British Cabinet (after General de Gaulle had turned down the idea of "a Western *bloc*") of the proposals advanced in the letter addressed in 1944 by the Head of the Spanish State to the British Prime Minister suggesting a common line of defence against Soviet Russia. In this once celebrated letter the Spaniard remarked that "history shows that it is not difficult to win the friendship and heart of Spain". But Churchill, in his considered reply,

---

entire medical and nursing staff. It stands on a prominence with glorious views of the wide *ría* and harbour of Corunna. There are beds for four hundred workers.

roundly declared: "I should let Your Excellency fall into a serious error if I did not remove from your mind the idea that His Majesty's Government would be ready to consider any *bloc* of Powers based on hostility to our Russian allies, or on any assumed need of defence against them." Yet that was precisely what the British and United States' Government did consider, and not only considered but were feverishly organising, before the memory of this correspondence had vanished from the public mind.

The previous year, in response to a suggestion from Count Jordana, then Spanish Foreign Minister, that they should exchange views on the European situation, the British Ambassador, delivered himself of this categorical pronouncement (dated 19th February, 1943):

> I am not accepting the Minister's view that Russia is the great danger to Europe. Nor am I accepting the Minister's view that Russia will embark upon an anti-European policy. . . . There is no reason to think that the alliance formed under the stress of war will not continue in the peace and provide a peaceful and stabilising force in European politics.

"Of course, Franco says now: 'I told you so'," the British Ambassador commented in the Madrid Embassy when I last saw him, "but how could he have seriously imagined acceptance of his proposals possible at a time when our people and all America were filled with admiration of the heroic achievements of the Red Army in defence of their country. . . . The position is different today."

In Italy and Sicily between the wars one used to see stencilled on the walls in country districts the boastful claim: "*Mussolini sempre ha ragione*" ("Mussolini is always right"). Although the majority of Spanish people may think the same of their *Caudillo*, and some of them occasionally say so, the nation does not record its belief in the Italian manner, but rather by means of such a verbal plebiscite as they gave themselves after publication of the Potsdam Conference decisions and the United Nations' resolution calling for the withdrawal of Ambassadors from Spain, when three hundred thousand citizens representing all classes gathered spontaneously in the great outer courtyard of the royal palace and chanted in unison their "*Franco, Sí!—Comunismo, No!*" . . .

Who are the key men in Spain today with whom the *Caudillo* has built up the new Spain? Any list must include Fernández Cuesta, Head of the Phalanx, whose name, with that of General Muñoz Grandes, the Minister of War, is sometimes mentioned as a possible successor to Franco; Señor Suanzes, who looks after the immense vested interests of I.N.I., the State industrial ventures; Señor Girón, the Minister of Labour, Spain's Bevan and like him in more ways than one; the Conde de Vallellano, a former Monarchist Mayor of Madrid and now Minister of Public Works, and Serrano Suñer who, though no longer holding any official position, is the man who has been in closer and more consistent touch with his brother-in-law ever since the Rising of 1936 than anyone else perhaps, with the single exception of Nicolás Franco.

Of the Cabinet of twelve, four Ministers only belong to the *Falange*.

The modern Cortes, the 'vertical' parliament evolved from the ancient traditions of the country, is entrusted with the mission of ensuring the collaboration of everyone in the performance of all State tasks, "through the family, the municipalities, and the syndicates".

"If you live long enough," says an Arab proverb, "you will see your enemy borne past your window". In the past five years the imperturbable patience, the Iberian tenacity, the Galician far-sightedness, and the essential statesmanship of Franco have been abundantly manifest. The new link with the United States grows in strength and effective collaboration from day to day (as I write Muñoz Grandes is in Washington as guest of the American authorities, by whom he was decorated on arrival with the Medal of Merit for his part in the conclusion of the Hispano-American pacts). The policy of Hispanity and the political and commercial understandings with the Arab States continue in full being, the Concordat with the Holy See has placed Spanish ecclesiastical affairs on a permanent basis satisfactory to both parties, while the award in 1953 by Pope Pius XII to the Head of the Spanish State of the rarely-bestowed Supreme Order of Christ was an advertisement to the world, not only of Franco's past services to Christendom but of the undeniable fact that he remains today, as eighteen years ago, its foremost champion against the Eastern menace. He has confounded his enemies and all the jeremiah prophets among the Spanish exiles. His position in the country is firm as a rock, and contemporary Spain, in the words of a visiting U.S. Senator, is recognised as "the most politically and nationally united country in Europe"—"no more Fascist than Communist, but Christian, Democratic and Syndicalist" according to Franco's declaration when opening the Cortes on May 14th, 1946.

Near the Alto del León Pass (where a group of young Spaniards died to a man repelling the advance of the Madrid Red militia in the first days of the Civil War), situated on the crest of the Guadarramas a few miles from the capital, the huge granite monument to the million Spanish dead, with its vast subterranean chamber three hundred feet long, nears completion, and while every country in Europe shows signs of internal tensions and political neurasthenia, "Franco's Spain" is an oasis of order, peace, prosperity and tranquillity in a world of fear.

Nothing seems less likely than that the Nobel Peace Prize will ever be awarded to the extraordinary Spaniard who has lifted up his country to such a lofty height from the ruin, chaos and misery into which it had fallen, and brought it triumphantly through international, economic and political persecution; nothing is more sure than that, on the whole basis of his enduring achievement on behalf of Spain, of Europe and of the entire free world, he has a just moral claim to it.

EPILOGUE

ONE DAY IN FEBRUARY OF LAST YEAR the Nobel Prize Winner, M. François Mauriac, in a signed leading article in his paper *Le Figaro*, described a visit paid him in his office in the Champs Elysées the previous day by a young man from Leningrad (or Stalingrad) who was spending some weeks of study in the French capital. The Russian had evinced no particular curiosity about the contemporary life, or the two-thousand years' history of Paris; what he wished to be enlightened upon was the meaning and purpose of religion. "What we have to realise," wrote Mauriac in his editorial (to which I refer from memory), "is that in the world today there are millions and millions of our fellow human beings completely and finally lost to Christian belief." Yet, as another French writer declared elsewhere at this time, "without the lives of the Saints, this world has no significance"— a modern echo of Shakespeare's "tale told by an idiot, full of sound and fury, signifying nothing". The same empty conclusion is at least hinted at by W. MacNeile Dixon in that extraordinarily erudite but thoroughly dismaying book, *The Human Situation.*

"Against souls the lie, against bodies violence," counselled the Slav apostle of world revolution Lenin, who 'honoured' Spain as the first country outside Soviet Russia to be subjected to the Marxist experiment. Stalin, the Georgian ex-postulant for the Orthodox priesthood, adopted a more subtle and even more sinister stand: "Why make war on Europe? Europe will destroy itself."

For a week or two in 1953 a news-reel was being shown with awe-inspiring shots, taken through the world's largest telescope on Mount Palomar Observatory, California, of explosions on the sun reaching a hundred thousand miles in height and "equal to the explosion of a hundred hydrogen bombs". "Judge of the spectacle!" apostrophised a Lucerne journal which I cut: "Man is beginning to sense that he is lost in an unintelligible Universe. But if only humanity could discover how to reconcile its tragic differences we might still find collective salvation."

The Spanish *enfant terrible* has said of the European dilemma, in face of the solid mass of the Red Army and the satellite forces: "A Europe convinced of its universal destiny would be converted automatically into a *'potencia terrible'*. . . . The nations of Europe have no other alternative but to unite or perish. . . . Communism is not one evil, but a compendium of all the evils."

Then what, in the name of God, do we think that we are doing about "this man" Franco? The T.U.C. and the Labour leaders, and Left-wing intellectuals who contribute regularly to *The New Statesman*, are still thinking of Spain in the terms of the "rebels" and the "legitimate Government", although at times during the Civil War there were five different Republics in being each refusing to recognise the passports of the other "but all collectively saluted by Britain as 'the legitimate Government' "—or of Mr. Attlee's clenched fist salute at a parade in Madrid of the Communist International Brigades who prolonged the war between brothers by three years and cost Spain a million dead. Moreover, the great majority of Spaniards believe, rightly or wrongly, that Eden is just as perversely prejudiced against the truth of the emergence of Spain from years of strife and chaos to its present nation-wide condition of peace, order and prosperity. Politically, they believe, Britain is still dancing to the Spanish tune called by Moscow. For our politicians swallow a whole caravan of propaganda camels from Moscow and in the Red China of Mao-Tse-Tung, and strain and reach at the benevolent gnat of contemporary Spain, despite Sir Winston Churchill's admonition, given with particular reference to Francisco Franco, that "there is all the difference in the world between the man who knocks you down and the man who leaves you alone."

Following the same train of thought, Mr. Colin R. Coote, Editor of the *Daily Telegraph*, pointed out in a leader-page article on Spain that "there is only one thing worse than hitting a man when he is down, and that is hitting a man when you know that he cannot hit back".

That is precisely what the European Division of the B.B.C. was doing for a dozen years and more in its Spanish Service political broadcasts, which have only lately become less venomous and partisan. Mr. James Cleugh refers in his conscientious and well-balanced work *Spain in the Modern World* (p. 213), which appeared in 1952, to "the persistent denigration of Spain which continues to characterise the policy of the B.B.C.", adding: "That policy was framed when . . . the Spanish section at Bush House was manned by Republican exiles. Spain continues to be the butt of this powerful organisation, the non-political character of which, as laid down in its charter, evidently does not extend to the criticism of foreign countries".

Moreover, staff suspected of harbouring a fairer and more balanced attitude ran some risk of being 'edged out'. The present writer happens to be acquainted personally with a former editorial member of the section who, after years of service, was thus dealt with for not 'toeing the party line', on false information proffered against him by a personnel officer with no third party present, and on a charge of 'inefficiency' by a superior who had previously signed a declaration of his professional competence. A protest memorial addressed collectively to the Board of Governors failed to reach its true destination.

"I am not at all surprised", was the voluntary comment made to another personal acquaintance by no less a person than the then Chief News Editor at Broadcasting House, "with the bunch of Bolsheviks they've got there."

Week by week, month by month, year after year, the millions of the B.B.C.'s listeners are regaled in the Third Programme with "The Soviet View", which, as all the world knows, can only represent the Soviet party-line view; but in no single instance is "The Spanish View" ever allowed to be heard, nor any individual non-partisan discourse on the actualities of contemporary Spain and the true origins of the Civil War.

On January 7th, 1955, the one hundredth "Town Forum" was broadcast and televised from Nottingham, and the *Radio Times* seized the opportunity to boast that the programme "has now been held 99 times in different towns and cities of England, France, Italy, Germany, Belgium, Holland, Norway, Sweden, and Denmark". But not in Spain. Why not? Spain is also part of continental Europe, west of the Iron Curtain—perhaps too far west for the tastes of Broadcasting House.

The time is long overdue for a reconsideration of "the Spanish problem", which, the Head of the Spanish State has affirmed a number of times exists only in the imagination of Spain's ill-wishers—not in the light of any evidence from supporters of the present régime or sympathisers with "this man", but from the published works of convinced and still loyal Spanish Republicans. A re-reading, for example, of such a strongly anti-Franco and anti-Nationalist book as the Republican, Colonel S. Casado's *Last Days of Madrid*, translated by Rupert Hart-Davis in 1939, would be likely to prove salutary for other 'sitters on the fence' as it proved to the present writer:

> In the first month of war a new organisation was created—the Commissariat of Army, Navy and Air. Its root was Sovietic, and its end Communism. The first General Commissar, Peoples' Army, was Señor Alvarez del Vayo* . . . just the man needed to stamp this office with Sovietic doctrines and procedure, and to secure as many militant communists as possible in the ranks of the Commissariat.
>
> They (*i.e.*, the Communists) confused the situation by recruiting thousands and thousands of women militant members of their party, with plans of the *coup d'etat* which they were preparing (p. 62).
>
> They (*i.e.*, the people) were perpetually fed on praise for Stalin, Vorochilov, José Díaz, La Pasionaria, etc. . . . with the approval of the Republican Government (p. 80).
>
> The people loathed this Government, to which the Communists gave the name of Dr. Negrín's Government of National Union. The title could not have been more inaccurate, since it was not a Government, there was nothing National about it, and Dr. Negrín was not at its head. It was an anti-Spanish dictatorship, ruled by the Communist Party (p. 281).

It needs to be re-emphasised that these unequivocal statements were made public immediately after the Civil War by a convinced Republican who had commanded the Government Armies on the Central Front and who, when he saw that the pseudo-Republican but actual Communist cause was lost in the peninsula, brought about an armistice in the face of the Communist *ultrancistas* who wished to fight to a finish at the expense of countless other lives.

Is it known that when the Nationalist *Alzamiento* took place in the summer of 1936 a Spanish Government Minister approached the British Ambassador in Lisbon with the request for active

---

* Afterwards Republican Minister for Foreign Affairs, and the author of *Freedom's Battle*.

British support of the Republican cause, and was informed: "But you have eight Ministers in the present Government for whose political views there is no elected representation in the Cortes, and other Ministers who are not even members of that body." Is it yet appreciated in freedom-loving Britain that the Government troops in Madrid were harangued by the Soviet Ambassador to Republican Spain, Marcel Rosenberg, in the same way as the populace of Prague were later harangued by the Soviet Vice-Commissar at the time of the Communist *coup d'etat* in Czechoslovakia?

*   *   *   *

It was only after the completion of the final chapter of this book that a copy at last came into my hands of ¿*Para Qué*? (see page 23 of Prologue), in the shape of a French translation by Jean Viet— "*Mémoires d'un Monarchiste Espagnol, 1931-52, por Juan Antonio Ansaldo, ex-Attaché de l'Air à Paris, Vichy et Londres*". This translation was published in 1953 by Editions du Rocher of Monaco.

Colonel Ansaldo, a valiant airman who holds the Laureada de San Fernando decoration for outstanding bravery in Spanish Morocco in 1923, was an early member of the *Falange* and commanded a Nationalist air squadron and later a brigade in the Civil War. He "*fut relevé de ses fonctions* (says the publisher's announcement) *en raison de ses sentiments antifranquistes; il s'enfuit au Portugal et après deux ans de relégation à Madère regagna Lisbonne . . . Il arriva en France en 1947*".

The outstanding point of interest of these memoirs lies in the fact that they provide the first factual account of the crash of the Puss-Moth in which General Sanjurjo, who was flying to Burgos to take over the supreme command of all the Nationalist forces, lost his life. Colonel Ansaldo was himself the pilot of the aircraft.

Again, it is an anti-Franco man, an extreme Monarchist, whose political sentiments proved embarrassing even to the Portuguese authorities themselves, who provides confirmation of certain key facts which Spain's and Franco's detractors find it convenient to by-pass:

> Nous sommes en l'été tragique de 1936 *et Franco ne s'est toujours pas décidé à participer á la rébellion.* . . . 'Avec ou sans Franquito, nous sauverons l'Espagne'. (p. 42—present writer's italics).

The following passage bears full translation:

". . . Calvo Sotelo, menaced, took on his broad shoulders, with a classic nobility, the responsibility to confront that which threatened the welfare of the country, and affirmed: 'It is better to die with honour than to live in shame'. It was then that Dolores Ibarruri, 'La Pasionaria', pronounced sentence of death, notifying him with a cynicism without equal that it was the last time that he would speak in that place (*i.e.*, the Cortes)."

The most sensational revelation is made in Chapter VII where Ansaldo recounts a visit to London with a Spanish aeronautical mission at the height of the Battle of Britain. On his return he states that he was instructed by the then Air Minister, a Germano-phile, to make a detailed report on his visit in the presence of the Head of the German Intelligence Service, Admiral Canaris (later executed on Hitler's orders) and other German functionaries, but that, being a man of honour deeply impressed by the gay heroism of the Battle of Britain pilots and the warm hospitality with which the mission had been received, he declined to give anything but a general description. "That request was not a very neutral act on the part of the Air Minister," the British Ambassador remarked upon the matter one day, with which summing up none will fail to concur.

The memoirs of the *Caudillo*'s brother-in-law, Ramón Serrano Suñer, Foreign Minister from 1940 to 1942, whose two brothers were barbarously assassinated by the Madrid 'militia', are in a different category. *Entre Hendaya y Gibraltar*, which is not yet available in English or French, is the book of a trained and acute mind, for the author is a barrister by profession, with a rapier-like quality of piercing to the heart of a situation, or the weakness in an opponent's argument. However *antipático* and *persona non grata* he may still be to the British Government (for in the United States the official attitude towards Spain has been reversed in the past two years), he has produced in this important work an indispensable source-book for future historians, and it is not without significance that today he is a welcome visitor to the British Ambassador's private residence, the identical house where he hobnobbed in wartime with Hitler's Envoy, von Stohrer, and that he maintains a close friendship with 'Don Bernardo', Mr. Bernard Malley, our Embassy's remarkable First Counsellor, to whom he pays extraordinary tribute in his book.

The essence of his arguments, both in their relation to the Civil War and to the 1939-45 War, is that, like his chief, the Head of the State, he acted throughout as a Spanish patriot whose principal and overriding concern was the welfare and greatness of his own country.

If we are able to understand the patriotism of the English (he writes in a key passage, of which I offer this translation) when they believe they are serving, and do in fact serve the interests of their great Empire, why were they not able to comprehend the strength and loyalty of our patriotism, to divine and serve the present and future interests of Spain? . . . What historical reasons, remote or recent, what hopes of liberty and prosperity, what stimulus did the Democracies then offer us that we should have made the decision to die for them? . . . We lived in times when to remain neutral it was not sufficient to say: Let there be a Balance of Power. A neutrality without words, without attitude, without gestures of friendship, would have been catastrophic for us. We should have succumbed.

He takes up Lord Templewood's statement in *Ambassador on Special Mission* that "open war" existed between the two men with the claim that he was serving the sole interests of Spain in his foreign policy, and in fact expresses an obviously genuine and sincere admiration for the "brilliance" of the British wartime Ambassador's achievements on behalf of his country and the Allied cause. He adds expressions of regret that, despite inevitable wartime differences, the ex-Ambassador obviously entertained no customary sentiments of diplomatic friendship for his 'adversary'. "The attitude," explained Malley to me one day in 1949, "is that of the traditional Spaniard who seeks the honourable friendship of one with whom circumstances have placed him, for the time being and in the vital interests of his country, in a different camp."

Serrano Suñer concludes:

. . . And without denying his merits—on the contrary—it would likewise be unjust to forget in all his actions the inspiration he received from the politician of the first magnitude who, from London, directed British policy and who, most valiantly, won a hard victory more valuable than an ill-woven legend. . . .

The late Professor Allison Peers has been several times quoted in this work, for he was an acute and balanced observer of the Spanish scene for over forty years. Here is one more of his profound observations, a truism he was fond of offering to British audiences: "Spain has more to teach us than we have to teach Spain". While George Orwell, who never realised his life-long ambition to see the real Spain, could declare after his disillusioning and distressing months fighting for the revolution of the Spanish proletariat:

> I have the most evil memories of Spain, but I have very few bad memories of Spaniards. . . . They have, there is no doubt, a generosity, a species of nobility, that does not really belong to the twentieth century.

Professor Carlton J. H. Hayes, the American historian and wartime Ambassador, writes in similar vein in his very balanced and objective account of his *Wartime Mission in Spain*, which, strangely enough, has never achieved a British edition:

> I liked Spaniards. I always found them, regardless of class or calling, extraordinarily courteous and charming. They are a very approachable and frank people, with a high sense of individual dignity and worth. It was patent to me that by habit and tempera-ment they were instinctively and stubbornly resistant to any such regimentation as obtained in Nazi Germany or Communist Russia (p. 43).

Contemplating the perilous condition of the present world, one is led to the conclusion that the fixed orientation of the soul towards its Maker—the characteristic Spanish attitude—towards the Queen of Heaven '*y todos los santos*', joined with a courageous defiance of pain and death, is the right human attitude in this "vale of soul-making," as Keats identified human life.

Cannot we other peoples of the Christian West at long last meet this innate spirituality, generosity and nobility of our Spanish brothers half-way, with friendship and understanding? Can we not let byegones (mostly of our own making) be bye-gones, and emulate the new realistic approach to "this morose people"* that the previously strongly prejudiced United States of America has made under the ægis of another army general who is proving his statesmanlike stature, President Dwight E. Eisenhower?

It might well be that the only dread alternative to the full

---

* More *Churchilliana*.

defensive unity of the West, *with and including Spain*, will prove to be that prophesied with apocalyptic vision by Shakespeare in *The Tempest*, presaging the 'Atomic Age' which is now upon us:

> *The cloud-capped towers, the gorgeous palaces,*
> *The solemn temples, the great globe itself,*
> *Yea, all which it doth inherit, shall dissolve,*
> *And, like this insubstantial pageant faded,*
> *Leave not a rack behind.*

January—December, 1954.

Dehesa de Pedrosillo, Avila—Madrid—London—Munich—Lenggries-Murnau, Oberbayern—Santillana del Mar—El Burgo, Corunna.

TRANSLATION

by *Sir John Balfour, K.C.M.G.,*

British Ambassador to Spain, 1951-54, and to the Argentine, 1948-51, of the Sonnet by Luis de Góngora on the poet's native Cordoba (see p. 20 of Prologue)

¡Oh excelso muro! Oh torres coronadas
de honor, de majestad, de gallardía.
Oh gran río, gran rey de Andalucía
de arenas nobles, ya que no doradas.

Oh fértil llano, oh sierras levantadas
que privilegia el cielo y dora el día!
¡Oh siempre gloriosa Patria mía,
tanto por plumas, cuanto por espadas!

Si entre aquellas ruinas y despojos
que enriquece Genil y Darro baña,
tu memoria no fué alimento mío,

nunca merezcan mis ausentes ojos
ver tu muro, tus torres y tu río,
tu llano, y sierra, ¡oh Patria, oh flor de España!

O lofty wall! O battlemented scene
crowned with all honour, brave in everything,
O mighty river, Andalucia's King,
with noble sands, once decked in golden sheen!
O mountain ranges, fertile pastures green
blest by the sky at dawn's illumining!
My native land whose fame shall ever spring
from quill of Poet and from sword-blade keen!
If midst these ruins and the spoils of war
Where Genil flows and Darro bathes the plain
thy memory doth not enrich my dream,
Never may I deserve to view once more
thy wall, thy towers, thy mountains, fields, and stream
O native land of mine, O flower of Spain!

SOURCE-BOOKS AND WORKS OF REFERENCE

A B C. Daily illustrated newspaper, Madrid.

Alcolea, R. *Le Christ chez Franco.* Paris; 1938.

Anonymous. *The Spanish Republic.* (Eyre & Spottiswoode; 1933).

Ansaldo, Juan Antonio, *Mémoires d'un Monarchiste Espagnol.* Monaco; 1953.

Arrarás, Joaquín. *Francisco Franco.* Translated by J. Manuel Espinosa, Ph.D. (Geoffrey Bles; 1938).

Belloc, Hilaire. *Many Cities.* (Constable; 1930).

Bernanos, Georges. *Les Grands cimetières sous la lune.* Paris; 1938.

Bertrán y Güell F. *Caudillo, Profetas y Soldados.* Madrid; 1938.

Bone, Gertrude. *Days in Old Spain.* With illustrations by the late Sir Muirhead Bone. (Macmillan; 1942).

Borrás, Tomás. *Chekas de Madrid.* Madrid; 1953.

Borkenau, Franz. *The Spanish Cockpit.* London; 1938.

Borrow, George. *The Bible in Spain.* (Collins Clear Type edition).

Brenan, Gerald. *The Spanish Labyrinth.* (Cambridge University Press; 1943). *The Face of Spain.* (Turnstile Press; 1950). *The Literature of the Spanish People.* (Cambridge University Press; 1951).

Brodrick, A. H. *Pillars of Hercules. The Iberian Scene.* (Hutchinson; 1950).

Buckley, Henry. *The Life and Death of the Spanish Republic.* (Hamish Hamilton; 1939).

Casado, S. *The Last Days of Madrid.* (Peter Davies; 1939).

Castro y Pedrera, Fernández de. *Franco, Mola, Varela.* Madrid; 1938.

Cherry, Jack. *Franco and the United Nations.* (Friends of Spain; 1947).

Ciano, Count. *Ciano's Diary, 1939-1943.* Edited with an Introduction by Malcolm Muggeridge. (Heinemann; 1949). *Ciano's Diary, 1937-1938.* Translation and Note by Andreas Mayor. (Methuen; 1953). *Ciano's Diplomatic Papers.* Being a record of nearly two-hundred conversations held during the years 1936-1942. (Odhams; 1948).

Cleugh, James. *Spain in the Modern World.* (Eyre & Spottiswood;1952).

Coles, S. F. A. *With Odysseus: Mediterranean Landfalls.* (Lovat Dickson; 1936). *Spain Everlasting* (Reprint). (Hollis & Carter; 1945-6). *Spain: Aspects of Truth.* (Anglo-Spanish League of Friendship; 1951). *Spain as an Atlantic and Mediterranean Power.* Lecture to N.A.T.O. Defense College, Paris; June, 1953.

Diego, Gerardo. *Soria* (poems). Madrid; 1948.*

Dixon, Sir Pierson, K.C.M.G., C.B. *The Iberians of Spain and Their Relations with the Aegean World.* (Oxford University Press; 1940).*

El Tebib Arrumi (Victor Ruiz Albéniz). *El Caudillo.* Avila; 1937.

El Campesino (Valentín González). *Listen Comrades. Life and Death in the Soviet Union.* (Heinemann; 1952).

Encyclopedia Britannica. 14th Edition. "Spain"—"Gibraltar".

Farquhar, G. R. *General Franco.* (Pallas Publishing Co.; 1939).

Ford, Richard. *The Handbook for Travellers in Spain: Parts I and II.* Ninth Edition. (John Murray; 1898).

Foss, William & Cecil Gerahty. *The Spanish Arena.* (Right Book Club, 1939).

Franco, Francisco. *Marruecos: Diario de una Bandera* (*i.e.*, Spanish Foreign Legion). Madrid; 1922. *Franco ha dicho* (three volumes). Madrid; 1948. *Palabras del Caudillo.* Madrid; 1943. *Speeches* (English translation). Madrid; 1947-49. *Statements to E. Knoblaugh.* Madrid; 1949.

Ganivet, Angel. *Spain: An Interpretation* (Idearium Español). With Introduction by R. M. Nadal. (Eyre & Spottiswoode; 1946).

Gannes, Harry & Theodore Repard. *Spain in Revolt.* (Gollancz; 1936).

German Captured Diplomatic Papers. *Documents on German Foreign Policy.* Series D, Volume III—*The Spanish Civil War.* (H.M.S.O.; 1951).

Hansard.

Hayes, Carlton J. H. *Wartime Mission in Spain.* (Macmillan Company, New York; 1945).

Hoare, The Rt. Hon. Sir Samuel, D.C.L., LL.D., D.Litt., Viscount Templewood. *Ambassador on Special Mission.* (Collins; 1946).

Instituto de Estudios Políticos, Madrid. *Cuadernos de Política Internacional.*

Jerrold, Douglas. *Georgian Adventure.* (Collins; 1937).

Hodgson, Sir Robert, K.C.M.G., K.B.E. *Spain Resurgent.* (Hutchinson; 1952).

Hughes, Emmett. *Report from Spain.* (Latimer House; 1947).

Informaciones. Evening newspaper, Madrid.

Jewish Encyclopedia.

Keesing's Contemporary Archives.

Koestler, Arthur. *Spanish Testament.* (Gollancz; 1937).

Loveday, Arthur F., O.B.E. *World War in Spain.* Foreword by Sir Arnold Wilson, K.C.I.E., C.M.G., M.P. (John Murray; 1939). *Spain: 1923-1948: Civil War and World War.* (Boswell; 1949).

Macaulay, Rose. *Fabled Shore. From the Pyrenees to Portugal.* (Hamish Hamilton; 1949).

Madariaga, Salvador de. *Englishmen, Frenchmen, Spaniards.* (Humphrey Milford: 1928). *Spain.* (Benn; 1943). *Spain and the Jews.* Lucien Wolf Memorial Lecture, 1946. (Jewish Historical Society of England).

Marañón, Gregorio. *Ensayo Biológico sobre Enrique IV de Castilla y su tiempo.* 6th edn., Madrid; 1947. (With Report by a Commission of the Spanish Academy of History on the exhumation of the king's remains at Guadalupe in 1946, which the present writer attended)*

Menéndez Pidal, Ramón. *The Spaniards in their History.* Translated and with an Introduction by Dr. Walter Starkie. (Hollis and Carter; 1950).

Millán-Astray, J. *Franco el Caudillo.* Madrid; 1939.

Ministerio de Asuntos Exteriores, Madrid. *Réplica a la publicación hecha por el Departamento de Estado de los Estados Unidos de América de documentos relativos a España.* Madrid, March, 1946.

Ministerio de Justicia. *Causa General: La Dominación Roja en España. Avance de la información instruída por el Ministerio Público.* Madrid; 1943. *The Red Domination in Spain* (English translation). Madrid; 1953.

Moss, Geoffrey (MacNeil-). *Epic of the Alcazar.* (Rich & Cowan; 1937) *The Legend of Badajoz.* (Burns, Oates; 1937).

New Statesmen, The. Files, 1936-1939.

O'Callaghan, Sheila M. *Cinderella of Europe. Spain Explained.* (Skeffington; 1951)

Oficina de Información Diplomática, Madrid. *The Spanish Controversy. Sixty-four Questions on Spain.* Madrid, 1953. *The Protestant Church in Spain.* Madrid, 1950. *Franco y la Cultura.* Madrid; 1947.

Oficina Informativa Española. *Las Reformas Sociales en España* (2a edición). Madrid; 1948.

Orwell, George. *Homage to Catalonia.* (Secker & Warburg; 1938).

Peers, E. Allison. *Spain: A Companion to Spanish Travel.* (Harrap; 1930). *Spain: A Companion to Spanish Studies.* 4th edition. (Methuen; 1948). *Spain in Eclipse.* 1937-1943. (Methuen; 1943). *The Spanish Tragedy.* 6th edition. (Methuen; 1937). *The Spanish Dilemma.* (Methuen; 1940). Studies of The Spanish Mystics.

Pereda de la Reguera, Manuel. *Santillana del Mar y Altamira.* Santander; 1953.

Petrie, Sir Charles, Bt. *Spain.* (Arrowsmith; 1934) *Spain in the Modern World.* Montague Burton International Relations Lecture. (University of Nottingham; 1952).

Piétri, M. François. *Mes Années d'Espagne, 1940-1948.* Paris; 1954.

Pritchett, V. S. *The Spanish Temper.* (Chatto and Windus; 1954).

Real Academia de la Historia, Madrid. *Documentos inéditos para la Historia de España.* Tomos, I, II, III, IV. Madrid, 1936, 1943-4-5. (Presentation copies from the President of the Academy, the late Duke of Berwick and Alba, K.C.V.O.).

Reguera Sevilla, Joaquín. *La Reconstrucción de Santander. El tratamiento jurídico de una catástrofe.* Santander, 1953.*

Revész, Andrés. *Wellington: El Duque de Hierro.* Madrid; 1946. *

Robinson, Philip. *Africa in Spain.* (Fortune Press; 1952).

Rotvand, G. *Franco et la nouvelle Espagne.* Paris; 1936.

Ruiz Morales, José M. *Relaciones económicas entre España y los Estados Unidos.* Madrid; 1945.

Salter, Cedric. *Introducing Spain.* (Methuen; 1953).

Schmidt, Dr. Paul. *Hitler's Interpreter.* (Heinemann; 1951).

Schonfield, Dr. H. J. *The History of Jewish Christianity.* (Duckworth; 1936).

Serrano Suñer, Ramón, *Entre Hendaya y Gibraltar.* Madrid; 1947.

Sitwell, Sacheverell. *Spain.* (Batsford: 1953).*

Sencourt, Robert. *Spain's Uncertain Crown.* (Benn; 1932). *Spain's Ordeal.* (Longmans, Green; 1938).*

Starkie, Dr. Walter, C.M.G., C.B.E. *Spanish Raggle-Taggle.* (John Murray; 1934).

Sutherland, Halliday. *Spanish Journey.* (Hollis and Carter; 1948).

Torrente Ballester, Gonzalo. *José Antonio Primo de Rivera* (Anthology). Madrid, 1943.

Timmermans, Dr. Rudolf. *General Franco.* (Verlag Otto Walter; Olton; 1937) German text.

Torre, Federico Carasa. *Presos de los Rojo-Separatistas Navarros, Guipuzcoanos y Vizcaínos.* Avila, 1938.

Trend, J. B. *The Origins of Modern Spain.* (Cambridge University Press; 1934). *The Civilisation of Spain.* (Oxford University Press; 1944).

Unamuno, Miguel de. *Del sentimiento trágico de la vida en los hombres y en los pueblos.* 7a edicion. (Espasa Calpe Argentina; 1945). *Antología Poética.* Madrid; 1932.

Valdesoto, F. de. *Francisco Franco.* Madrid; 1943.

Walsh, W. T. *Philip II.* (Sheed and Ward; 1938).

Wild, Sam. *Franco the Fascist.* (London; 1944).

Ya. Evening newspaper, Madrid.

(and various other works pertaining to Spain).

---

* Presentation copy from the author.

INDEX